Praise for

BIRD'S EYE VIEW

"A masterfully written and captivating tale with heartbreak as the catalyst to change the course of life. *Bird's Eye View* shows us a woman's strength and resilience as author Jan Capps weaves the past and the present using the concepts of an ancient culture. You will become lost in this quest for love, peace, and self-acceptance, with fascinating storylines and an air of mystery as we learn the intricacies of the Maya world. A fantastic read that will not leave you for some time."

— **Dianne C. Braley**, Author of *The Silence in the Sound* and Winner of the NYC Big Book Award for Women's Fiction

"Infused with insights, adventure, mythology, and parenting foibles and triumphs, this memoir of a year in Guatemala as a single mother is a delicious combination of hard-won wisdoms, sometimes painful moments, humor, and Maya folklore. Jan Capps is a natural storyteller with a keen eye for detail. *Bird's Eye View* is thoughtfully perceptive and funny as Capps fearlessly brings us along to explore literally and figuratively everything. A perfect mergence and a page-turning read."

—**Susanna Block, MD, MPH,** Pediatric Hospitalist, Seattle's Child Columnist, Founder of Rise Up and Read Refugee Library Literacy and Attachment Project

"*Bird's Eye View* is a story about an extraordinarily capable woman trying to reorient the trajectory of her life after a painful divorce and find purpose as a clinic director in remote Guatemala. In doing this, she's living out a longtime dream; however, she is accompanied by her ten-year-old daughter, who dreams of returning to Seattle. Jan tries every way imaginable to wrap her daughter in love as they face challenges from all directions. If you have ever navigated another culture, been heartbroken, or taken great risks to make a new start, this book is for you."

—**Jeff Hassell**, Former Executive Director of Organization for the Development of the Indigenous Maya

"In *Bird's Eye View*, author Jan Capps embarks on a profound journey of self-discovery. A single mother, she courageously decides to step into the unknown, leave her old life behind, and enter a new world that will change her forever. This is really a book about life and how our purpose is really the exploration of it."

—**Ryan Lindner**, Author of *The Half-Known Life: What Matters Most When You're Running Out of Time*

"*Bird's Eye View* is a remarkable, captivating book. Memoir, travelogue, anthropological essay on Mayan cosmology, and indictment of Guatemala's corrupt political system and feckless state, Jan Capps's highly entertaining work overflows the boundaries imposed by simplistic genre labels. With candor, wit, and rich detail, she invites us to accompany her on her personal journey to make a difference among Guatemala's marginalized Maya population, to make sense of her failed marriage, and to overcome the challenges of parenting her young daughter far from the comforts, predictability, and security of home."

—**Paul W. Posner, PhD**, Professor of Political Science, Clark University

"*Bird's Eye View* is a compelling read. Jan Capps artfully weaves together her post-divorce struggles to raise a preteen child alone in a foreign land with her understanding of Guatemalan history and Mayan cosmology. As she courageously reveals her innermost fears and failures, Jan's love for the people of Guatemala and their impact on her life shine through."

——**Ron W. Wilhelm, PhD,** President, ODIM Board of Directors, Professor Emeritus, University of North Texas

"A spiritual journey and in equal parts a story of a single mother guiding her daughter while they live in Guatemala and providing leadership to a nonprofit health project. A worthy read."

——**Sue Hammerton, ARNP,** Professor Denver School of Nursing and Advisor to San Benito Health Program

"A humbling piece of introspection, interwoven with rich cultural context and symbolism. Jan bares her inner world to the reader, inviting us to accompany her on her quest for meaning and belonging."

——**Holly Hayes, MSc,** International Humanitarian Worker

"In her mesmerizing memoir, Jan Capps unfolds a captivating narrative that transcends the conventional tale of heartbreak and resilience. Against the backdrop of the picturesque Lake Atitlan in the Guatemalan highlands, Jan immerses herself in the local community, runs a health clinic, and raises her daughter in this colorful and sometimes dangerous new world. Jan's narrative unfolds as a rich tapestry, seamlessly blending her Southern Baptist roots, her pursuit of social justice, the complexities of love."

——**Jonathan Scheffer, MD** Emergency Medicine Physician, Kaiser Permanente

Bird's Eye View
by Jan Capps

© Copyright 2024 Jan Capps

ISBN 979-8-88824-201-8

All rights reserved. No part of this publication may be reproduced, stored in a retrieval system, or transmitted in any form or by any means—electronic, mechanical, photocopy, recording, or any other—except for brief quotations in printed reviews, without the prior written permission of the author.

Published by

köehlerbooks™

3705 Shore Drive
Virginia Beach, VA 23455
800-435-4811
www.koehlerbooks.com

BIRD'S EYE VIEW

JAN CAPPS

VIRGINIA BEACH
CAPE CHARLES

To the Sun-Woman-King.
Thank you for the light you bring to the world.

TABLE OF CONTENTS

Introduction 7

Part I 11

1: Leap of Faith 12

2: Landing 20

3: Kaxlán 28

4: Outings 41

5: How Did I Get Here? 43

6: Everything Has a Spirit 49

7: Inside These Walls 53

8: Finding My Flock 62

9: Assembling the Nest 70

10: El Cambalache 78

11: What Is Your Plan, Jan? 83

12: For Our Families, for Ourselves 91

13: Clara 97

14: Bach Flowers 101

15: Smoke Signals 104

16: Pena 111

17: Trees 117

18: The Sun, the Earth, and the Sky 121

19: Tikal 126

20: Search for Home 138

21: From the Center of the Earth to the Top of the Sky 144

22: Bands 152

23: Crushed 155

24: Go in Peace 166

25: Spiral 169

26: Clashes, Crashes, and Quakes 177

27: The Push 190

Part II 197

28: Najit 198

29: Values 204

30: *Nuevo Amanecer* (New Dawn) 211

31: Happy Home 220

32: Weaving 225

33: Floating 230

34: Heart of the Earth, Heart of the Sky 234

35: The Long Count 243

36: El Don 249

37: Somewhere in the Middle 254

38: Hidden Treasures 260

39: Rogelio 265

40: The Other Side of the Hill 270

41: Blood on the Floor 275

42: In What World? 282

43: Dance of the Moors and the Christians 290

44: Holy Week 300

45: Bringing Light into the World 314

46: The Fall of the Puffed-Up Plumed Bird 322

47: What Lies Between the Sea and the Sky 329

48: Sick and Stunted 333

49: Fish-Eye View 343

50: Birdsong 344

51: Feria de San Juan 349

52: Confianza 352

53: There Is a Light That Never Goes Out 359

54: Bird's-Eye View 368

55: Fairy-Tale Mashup 373

56: Leaving 375

Acknowledgments 378

Additional References 379

INTRODUCTION

A FEW MONTHS before we were to embark on the Latin American odyssey that we had been planning for years, my husband backed out of the trip. Weeks later, he backed out of our marriage.

"Write it down" was the advice I received as a means to cope with my feelings after my divorce. At the time, I had a job in public health finance in a large Seattle office building. My days were spent in front of a computer, categorizing and sorting thousands of lines of data in spreadsheets. My nights were also spent in front of a computer as I tried to type the feelings out, but they just didn't compute. My mind went over thousands of data points, categorizing and sorting, trying to decipher the factors that led to this, but I couldn't insert a pivot table to reveal an answer. The events and evolution of emotions did not equate. The whole did not equal the sum of its parts. How did I meet the man I had been searching for, fall in love, start a life, build a dream, and then lose it all with what seemed the push of a button? This could not be merely a formulaic midlife crisis.

I decided to continue the journey two years later without my husband but with our ten-year-old daughter. I took a position as a clinic administrator for a small nonprofit organization in rural Guatemala. As a single mother working full-time as an immigrant in a poor country, I was faced with my dueling commitments to the clinic and to my daughter, the paradox of privilege when trying to assimilate, and what it means to have dreams change.

In Guatemala, I learned the Mayan Tz'utujil[1] word for computer is *kemooneem* (weaver of words), which offered a different way of looking at the machine I touched every day. After this, while writing, I took a step back and let my narrative slide through my fingers as I spun my story, like cotton to thread, along with Maya[2] mythology, Guatemalan history and politics, and anecdotes of people I met there. Looking sideways at the sun is the only way not to be blinded.

I also learned that the Tz'utujil consider the dream world to be as important as the physical world. Dreams must be interpreted in a spiritual context and influence every decision. As such, I had to discern the illusions from the dreams that were connected to my soul.

What I write about me is real—real to me, at least. What I write about others comprises my interpretations and assumptions of their feelings, thoughts, and behaviors and includes changed names, amalgamated characters, and fudged identifying details. What I write about Guatemala and its community life is based on what I saw, heard, or read. In other words, I don't know for certain what the truth is about what is not me.

The Maya worldview includes the concept of duality. There cannot be light without the dark, joy without pain, or loyalty without betrayal. I set out to show this duality, the good and bad in Guatemala, both in my experience and in myself.

---

[1] Guatemala has twenty-three recognized ethnic groups. These consist of Ladinos, who are of mixed European and Indigenous descent, speak Spanish, and identify with Western culture; the Garifuna people, of mixed free African and Indigenous American ancestry, who speak Garifuna, an Arawakan language; and twenty-one Indigenous groups collectively referred to as the "Maya." Each Indigenous group has its own language, collectively referred to as "Mayan." Approximately half the population of Guatemala is Maya and speaks Spanish as a second language, if at all. In this book, the Maya groups referred to most often are the Tz'utujil, Kachiquel, and K'iche'.

[2] Ancient Maya civilizations and their descendants stretch across southeastern Mexico and Central America, including Guatemala, Belize, El Salvador, and Honduras. The word "Maya" comes from the name of the ancient Yucatán city of Mayapan, the last capital of the Maya kingdom in the Postclassic period.

I strive to tell my story in a Tz'utujil way, with repetition, subtle hints of meaning, and hidden clues of what is to come. In telling my story, I use poetic and literary devices from the *Popol Wuj*, the sacred text of the K'iche' and the origin story of all Maya people. Like many numinous texts, the *Popol Wuj* isn't told in a strictly linear fashion. It relays the world order, misadventures of the gods, and the creation of humans through a series of parallel occurrences, flashforwards, and flashbacks. Essentially, it suggests that if one wants to understand who and what a person is, and why that person is the way she is, it's necessary to understand where she came from.[3] This is why I included much of my past to explain—or, better said, to help me understand—my present.

Likewise, while this book moves forward in story and theme, it is far from linear. I flash back to different people and parts of my life to explain how I wound up where I did. I mix my all-too-human story with that of the gods, and I look for signs where no one else can see them. In doing so, I hope to show how looking through the prism of another culture, another set of myths, can help us understand our own lives and the myths we have unwittingly followed. I also hope to show the compassion, intelligence, and resilience of the Guatemalan people who have supported and inspired me.

---

[3] Tedlock, Dennis. *Popol Vuh*. LitCharts.com 2023. https://www.litcharts.com/lit/popol-vuh/themes/origins-customs-and-the-mayan-culture

Part I

1
LEAP OF FAITH

MY HUSBAND, WADE, and I had talked about sojourning in Latin America since we started dating. This ongoing conversation evolved into a vision I thought we shared. Our daughter, Lucia, would have a wondrous educational and cultural experience. I hoped that living in another country would inoculate her against the worst of middle-class American materialism and middle school drama. Wade would dedicate himself to his advocacy for fair trade coffee. I would return to the type of community work I had done in Guatemala just before we met, which had been the most meaningful and challenging of my public health career.

By June 2013, our daughter was eight years old, our years of planning had paid off, and we were set to move at the end of summer. We settled on going to Bolivia because he had family there, and it was relatively safe and stable.

On a warm afternoon, I was happily preparing my resignation letter in the kitchen while Lucia played outside. Wade came home from work and said we needed to talk.

"I'm worried that if we are on our own in Bolivia, without any support from family or friends, we will have trouble."

"What do you mean? Your cousins are there. We can call them if we need help with anything. Also, it's easy to Skype with people back in the States. Of course we'll have support," I responded.

"What I mean is that I don't think we should do the trip because I don't think we'd make it as a couple."

I thought I must have not heard correctly. "As a couple? Of course we can do this. Lucia will have both of us to depend on."

I looked more intently at his solemn expression, and tidbits of the conversation registered: *"Trouble." "Not make it as a couple." Oh, shit.* I'd completely misunderstood. He didn't mean that we might have some travel mishap and would be stranded with a young child; he meant that our marriage would not survive.

This was the first time he had ever mentioned doubts about our relationship, so the concept took me a while to comprehend. The tear in the corner of his chronically dry eyes finally made me see what he was trying to say. I ran upstairs and hid in our bedroom closet so Lucia would not see me cry if she came back into the house. After a few minutes, he followed the sounds of my sobs and opened the closet door.

"Jan," he said softly.

"I don't understand. You think we might be in trouble? Don't you still love me?"

"Yes," he reflexively replied.

"But we've been talking about this for years. I thought this is what you wanted too."

"I don't know what I want."

The next day, after I had time to absorb the shock, I told him, "We can table the move. Our family is the most important thing in the world to me. We can go to counseling to address whatever problems we have."

But there was no counseling and no calling upon the family and friends he claimed were our source of support. Instead, around the time we were to move to Bolivia, he moved out because he felt "disconnected, disinterested, disengaged."

A decade before, I had relocated to Seattle from my home in North Carolina to live with Wade after two years of transcontinental dating. We had met while he was residing in North Carolina but planning to move back to the Seattle area where he was from. I thought Seattle was merely a stepping stone for us. It was a place where we would save a bit of money, and after we had our daughter, she could have a stable early childhood until we were able to embark on a new adventure.

Since my childhood, I'd felt a call from God to help others. I viewed God as "the Great Compeller"—the force beckoning me to go into the world to do good, which was part of the reason I wanted to go on this peregrination. My religious upbringing also influenced my view of an intimate relationship. I'd learned that Adam and Eve were made to be helpmates as well as companions. They were tasked by God to tend Eden together. When they failed to focus on their duty, they were banished. There was a time in my parents' marriage when I saw them work together as a team; they raised a family and built a business. This was what I yearned for—a partner to do this work with, my helpmate in making this new Eden.

When I met Wade, he seemed to share many of my values, albeit from a secular perspective. I thought I had found my Adam. With Lucia, we would be—as described in the Bible—a threefold cord that was hard to break. Together we would leave flowers in our footprints.

Instead, it appeared the cord had unraveled, the call would remain unanswered, and no footprints would be made.

Two years after our separation, my life had stagnated—or, rather, had come to a screeching halt. I felt like I was barely getting by. I feared I would be trapped in Seattle forever, slogging away at a loathsome job in finance that I had stayed in to save money for our trip. I questioned my purpose, my worth, and where I was headed.

To compensate for canceling the trip and to fill what I thought was a void, I enrolled Lucia in violin lessons, choir, the school newspaper, soccer, theater, and Girl Scouts and even enlisted her in helping me volunteer with homeless families. In wanting my child not to be deprived of enrichment, I overwhelmed us both. Still, I longed to travel with her, thinking that we both needed space to be open and decompress.

A friend suggested I look for an opportunity to work abroad through the church. Ironically, though my faith had influenced my path, I had not considered searching for a job that way.

When I was growing up, my Southern Baptist church was the center of my small-town social life. Sunday school was followed by morning worship, youth group, and evening worship. Tuesdays were for Girls in Action and then choir, and Wednesdays consisted of fellowship and family supper. Revival was every spring and vacation Bible school every summer. My family went to the same congregation my father had grown up in, as did his parents and, I assume, their parents as well. Everyone knew my family and me. We belonged.

The messages I read in the gospels to heal the sick, help the poor, care for widows and orphans, and befriend the stranger inspired me. These teachings, which I marked in my Children's Bible with a pink highlighter, were also marked in me. I interpreted the phrase "thy kingdom come, thy will be done, on earth as it is in heaven" from the Lord's prayer to mean that we must endeavor to fill the earth with God's grace. Rather than saving souls from hell and sending them to heaven, we should recognize that hell already exists here for many people, and we should strive to bring heaven to earth.

However, the sermons I heard in church did little to inspire me. I thought that terms like "sin," "righteousness," "judgment," and "salvation" separate us from God and each other. I dubbed such preaching as "Jesus-speak" and considered it an abstruse language. Other churchgoers who communicated in this Jesus-speak measured a person by creed, yet I saw them practice the commandment to "love thy neighbor as thyself" only with their immediate neighbors: other White Christians.

These people made me uncomfortable and twitchy. I felt like a nail sticking out of a board that needed to be hammered into place for not subscribing to their dogma. When I expressed my views, I was told, "You are not the right kind of Christian because all you want to do is help people. You're not trying to save them from hell." So, I dropped out of church for most of my adulthood and explored theology on my own. My work in public health on behalf of immigrants, farmworkers, victims of violence, and the poor became my mission.

Within that, in 1999, when I was in my early thirties, my desire to improve my Spanish and to learn about the social reality in Central America so that I could better serve immigrants in North Carolina led me to take a two-year position with a small, American, nongovernmental organization (NGO) as a community organizer for a health program in Guatemala.

The NGO that employed me had ties with the Catholic Church, so, though I did not proselytize, I was officially there as a lay Catholic missionary and lived on a church property with my colleagues. Our sponsor, of sorts, was Padre Cirilo, a chain-smoking Spanish priest who, with his wild white hair and beard and long, pointy nose, looked like a figure from an El Greco painting.

Cirilo was part of the liberation theology movement within the Catholic Church, which is based on unapologetic alignment with the poor against the power structures that oppress them. He and the other parish staff organized political debates and openly criticized the government—actions that led to the murder of dozens of Catholic priests, nuns, and church workers in Central America by authoritarian regimes in the name of anti-communism. I heard the regional director of the Ministry of Health criticize the parish's social outreach for encroaching on the government's program and urge Padre Cirilo to yield to the government's plans. Cirilo argued back, "Governments come and go, but the church is here to stay. We will not abandon the people."

When I heard Cirilo talk plainly about the "dream of God," which is that "all people should have a life of dignity that includes health, education, decent housing, gender equality, and economic opportunity" and that as the "face and hands of God" we were to create that reality, I was hooked. I bought into this pure and potent way of thinking.

After my two-year stint in Guatemala was completed, I returned to North Carolina and rallied my compatriots to change their views and my government to change its laws about immigrants and policies about Central America. However, by the time I was in my forties, my zealousness had faded, and my focus had shifted to marriage and motherhood.

Though I had stepped away from church for twenty years and pursued my mission elsewhere, when Lucia was in kindergarten, I started looking for a spiritual home. I wanted my daughter to have the positive experiences I had as a child. After much searching, I found a Methodist church with a children's program and an enlightened theology that aligned with mine. Wade oscillated between apathy and antipathy toward religion, so Lucia and I attended on our own. She felt the belonging I wanted for her, yet I couldn't imagine her highlighting her favorite Bible passages. It was not that kind of church, and she was not that kind of kid.

During my separation and divorce, this church sustained me. The weekly ritual of attending service where I would see welcoming, familiar faces, hear that "despite all, you are loved," and quietly reflect grounded me and, at the same time, pushed me along. It was through the United Methodist Church website that I found a job as a clinic administrator for a small NGO in Guatemala: the Organization for the Development of the Indigenous Maya (ODIM).

My interest in the job was piqued. It was located in the *departamento*[4] Sololá, which had the second highest poverty rate (80 percent) in a country with one of the highest poverty rates in the Western Hemisphere and thus had an immense need for health care. I felt it was a place where I could be of service.

Like my first time in Guatemala, I would be collaborating with *comadronas* (midwives) and *promotores*.[5] These women and men had welcomed me into their homes and lives, tolerated my idiosyncrasies, and helped me understand their reality. Unlike my previous job in Guatemala, which required overnight outings to search for hamlets of war refugees, I would be in a clinic from 9 a.m. to 5 p.m., which would allow me to be available for my daughter.

ODIM had two clinics, one each in the villages of San Juan La Laguna

---

[4] Guatemala comprises twenty-two *departamentos*, which are political units similar to US states.

[5] *Promotores* (promoters) are noncredentialed personnel who work in fields such as health, education, or human rights, where professional staff and infrastructure are lacking. They are generally well respected and viewed as community leaders.

and San Pablo La Laguna, both of which lie on the shores of Lake Atitlán, a turquoise lake surrounded by three dormant volcanoes and a dozen Indigenous Maya communities. Located in the temperate highlands, a sylvan and serene region known as the "land of eternal spring," the lake is a popular tourist destination. As such, there is basic infrastructure, including running water, electricity, telephones, and internet access.

As I contemplated my future, I listed all the reasons I could not follow my dream to move to Latin America: I was middle-aged. My Spanish was rusty. I needed to save for retirement. I couldn't afford it. I wanted my daughter to have a good relationship with her father. He would never approve. I wouldn't have health insurance. Lucia would fall behind in school. It would be too hard to get a job when I returned. I needed to provide a decent living for my child. If something happened to my father in North Carolina, I wouldn't be able to swiftly get to him.

These reasons for not going were cages I created. When I crossed out all those that were based on my fears rather than my values, only two remained: "I must provide a decent life for my daughter," and "I want my daughter to have a good relationship with her father." As long as I fulfilled these two requirements, I could do anything I wanted.

I applied for the position in April, and by May, I was interviewing in Guatemala. I visited viable schools, chatted with locals and expats on the street, toured the clinic sites, and talked for hours with Kenneth, the director, and the rest of the staff. When I asked Kenneth what led him there, he said that in his past role as a Methodist minister, he had not felt authentic. He had denied his call to "learn Spanish and build" for years. Once he sacrificed the stability of being a privileged pastor, he finally felt that he was being his true self. His reasoning resonated with me; I had felt for years that my life was not the one I was supposed to be living.

After my site visit, I thought it would be a positive place and secure situation for my daughter, though I knew we were not immune from reckless drivers, capricious acts of violence, or contagious diseases in Guatemala, in Seattle, or anywhere. Still, I would have to build a support system for my child and teach her the country, the language, and how to have a life there. I was terrified that I couldn't do it—but even more scared to turn away from this opportunity.

By June, nearly two years to the day after Wade canceled our trip, I accepted the position. After much negotiation with Wade, I explained to Lucia that I had taken a job in Guatemala and we would be going together. I replaced the books on Bolivia with back issues of *National Geographic* containing articles on Guatemala. By July, I had sublet my house and packed our two suitcases, one with books, art supplies, and a few small dolls, and the other with summer clothes that Lucia would soon outgrow and thrift-store dresses for me that I had accumulated in anticipation for our relocation to Bolivia.

I held my breath and leaped off the cliff.

2

LANDING

WHEN LUCIA SAW that we were going to have opposing aisle seats on our overnight flight to Guatemala City, she protested. "How are you going to read to me? How am I going to sleep if I can't lay in your lap?"

"Lucia, you're ten now. You don't need to be on top of me to sleep. You can do this on your own," I responded.

Her face scrunched up in disapproval.

"Here, why don't you take Julie," I suggested, referring to her American Girl doll, which was wearing a matching pink tutu. "You can hold on to her while you sleep."

After a long flight and a restless night, she was grumpy and groggy, but I was full of adrenaline. When we landed, Lucia clung to me as we walked through the airport. I collected our luggage and moved us briskly through immigration and customs.

"We need to stop at this kiosk to exchange some money before we leave the airport," I explained to Lucia.

"But I'm hungry. Can't we get something to eat first?"

"Honey, I need the cash to buy food. A lot of vendors here don't take credit cards."

When I counted my wad of quetzales[6] after handing over a few hundred dollars, I moaned, "Ugh, I should have remembered that airport

---

[6] Quetzal, the Guatemala currency, is often abbreviated as "Q" in the manner that the US dollar is abbreviated as "$."

exchange rates are awful. And the fees they charge are ridiculous! I can't believe I spent so much money just to get money."

Among the dark, diminutive Guatemalans waiting outside the terminal, I spotted the towering, silver-haired man as quickly as he spotted the two blonds. Kenneth, my new boss, greeted me with a bear hug.

"Welcome to Guatemala! This must be Lucia," he said as he knelt to greet her. Lucia wrinkled her forehead and turned away, and Kenneth, in turn, pulled back from her. Noting the mere glance, the glare they shared, I surmised that this dynamic would be challenging to navigate.

As Kenneth loaded our luggage, he said, "It's a good thing you got here early. Hopefully, we can get out of the city before the streets are barricaded."

"What? Do they close the roads for construction on the weekends?" I asked.

"For the protesters, actually. Every Saturday, the streets are flooded with people who are angry about the corruption. The government thinks that barricading the streets will stop them, but the demonstrations are getting bigger every week. They jailed the vice president for taking kickbacks from businesses to lower duties on imports. Now they are going after the president, who was also involved. They stole millions."

"Wow, I'm shocked. I mean, not about the corruption, but that they actually tried and convicted the vice president. I thought impunity was as common as corruption here. Are there protests in Antigua?" I asked, concerned about Lucia's introduction to the country.

"Oh, no. With so many tourists there, no one wants a ruckus."

After we boarded the shuttle, I searched for a more congenial topic to build rapport with Kenneth.

"Where's your favorite place to eat in Antigua? Do they still have all the food kiosks in the Plaza Merced at night? I used to love sampling *mole con plátanos* and enchiladas there."

Lucia, who had wedged herself between us, interjected, "Food? I'm hungry!"

"I just gave you a snack. Here, you can have another protein bar, but don't eat them all. I only brought a few, and they'll have to last a long time," I said, at which Lucia grumbled. I kept trying to engage Kenneth by asking about other activities in the area—trekking volcanoes, touring coffee cooperatives, surveying Maya and Spanish colonial ruins.

Lucia wiggled so that Kenneth and I had to strain to see each other. "Mommy, how much longer? Can we play a game? Can you read to me?"

"No, I can't read now. We'll be there soon." I thought if I switched the topic of conversation to the clinic, Lucia would feel less threatened and calm down. "How has the week been with the volunteer group that's here now? Did they bring all the medicines and supplies you need, or do we need to stop and buy any before going to San Juan? What kinds of trainings have you been doing with the promotores? Do the local churches object to the clinic providing birth control?"

Nevertheless, Lucia persisted in cutting off our conversation, so Kenneth discreetly sighed and turned to look out his window.

I put my arm around her and said, "I know you're tired. You can nap when we get to the hotel. Until then, let's look out the window together."

The landscape was covered with propaganda for the following month's elections. I pointed out the billboards as we passed them.

"I remember Berger; he used to be president, and it looks like now he's running for Congress. The woman is the daughter of another former president, Rios-Montt; he was responsible for killing thousands of peasants during the war. That other woman, Sandra Torres, is the ex-wife of the ex-president, Colom. And that man, Baldizón, I used to rent a house from his aunt, who I think was in the mafia."

I turned to see that my daughter's eyes were closed, her head bobbing up and down. Apparently, the way to quiet her was to bore her.

As I peered out my window at the familiar panorama, I thought about how the same old cast of characters in politics had just swapped roles since I had last worked in Guatemala. I wondered what else would be the same or different this time.

When I first landed in Guatemala in June 1999, I was thirty-two years old, single, and spoke marginal Spanish. My only experience in Latin America had been the six months I lived in Mexico after I finished graduate school in the early 1990s with my then boyfriend and future fiancé, Stuart.

At that time, three years had passed since the end of a thirty-five-year civil war and since the end of my engagement to Stuart, a man I once thought was the love of my life. The country and I were still reeling from the devastation, both in need of healing.

I had imagined that the village where I would be living, Las Cruces, would resemble those picturesque pueblos I once visited with Stuart. The town center would have a stone plaza flanked by an adobe church, restaurants offering rich cuisine, and brightly painted buildings. Innumerable tropical fruits would be sold on the corners and made into *paletas* (Mexican popsicles). Rows of street vendors would be selling their wares, children would be playing in the fountain, and young couples would be cuddling on the benches behind jacaranda trees.

Instead, Las Cruces was more like an outpost. It was in Petén—the largest of Guatemala's departamentos, filled with hot, sticky jungle and dry, dusty farmland, only linked to the rest of the country via a serpentine dirt road. Occupied by political and economic refugees, drug and human traffickers, and a few wealthy landowners, Petén was the Wild West. The state had limited presence, the rule of law was nearly nonexistent, and vigilante justice was common.

The town center included half a dozen sparsely filled farm-supply and food stores that carried only withered carrots, potatoes, and green beans. Las Cruces had no running water and no telephones, so we had to collect rainwater and use a latrine and drive an hour on a dirt road to a church to make calls. The town had gotten electricity only the previous year, and most households still did not have access. Horses, pigs, and fowl freely roamed the streets. Barefooted children with bloated bellies stared blankly at me as I walked by.

I can survive without modern conveniences or many possessions, so living materially poor was not difficult. It was everything else that goes with living in a society that created the poverty—the injustice, violence, and the worthlessness of life—that distressed me. In this postwar country, despair, death, and distrust were ubiquitous. Within the first few months of my time there, I was sickened by malaria, giardia, and hives. However, I was blessed by the deep, lifelong friendships I formed with Guatemalans and other international volunteers and was transformed by being part of "God's dream" that Padre Cirilo had described.

During that time in Guatemala, I had visited Antigua a few times. Looking out the window now, I saw that Antigua had undergone many changes. Internet cafés, bookstores, and photo-developing kiosks were now spas, salons, and shops. The backpackers were younger—I was certainly not older! The sounds of tweeting birds were drowned out by the honking car horns of Guatemalans eager to escape the city for a tranquil weekend.

Antigua's proper name was Antigua Guatemala (Old Guatemala) because it was a previous site of the capital city, though not the first. The K'iche', Kachiquel, and Tz'utujil—three related Maya groups—are thought to have migrated to the western highlands in the thirteenth century. These groups alternately formed and dissolved alliances, coexisted and conflicted over land, and built their capitals: Q'umarkaj, Iximiche', and Chuitinamit, respectively. Their cities had kings and priests, palaces and pyramids, jade and precious metals, and ball courts and plazas.

The K'iche' were the first of these to engage with the Spanish invaders, who were led by Oscar de Alvarado in the early sixteenth century. Defeated after a protracted resistance, the K'iche' invited the Spanish conquistadores into Q'umarkaj. Doubting the sincerity of their surrender, Alvarado captured their lords, burned them to death, and then burned the entire city.

The Kachiquel, depleted from their ongoing battles with the K'iche' and diminished by the smallpox the Europeans had brought to the Americas, agreed to aid the conquistadores in wiping out the remaining K'iche' resistance and to align against the Tz'utujil. The Kachiquel invited the Spaniards into Iximiche', and soon thereafter, Alvarado demanded excessive tribute from them. The Kachiquel refused and left their own city rather than comply. In return, Alvarado declared war on them and named Iximiche' as the capital of the Kingdom of Guatemala, a new territory of Spain.

The Kachiquel did not relent, though. After they repeatedly attacked the squatters in their former home, the Spaniards relocated their capital to a new site—which was destroyed by a volcanic mudflow within a few years. Once again, the Spaniards moved their capital, to the valley where Antigua is now. After three devastating earthquakes and foiled attempts to rebuild over the course of two centuries, they shifted the capital to its current location of Guatemala City.

Despite the constant conflict and natural and man-made disasters, the people of this place are full of resiliency.

Kenneth announced we would be at our hotel soon, pulling me out of my reverie. After checking into our hotel, a quick message to Wade, and a nap, I was ready to inaugurate our adventure.

"Come on, let's get out and see the town."

"But I'm still tired," Lucia responded. "Can't we just stay in the room and watch a movie?"

"No. We only have this afternoon to look around. Tonight, we have to have dinner with the volunteer team who just finished up the week building houses with ODIM, and we leave early tomorrow morning to go to the lake." Noting her disgruntled expression, I added, "I'll take you to a nice restaurant first, and you can order anything you want."

Always willing to be bribed by food, Lucia agreed and added, "Even dessert?"

"Yes, even dessert."

My strategy for helping Lucia adjust was to keep her belly full and her attention occupied. She was only willing to venture out a few blocks from the hotel, but I tried to cram in as much as possible. We watched a parade in honor of the apostle Santiago (James), Antigua's patron saint, visited an arts festival, and splurged on a pony ride.

I took Lucia to an emporium of *artesanías* (crafts) from across the country.

"Look there," I said, pointing to the back wall. "See the clothes hanging with the names of the regions below? That is what Indigenous women here wear. The skirt they call a *corte* is a long, rectangular cloth that they wrap around, and the wrap belt is called a *faja*. On top, women either wear a *blusa* [blouse] or a *huipil*.[7] Those designs sewn into the huipiles that look like geometric patterns are symbols from Maya mythology. The embroidered flowers and birds are native to the region where the huipiles are made. Each region has a set they call their *traje típico* [typical suit]. People used to be able to tell where a woman was from by the clothes she wore. That huipil is from Sacatepéquez, and that one is from Huehuetenango."[8]

"Hmph, you only know that because you read the labels on the wall, right?"

"Well, I said people can tell what region they are from, not that I can."

Rather than listen to my lecture about the artesanías, Lucia preferred to dart between rows of masks, weavings, and painted figurines and touch them all. In our many Latin American vacations, Wade and I would stand by and watch as Lucia ran around in the markets, parks, and plazas. Everything she saw was an amusement to her, every child a potential playmate. However, this was different from our family vacations. We would be building a life here, and Daddy was not with us.

Daddy.

I couldn't help but wish that he were there to share these experiences with her, watch her thrive in a new environment, and reassure her.

---

[7] The huipil is a traditional garment worn by Indigenous women in Guatemala and other areas in Mexico and Central America. It is a loose-fitting top made from two or three rectangular pieces of woven fabric that are sewn together with openings for the head and arms.

[8] Sacatepéquez and Huehuetenango are *departamentos* of Guatemala.

Becoming her parents had been woven into our relationship as lovers. We took turns holding her during our wedding, passing her back and forth as we said our vows. I often joked with her that the three of us were married.

Though I had been a capable, single woman for nearly twenty years before we met, while we were together, our lives intertwined, and we were able to rely on each other's strengths. We complemented each other in our care of Lucia. He bought warm jackets and comfortable shoes and kept the refrigerator stocked. I interacted with the teachers and coordinated all the activities and playdates. I would come up with the grand ideas, and he would do the practical work of making them happen. Lucia saw her parents as a unit ("Mommy-Daddy" was her name for us both), and I saw the three of us as a unit. I still could not think of him without me, her without him, and me without her.

When we divorced, I wrestled with teasing apart being his wife and the mother of his child. I told him what Christmas gifts to buy, what parenting books to read, and how to talk to Lucia about problems with friends or school. I think he only feigned listening to me.

When I was planning the move to Guatemala with Lucia, I welcomed him to visit her there as often and as long as he liked. I advised him on how he could continue to have a relationship with her while we were away: they could video chat every day; he could read to her at night on the Kindle; he could help her with her math exercises. While he welcomed the first suggestion, he dismissed the last two. He would need to find his own way without my being the glue that connected them—or, perhaps better said, I needed to back out of their relationship. He would have to figure out how to do this on his own. And so would I.

3

KAXLÁN

THE NEXT DAY, we piled into a tourist shuttle with Kenneth and headed to Lake Atitlán. Lake Atitlán is nestled in the crater of a mega-volcano that exploded tens of thousands of years ago. Two volcanoes on the southern side of the lake form eastern and western bays and have a channel of water between them. There, the Tz'utujil established their capital on a large, rocky hill and named it Chuitinamit.

According to legend, when the tribes of the Maya were formed, Ajaw (the great god) sent the Tz'utujil to look for their promised land, a large puddle with mountains. The puddle they found was Lake Atitlán, and the mountains were the surrounding volcanoes.[9] The lake became their mother, gave them life, and protected them, at least for a while. They established deep roots and became connected to the land and water, the plants and animals, and even to the stones. They roamed the expanse of their kingdom, which ranged from north of the lake down to the Pacific coast and beyond, to trade their cacao beans and fruits.

Centuries later, the Tz'utujil villages on the eastern side of the lake would attract foreign tourists and expats seeking a relaxed pace. The villages of San Juan and San Pablo had a handful of international NGOs, and the

---

[9] This legend, along with many others, was told to me by Nehemias, my Tz'utujil-language teacher toward the end of my time in Guatemala. Nehemias is also an artist, entrepreneur, and amateur anthropologist. Much of the spirit of this book was influenced by him. He appears as a character in chapter 34, "Heart of the Earth, Heart of the Sky."

larger neighboring town of San Pedro was full of cheap Spanish schools.

The plan was that Lucia and I would live for two weeks with a host family in San Pedro, a town adjacent to San Juan and San Pablo, to study Spanish before we started school and work. Lucia had gone to a bilingual school in Seattle, but she was not accustomed to real-life interactions in Spanish, and it had been fifteen years since I had spoken the language on a daily basis, so we both needed to get up to speed.

After a three-hour journey, we turned to make the one-hour descent into the crater on a narrow, unpaved road with no less than seventeen switchback turns. We saw thickets of ancient, lush, flora-covered lava flows and waves of silver- and rust-covered *lámina* (corrugated tin) roofs that sparkled like the water nearby. The turns oscillated in exposing San Pablo and San Pedro. San Pedro, the largest of the towns on the western shore, was filled with numerous two- and three-story cement-block buildings and dotted with avocado and mango trees. The *fútbol* (soccer) stadium and a large, ornate, white church that looked like a wedding cake signaled the community's wealth. In contrast, San Pablo was tightly packed with small adobe buildings and had no distinguishing structures or vegetation.

After the descent, we turned onto the main road in San Pablo. Kenneth pointed out the window.

"That alley leads to Chuitinamit," he said, referring to one of ODIM's two clinics.

"Chi-what?" I asked.

"Chui-tee-NA-meet," he pronounced slowly. "The staff named it that when it was built a couple of years ago. It means 'top of the hill' in Tz'utujil."

We turned right at the bottom of the main road in San Pablo to go to San Juan, where ODIM's other clinic, duly named *Sanjuanerita*, was located. The shuttle bumped along the dilapidated road until it came to a sudden stop. I looked out the window to see branches blocking the way and panicked that this might be a booby trap laid for a robbery, as occasionally happened in Petén. Tuk-tuks, little red vehicles that look like a cross between a golf cart and a motorcycle, lined the road. *Is this how the thieves would get away?* I wondered.

Our driver rolled down his window, talked to a man in Tz'utujil, and then handed him some money. I clenched the back of the seat and whispered to Kenneth, "Oh, God. Do you think we'll be okay?"

"Uh, sure," Kenneth said with a confused look. "We just have to wait a few minutes until the tuk-tuk drivers finish fixing the road."

"What do you mean?"

"Well, the government has been promising for years to pave this road, but no one believes them. The tuk-tuk drivers pool together to fill the potholes with gravel. They are asking donations from shuttle drivers to help pay the cost."

"Do you understand what they're saying?" I asked.

"Oh, no! There's no way I could learn Tz'utujil. Learning Spanish has been hard enough. I just know this because it happens every few months."

I was ashamed of myself for how hastily I had misjudged the situation. My first time in Guatemala, I had struggled with my mediocre Spanish to comprehend the Ladino[10] culture. This time I would need to grasp the meaning of a culture and language even further from my own—not to mention doing so with my child while working full-time.

When we dropped Kenneth at his home outside of San Juan, it hit me that now I was alone with my child and no other English speakers for two weeks. *Would I be able to do this?*

After passing through San Juan, we headed to San Pedro. The driver dropped off the other passengers at a bustling intersection with a travel agency, Irish pub, organic food store, and a souvenir shop on each corner. Placards in English pointing to kayak rentals, hostels, and horseback riding were displayed on the sidewalk. Down the street was a dock where *lancha* (motorboats for about twenty passengers) pilots milled about while their

---

[10] As noted in the introduction, "Ladino" is the term used in Guatemala to describe Guatemalans who identify with Western culture by speaking Spanish as their first or primary language and, for women, dressing in Western clothes. Many Ladinos are of mixed Indigenous and Spanish heritage, and some deny their Indigenous roots and embrace Ladino culture to avoid facing state-sanctioned and social discrimination against Indigenous groups.

assistants hurriedly directed the passengers, mostly tourists, and collected their fares. This did not seem like the quaint village I had visited years earlier and lacked the authentic ambiance I was hoping for in our life at the lake.

"What do we do now?" Lucia asked. "Can we eat? I'm starving."

"First, we need to go to the school so we can find our host family." I waved down a tuk-tuk whose driver may have been one of the men I had feared only minutes before and asked him to take us to the school. From the base of Volcán San Pedro, for which the town was named, we puttered up a steep hill to the school.

After hours of missed calls and miscommunication (and the ample lunch I had promised), we finally connected with our host family. Balvino and Josefina Cox, their two sons, Marlon and Anders, and their daughter, Piñita, were lined up at their home to greet us.

Balvino told us that in addition to hosting Spanish students, he operated his own shuttle service, and Josefina had a kiosk in the town center where she sold household goods. Extroverted Marlon explained in detail that he was a Spanish teacher with another school, and when he had enough money for tuition, he studied law at a university. Introverted Anders gave us a perfunctory greeting and excused himself, so Marlon shared that his younger brother studied computers in high school. Eleven-year-old Piñita said that she was in her last year of primary school and happy to have a new friend in the house.

They were warm and welcoming, yet I wondered about their sincerity. *How often do they do this? Do they tire of having to constantly explain themselves and have strangers in their home?*

Josefina showed us our rooms and gave us a tour of the property. The postage-stamp-sized patch of grass by the front door was neatly trimmed. The two-story house had four bedrooms in addition to the two provided for Lucia and me, as well as a kitchen with an electric stove and color television. They represented what I thought must be the Maya middle class.

When Josefina showed us the pila, a large concrete basin flanked by two scrub boards, I said to Lucia in Spanish, "Look, that's where we'll do our laundry and wash our dishes."

Hearing my comment, Josefina suggested to Lucia, "You and Piñita can wash clothes together."

Lucia swung her head to me with a confused look. I tried to assure her by saying in English, "Don't worry. You won't be washing their clothes in the pila." Lucia sighed with relief. In Seattle, her chores didn't extend much past clearing the table and cleaning her room. "You'll just be washing ours."

"Mommy, no!"

I laughed and said, "Come on, now. Let's go unpack."

Before we turned to go to our rooms, Josefina informed us, "Since today is Sunday and my day off, no dinner will be provided. We're leaving in a few minutes to go to church, so do you have any questions before we go?"

I quickly assessed the situation. Lucia would be hungry again soon. The markets were closed. It was getting dark, so I didn't want to venture out to find a restaurant. I fretted about going through all our protein bars in the first days.

Probably noticing my frown, Balvino followed up with "I know most students aren't interested in attending church, but you can come if you like. There will be a celebration afterward with coffee and tamales."

I recalled living on the Catholic church property in Las Cruces. The four evangelical churches that surrounded us took advantage of the newly connected electricity by blasting their services day and night. The shrill singing and shrieking sermons were enough to keep me from ever setting foot in an evangelical church there. However, I knew that worshipping under the same roof was a way to become acquainted with the people and build a community. I also thought this might be our only opportunity to eat that night.

"What type of church is it?" I asked, hoping that perhaps it was a more somber denomination.

"Wesleyan," he answered.

"Ah, yes, I know this type of church." John Wesley was the founder of the Methodist Church, the mainline Protestant denomination that Lucia and I attended. The little I knew about Wesley was that he valued liturgy more than preaching (okay, no long sermons), encouraged itinerant rather than permanently placed ministers (okay, no demagoguery), and his followers were active in the abolitionist and prison-reform movements (okay, socially progressive). Sounded safe.

"We would love to go," I said.

Lucia was not thrilled. She wanted to rest in our room and watch videos on our tablet. I encouraged her to accept Piñita's offer to lend her a set of típica clothes to make going to church feel more like a fun outing. Josefina helped her dress, wrapping and folding the corte around her and tightening it firmly with a faja.

After her makeover, Lucia asked, "Do I look weird?"

"Asks the girl who was wearing a pink tutu yesterday," I responded.

As we accompanied the Cox family to the church, we passed through a plaza with an open-air market, Catholic church, and municipal building—the type of Latin American town square I had mistakenly assumed Las Cruces would have. Children were queuing for *licuados* (smoothies) at a kiosk; women dressed in elaborately embroidered huipiles were chatting in a huddle; and men with their best hats were quietly reclining on the benches. All were enjoying the last moments of their afternoon before heading to their respective churches for evening services. Lining the streets were pharmacies, fabric shops, and school supply stores, all with metal gates covering their doors, closed for the Sabbath.

"This is nothing like the area where we were let off today," I commented to Balvino.

"Near the dock? That is just for the Kaxlán. Uh, I mean the tourists."

"Kaxlán?" I asked.

Balvino explained that "Kaxlán" is the Tz'utujil pronunciation of the word "castellano," the name and language of the conquistadors.[11] I wondered if the Tz'utujil see all of us Kaxlán as invaders.

As we continued across town with the Cox family, I noticed the brightly colored murals of Maya culture and legends, including a hummingbird

---

11   In the fifteenth century, what is now known as Spain included multiple kingdoms and languages, of which the kingdom of Castille was the largest, and thus the language castellano was the most commonly spoken. The Tz'utujil now use this slightly derogatory label for anyone not Maya, including Ladinos.

kissing a girl, a man springing from corn, and a woman's dreamscape filled with pyramids and hieroglyphics. Intermixed with these were murals of biblical scripture and Christian sayings. Had the religions brought by the Kaxlán, which disavowed Maya beliefs, likewise divided the people?

Shortly down the side street, we reached the church, a cinder-block hall. About fifty or so congregants were seated in plastic chairs, and the only man in the room wearing a suit was installed on a velvet, gilded chair on the dais that also supported a podium and stereo speakers as tall as Lucia. Before we found our seats, the Cox children excused themselves. Marlon and Anders were going to assemble with their band, which would be performing during the service, and Piñita was going to a children's meeting and choir practice.

"Why don't you go with Piñita," I suggested to Lucia.

"Do I have to?"

"Well, it's a chance to meet other kids. If you stay with me during the service, you'll probably be bored, don't you think?"

With a sigh of resignation, she said, "Alright, then," and followed Piñita out the sanctuary door.

With some opening words in Tz'utujil by a man on the dais, the congregation stood and began singing in Spanish. I looked around to see several people singing from hymnals, so I asked Josefina, "Where are the hymnals?"

"You have to bring your own. Here, you can use mine," she said and handed over the book.

"Are you sure?"

"Of course. I know all the words by heart."

"And the melody?"

"I can't read the music."

After an hour of discordant singing accompanied by beginner-level bands, Lucia marched in with the other children to perform in front of the church. She shot me a look of such anger, betrayal, and annoyance that it made me want to hug her and hide from her simultaneously. When the children's one song was over, Lucia ran straight toward me and refused to rejoin the children, who were going back outside.

This Sunday, the congregation was celebrating Pastor's Day to honor and thank their leader, who had been with the church for sixteen years. For another hour, a guest minister preached about how a pastor was to use his staff not only to guide the flock but also to correct them if they strayed. *Long sermons and demagoguery after all*, I thought.

The third hour was more singing. A mere thirty-six hours had passed since landing after that red-eye flight, and three of these were spent in this church with sound waves shearing the sin off me. Despite the blaring sound, I kept dozing off. I knew that if I was tired, Lucia must be wiped out. We couldn't leave, though, because we wouldn't be able to find our way home.

When the service was finally over, we gathered in another large hall nearby, lined up to receive our rations—one corn tamal and a cup of thin, sweet coffee—and sat at long tables.

Balvino leaned over to tell me, "This is our communion." Noting my confused look, he added, "In your church you have bread and wine, right?"

"Uh, yeah."

"Well, we eat maize because we're made of maize. You've heard of the *Popol Wuj*, right?"

Indeed, I had heard of the *Popol Wuj*, the origin story of the Maya K'iche', which describes how man was made from maize. After leaving a three-hour Christian service, I had assumed he believed the creation account in Genesis.

"So, you don't believe that the people were made from earth, as told in the Bible?"

"Of course. Maize comes from earth." Though the Cox family was fervently Christian, it did not stop them from being Maya.

At the reception, the people were kind, friendly, and curious to see a foreign mother and daughter attend their church. Josefina and Balvino proudly introduced us to their friends, who related the church's activities to engage children and youth, the outreach to the poor, and the pride they had in their pastor because he was one of the few religious leaders who preached in Tz'utujil. I felt a twinge of contrition for my snarky thoughts.

Instead of being treated as interlopers taking advantage of a free meal, we were treated as guests at the banquet.

Lucia and I started our Spanish classes the next day. The school paired students with teachers for one-on-one instruction held in mini-cabanas on well-manicured grounds. Lourdes, a petite, soft-spoken young woman, was tasked with getting me to a decent level of Spanish so that I could manage a medical clinic in just two weeks.

From the onset, she used *usted* (the formal version of "you"), which recognized our social distance. She escorted me to our little hut, and we sat at a nightstand-sized table where she suggested we begin by conversing about our lives. In what sounded like a pat talk, she shared that she was married to a tuk-tuk driver, had a five-year-old daughter, and had been teaching for five years.

For me, though, sharing my story was cathartic. Perhaps it was that my inability to talk privately with friends without Lucia eavesdropping or just the reality of my situation was hitting me, but I found myself confessing my insecurities and fears, confiding about the dissolution of my marriage, and complaining about the lack of support I was feeling from Wade. Though I imagined a woman half my age and a world away from my upbringing would not understand my burdens, she listened attentively and, in turn, confessed her burdens and her dreams to me. She wanted to study law and go into politics, but the money to do so was limited. More than once, as one of us was pouring her heart out, we heard Lucia's singing waft out of her classroom hut, and our seriousness was broken by laughter.

During the midmorning breaks, the students converged on the terracotta-tiled terrace up by the main building to chat in English and snack on treats provided by the school—sugary breads made of white flour that were considered luxuries for Guatemalans. Meanwhile, our Spanish-language instructors used their free time to gather below on the concrete slab where the gardening tools were stacked, speak in Tz'utujil, and eat tortillas ground from corn. There we were, attempting to integrate with the locals, but would we ever really be able to do so?

Gradually, Lucia became more accustomed to her new surroundings and started clinging to me less. She befriended a pair of American boys at the school. She worked up the nerve to cross the street with them to order strawberry licuados from the *tienda* (shop) during the breaks. After a few days, she could walk up the alley to the Cox's house alone as I finished my last hour of class.

I hoped that being able to dress like the local girls might make Lucia feel like she fit in, though I knew her clothes weren't the only thing that made her stand out. When I learned Josefina had skills as a tailor, I asked her to help me assemble a decent traje. She attempted to hide her surprise when I offered fifty quetzales (about seven dollars) for her services. I later realized that what I thought was just a little better than a fair price was much more than she was usually offered.

To gather the materials, she took Lucia and me through a labyrinth of alleys to the home of an old woman. On the floor, the woman had a stack of a dozen bolts of cloth for cortes. Lucia, only a few days out of the pink tutu, giddily pointed to a magenta-and-black pattern with streaks of blue and white.

"That's the one I want."

I asked Josefina to negotiate the price. She had a few exchanges in Tz'utujil with the woman, first soft and deferential in tone and then louder and more forceful. The woman had told Josefina that my seventy-two-pound ten-year-old would need as much cloth to wrap around her waist as Josefina, who was more than double her size. Josefina wrapped Lucia in the fabric to prove the number of meters required and haggled the price down—or at least I assumed so, since I could not understand. For the blusa, we went to a fabric store, where Lucia selected a white polyester cloth with pink flowers and black lace for the trim. Josefina then introduced me to her neighbor, who sold fajas, to complete the ensemble.

I asked Josefina to also make a matching outfit for Lucia's doll, Julie, thinking that would make having traje típica more appealing to Lucia. The little girl still inside Piñita emerged when Lucia showed her Julie. Piñita had never had a doll with hair. She sat for hours with Lucia, brushing and braiding Julie's blond hair, dressing and redressing her. I thought about the contrast between the carload of toys I had donated to Goodwill before leaving Seattle and the one plastic doll that Piñita had. *Was I dressing Lucia like a doll, playing with her, and playing out my own story? Was I treating Lucia like my Julie?*

Having acquired some familiarity with the tastes of foreign students after hosting scores of them, Josefina attempted to prepare varied breakfasts of fruits, eggs, and pancakes. Dinners were usually a dollop of beans or greasy chow mein—a favorite Guatemalan dish that is a loose interpretation of the Chinese version—served on a saucer. Desperate for vegetables, we longed for anything green. At a dinner organized by the school, we devoured the chicken *pipián* with chunks of carrots and green peppers. Still, mealtime was about the family, not the food.

I tried to facilitate a friendship between Lucia and Piñita by inviting Piñita to join us kayaking and horseback riding. Though she was able to navigate the town center independently, she had rarely descended the steep hill into the tourist zone by the water. The tourists were considered dangerous to children because they brought drugs to the community. Also, paying a half day's wage (seven dollars per hour) for entertainment was an indulgence.

In turn, Piñita invited us to *bañarse* (bathe) in a non-touristy part of the lake. Rainwater slides into the lake from the surrounding slopes. The lake has no outlet, and whether its bottom has fissures for the water to recede is unknown. Water levels are said to rise and fall over decades-long cycles. The Indigenous population knows this and so builds up on the hills, whereas the Kaxlán, who want scenic views and easy ingress and egress, build on the shore. Their shortsightedness led to the inundation some years ago of their hotels, restaurants, and homes when the lake rose around twenty feet. Perhaps the Maya wait until the water washes us away.

At the spot where Piñita brought us, I saw reeds and lily pads, ducks and cranes, fish and crabs, and frogs and snails, which formed an ecosystem. Women stood knee-deep in the water, slapping their laundry on rocks, their small packets of detergent scattered on the shore. Nearby, the tops of the submerged buildings, formerly owned by Ladinos and foreigners, peeked out of the surface. We climbed onto a cement roof with rebar sticking out like artificial trees. I imagined the lives once lived beneath our feet, the livelihoods that had been consumed by the rising tide. This was a place of life and death, of cleansing and purification.

While Lucia and I sported swimsuits and swam, Piñita wore her shorts and a T-shirt and, not knowing how to swim, just splashed around. To not abandon Piñita, we stayed in the shallow part and taught her our game of mermaids. We crawled on the lake bottom with our hands while holding our legs together, flopping them around like a fishtail.

Before we headed back, Piñita soaped her body and long black hair with shampoo and rinsed by dunking into the water. On the many days that water is cut off in the city, this section of the lake is the only place where people can come to bathe, wash, and drink. She told me that it was a relief not to carry loads of laundry with her during this visit to the lake, as she often had to do.

Unfortunately, all the washing, draining of sewage, and zipping around in lanchas had led to the depletion of oxygen and blooming of cyanobacteria in the lake. On our walk home, I was overcome by nausea and vomited in the street. I had to let the sickness out so it wouldn't eat me inside.

Within the next few days, Lucia insisted that she was too tired to go to class. Josefina agreed to watch her at home so I could study in the morning. When I came home for lunch, I found that the swim had sickened Lucia as well. She had a low fever, was listless, and hunkered in our room, surrounded by her *National Geographic Kids* magazines. Her body and mind were overwhelmed. Fortunately, I had brought some children's Tylenol, which cooled her, but it took watching movies with Mommy to soothe her.

Late in the evening, Lucia's fever rose, and my supply of children's Tylenol ran out, so I went to find a pharmacy in the nearby center of town. There instead, I found a dispersing political rally. The crowd was loose, uncontrolled, and I couldn't find my way. Through the blaring music and *bombas* (noisemakers), I heard someone call out my name, and I turned to see Lourdes holding her sign. At that moment, we were not student/teacher or customer/vendor. We were two mothers who knew what it was like to stay up all night distressed about a sick child. She grabbed my hand, guided me to the pharmacy, and waited until I found the right medication.

The following morning, I walked down to the tourist section by the water. Alone for the first time in days, I found myself sitting on the dock where the lanchas come and go as they ferry tourists and locals.

Since it was early in the day, the lake's surface was still calm, but by the late afternoon, the western Pacific winds would stir the water, making it so choppy and dangerous that the lancha pilots would have to avoid the smaller docks along the rim of the lake. Even at this hour, I saw a woman in a tightly wrapped corte and flip-flops struggle to embark on a rocking boat. She had a large basket of oranges on her head, one child in her arms, and another by the hand. One slip, and everything she loved would crash into the water. *How does she balance it all?* I wondered.

As did the Tz'utujil centuries before me, I had migrated to this part of the world searching for a promised land, hoping for healing from this place. I appreciated the kindness and generosity of the people, yet I was disquieted that we would remain Kaxlán and not be accepted. I did not want to be an invader. The only thing I wanted to conquer was the roiling emotion inside me. I could not be engulfed; I could not crack. I had to hold the weight of the water in me. The water soothes, settles, subdues, but it can also submerge, suffocate, sicken.

4
OUTINGS

LOURDES ARRANGED A couple of field trips so that I could become acquainted with the community. For the first outing, we took Lucia with us to donate food to three households of poor families that the school supported. At each home, Lourdes knocked on a nondescript door, and out came a withered woman who humbly accepted the carton of eggs and bags of beans we offered.

This type of charity contrasted with what I had learned in Petén. There we strove to mobilize people to change the social, economic, and political conditions that caused poverty, not to merely pass out bread to someone who would be hungry again the next day. But how could I possibly critique this action when my belly was full of sweet bread?

For the next excursion, Lourdes and I went without Lucia to a school and therapy center for children with disabilities. Leticia, the director, started our tour of the spacious and apparently new facility by explaining, "The government paid for the building but doesn't fund operating expenses. We have donated equipment, but there is no money to hire or train staff to use it, so it just piles up." She pointed to medical equipment shoved against the walls and assistance devices piled in the corners.

She showed us a room of about fifteen deaf children, some also blind, and one teacher. The class was in pandemonium. Most of the children were crawling on the floor and crying. Only a couple were at the teacher's knee, practicing signing gestures.

"How does that one woman manage all those children on her own?"

I asked.

"Sometimes we have tourists who help for a day or a week."

"But isn't that hard for the kids to have to get used to new people? Do the volunteers even know sign language in Spanish?"

Leticia responded with a despondent shrug. I saw that one of the two windows in the classroom was broken.

"Isn't that a hazard?" I asked.

"We don't have the money to fix the window. The government said they would pay for building the facility, but not for the repairs."

At that moment, I heard a crash. One of the children had crawled onto the windowsill and banged against the glass. Now both windows were broken, and shards lay on the concrete playground outside the class. Having only one teacher for such a large group of special needs children would surely result in more hazards and cost.

Leticia shared that she had recently begun her position and had no experience running an organization. She claimed that she was selected because in high school she'd studied how to be a teacher and the other parents trusted her since she had a disabled child. I wanted to tell her that I could teach her how to develop a budget, write grants, recruit, and train staff—all the skills I used in the US and planned to use in my new job—but I knew I would be lying. I knew I would be spending my precious free time with my daughter.

These outings outed me. I began to see the dissonance between the values I purported and those I practiced.

5

HOW DID I GET HERE?

A MAYA BELIEF IS that we receive more than genes or blood from our ancestors. Our temperament—how we relate to the world—comes from our parents. Our dreams include their memories, not just memories of them. We inherit their insights and experiences gained during their lives, which we are to hold, to honor, and to pass on to others. Our present is their past.

One of my first memories as a girl was watching Disney's animated *Cinderella* and wanting to be like her. Perhaps the draw was that she was a blue-eyed blond like me. Or possibly because, like me, she would rather daydream than do housework, and she searched for a dark-haired prince to take her away from the drudgery.

I had a wristwatch with Cinderella dressed in her blue ball gown on the face. Her arms were the watch's hands. I would dance around the house and spin with my arms in the air to mimic Cinderella's swinging arms while my mother pled with me to do chores.

Despite her obsessive tidying, my mother, Virginia, loved dancing and silliness. She showed off her footwork from her favorite dances in the 1960s, but try as she might, she could never master the 1980s moonwalk. She would jump on my father like a flea and challenge him to practice a new wrestling move they saw on TV.

Sadly, she had a miserable childhood and, perhaps like many mothers, wanted to live vicariously through her children. Deprived of material goods and maternal oversight as a child, she overcompensated by showering, by drowning, her daughters with both. When I still lived at home, she wanted to know every detail of my social life. Who liked whom? Who was popular? Who was wearing what? What former best friends had a falling-out?

She measured success in terms of financial gains, stability, and structure. She adorned herself in gold and jewels before bling was a thing. A chronic shopaholic, when she died, armfuls of never-worn clothes were hanging in her closet, tags still attached. My childhood Christmases were bestrewn with presents. As young children, my sister and I received mounds of toys from Santa Claus and then mounds more from my mother. As a teen, I received "heirloom" jewelry: monogrammed charm bracelets, add-a-bead necklaces, and matching pearl sets. One Christmas, my father played a joke on her by hiding a diamond bracelet under a cheap trinket in a box. When she opened the gift to find the dime-store ceramic, she threw it across the room. Only after my father insisted she look deeper into the box did she find the real gift.

Her aspirations for me were to secure my position as an educated, upper-middle-class wife and mother. An elementary school teacher had told her that I wasn't very bright but not to fret because I was "pretty and could find a good husband to take care of [me]." She reinforced this message by telling me, "You can love a rich boy just as good as you can a poor boy." After that, I chafed at my mother's efforts to impart her homemaking skills to me. I never learned to sew or cook. I loathed cleaning and preferred exploring the nearby woods over playing house.

In my tween years, I heard stories of female missionaries in my Southern Baptist Girls in Action classes at church. Lottie Moon, a nineteenth-century woman, captured my imagination. Highly educated, she spoke seven modern languages and read several other ancient ones. She traveled to China to be a missionary as a single woman at thirty-two. At first, she was relegated to being a teacher, but later she broke away to start her own ministry. With only the respite of a couple of furloughs over forty years, she suffered the same famine, poverty, and war as the people she was called to serve. Giving away nearly all her food and money, she wasted away and died en route to the US for medical care.

Though I now understand that like Catholics in Latin America, Protestant missionaries in Asia were linked with Western imperialism, as a young girl who had only left her small town to go to the mall thirty minutes away, these stories of travel were romantic.

As good Southern Baptists, my family annually donated to the Lottie Moon Christmas offering for foreign missions. When I was "saved" at eleven years old, I decided to follow her example and become a missionary. I had no interest whatsoever in converting or "saving" anyone, but I felt a pull to go into the world to minister somehow. Naturally, my parents praised my "salvation" and baptism, but being a missionary? Absolutely not! That was what we gave money for; that was certainly not what we did.

Everyone with whom I shared my dream gave me a quizzical look and asked, "Are you serious?" or sneered, "But you're not that religious." Consequently, I succumbed to social pressures and suppressed my dreams.

In high school, I learned about Jane Goodall from a public television documentary. She presented a whole new way of going into the world. Coming of age in post–World War II England, she was fascinated by Africa and animals. She traveled by boat to Kenya to visit a family friend's farm. From there, she began her fifty-plus years of studying chimpanzees in the jungles of Tanzania. Watching her squat barefoot with her long blond ponytail draped over her shoulder while grooming chimpanzees, I thought she embodied what I then wanted to be—a woman of science, a woman of adventure.

In college I majored in biology, concentrating on genetics, telling myself and everyone else that I wanted to be a genetic counselor. Since I needed laboratory experience to pursue that career, I applied to be a student intern at a large federal research agency. I had heard that at this agency, biologist Bibba Goode was doing cutting-edge research on transposable elements in *Drosophila melanogaster* (i.e., jumping genes in fruit flies). In the days when someone could stroll into a federal building without being checked for ID, I showed up in Bibba's lab and asked for a job.

She was leery of taking me on because she didn't want the hassle, but said she would, "only because you are a woman." Bibba was an ardent feminist, the first I had ever met. She served as the state chapter president of the National Organization for Women, opened a feminist bookstore, and talked about wishing abortion were legal when she was young. She spoke openly about her struggles to balance her role in shaping her children's development with her own education and career. I did not know this was a dilemma for women.

In 1988, with my Daisy Duke shorts, I was the last person one would imagine as a feminist. Rather than writing me off or underestimating me as my professors had, she treated me like I was competent and filled with potential. She oriented me to a compendium of protocols and told me, "If you can cook, you can do molecular biology." Well, I never learned to cook and never really understood molecular biology. Nonetheless, she praised my successes and made me realistically accept responsibility for my failures.

My failures were not few. Toward the end of college and for the first few years after graduating in my next job, I floundered as a laboratory technician. Rather than being a methodical and meticulous scientist, I experimented with my experiments, substituting solutions and steps. I rarely wrote notes, haphazardly handled radioactive waste, and ruined equipment. Being a lab rat was a terrible fit for me.

When my job sponsored me to take a genetics course at a local university, I regularly passed the building housing the School of Public Health on my way to class. Curious about this field and wanting to check it out, I took a detour through the building one day and wandered the halls. On the walls, I saw posters about fascinating projects: radio campaigns to reduce AIDS in Africa, Black churches in the US South using peer networks to detect breast cancer, and efforts to stop the spread of cholera in Haiti. This melding of science and mission seemed perfect for me. I thought public health would take me out of the lab and into another realm, so I applied and was accepted to graduate school.

While still in my laboratory job during the summer before beginning graduate school, I began teaching English to migrant tobacco farmworkers at night. This job did indeed take me to another realm. Visiting the workers in their labor camps, joking with them in my broken Spanish, and dwelling momentarily in their reality was as different from being in a laboratory as I could imagine. I loved it so much that I taught part-time for seven years, all through graduate school and thereafter while I worked public health during the day.

Though raised surrounded by tobacco fields in eastern North Carolina, I was a townie and knew nothing of farmworkers' conditions. My summer jobs involved doing yard work for my father's real estate business, with breaks for Hardee's ham biscuits and Mountain Dew, not toiling in an open field and picking a poisonous leaf. The farmworkers wore long sleeves and gloves because, on contact, nicotine sickens a person with headaches, dizziness, and vomiting. They would have to dose themselves with Benadryl and wait a few weeks until the nicotine fully absorbed in their blood and bodies, building a resistance to the sickness while creating an addiction to the poison. In some cases, they lived in dormitory-style housing, and in other cases, they were in shacks that had been inhabited by enslaved people or sharecroppers a century before.

The camp where I taught that first summer consisted primarily of young single men from Mexico. When they were not in class, they behaved like any group of young guys living in the middle of nowhere: lots of drinking, sports, and looking for girls. Also living in the camp were a married couple in their early forties, Flavio and Estela Arias, and their three teenage sons. To me, they were the model of the ideal family because they banded together to work hard for each other. They were caring and compassionate, not only within their family but also toward other immigrants and Americans in need.

During this period of my life, my parents divorced, and my relationship with my mother became strained. I talked with Estela about the problems in my family, and she welcomed me into hers. Every time I showed up for class, she offered me food she had prepared or something from the garden. As summer ended, rather than going back to Mexico or moving to the next farm like the other workers, the Arias family stayed and insisted that their sons go to school.

Reeling from the disintegration of my family, I folded into this one.

I enrolled their kids in school, took them to medical appointments, and taught them English for several years. We celebrated Christmas together on December 26, after I could shop for deep discounts at the K-mart to enable me to show up at the Arias household with an armful of toys. Eventually, I brought my experience working with the legal, social, and health systems on behalf of this family and other families to my work in public health.

I somewhat reconciled with my mother after my daughter was born. When Lucia turned one, I told my mother that I understood how difficult it was to be a mother and how strong the urge was to give your child a better life. Still, when she sent Lucia a Cinderella Polly Pockets playset, I bristled at the anti-feminist fairy tales that might indoctrinate my child, despite my own love of Cinderella as a child. I told her I wanted to show Lucia examples of positive female role models, but my mother had no idea what I meant.

Sadly, she died just before Lucia turned three. She was not alive when I was going through my divorce. She did not see me when the clock struck midnight and the magic melted away. She did not get to hear me say that I understood what she went through. I had no idea what she had meant to me.

When I got the job as a clinic administrator for ODIM in Guatemala and moved with Lucia, I felt I had finally freed myself from the drudgery of my cubicle. Once again, I was doing the work that I was called to do. I would be able to combine science, public health, and Latin America into one job to help people. I would be a "missionary" on my terms and, in doing so, would be giving my daughter an experience that I could not have imagined as a child. I felt the lives of the women who influenced me, real and imagined, continue through me. Their past was in my present.

6
EVERYTHING HAS A SPIRIT

IN AN ANIMISTIC cosmology such as the Maya worldview, the natural and supernatural realms comingle, and all things are imbued with a sacred essence. Everything has a spirit—the rocks, the lake, the trees.

The spirits of trees are evidenced by the fact that they grow back when they are cut down, so it is forbidden to sit on a stump because that would be sitting on a spirit. Also, because the tree has a spirit, before cutting it or using its wood, one must ask permission of nature and wait until a full moon. If not, the tree's spirit can harm the logger or his family.

In San Juan, I heard of a man who wanted to clear the land but did not recognize the hallowedness of the tree spirit, did not consult the guardian of nature, and did not wait for the full moon. Instead, he capriciously chopped what was in his way and stepped over the stump. The trunk tumbled, the branches broke, and the crown collapsed. Rising from the stump was not a spirit but rather a ghost. The man only wanted to clear the land for his crops. He did not care for the wood he left on the ground, so he burned the stump and left the trunk to rot. The stump's ashes turned to mud, and its ghost haunted him.

If all natural objects have spirits, do intangible things such as relationships have them as well? If so, how had my relationship with Wade sprouted? How had it grown? How had it died?

After years of emotional drift, when I moved back to North Carolina from Guatemala in 2001, I was ready to set down roots. My dream job coordinating a program to help battered immigrant women was waiting for me. I was going to share what I had learned in Guatemala. I reconnected with my friends and family and enjoyed spending the weekends with my nieces. I bought a little house, delved into countless projects, and planted my garden. Still, I felt a hole in my life. I saw that my sister, my friends, and even my divorced parents, both remarried, had someone else in the center of their lives. Though I certainly felt loved, I was not in anyone's center.

Within a few months, I met Wade, who was in the process of ending a relationship. From the beginning, he wanted to move back to the West Coast to be closer to his family and friends in Seattle. I told myself that once he fell in love with me, he would give up his desire to move and settle with me in my little house.

We talked for hours about our shared ideas, supported each other in our respective careers, explored other countries, and imagined new adventures. He rehinged my back door that I had haphazardly hung so that I could sleep securely at night. He played tag with my young nieces. Every week, he called his mother and spoke tenderly to her in his spotty Spanish. He showed so much care for me and our respective families that I was sure he would care for our family yet to come.

I thought he might fill that hole in my life and move me to the center of his life. I unearthed the most buried parts of me. Our mutual respect and shared values grounded us, and our dreams of exploration and mutual exploits pushed us upward. We grew closer, but despite my best attempts, rather than placing me at the center of his life, he chose to move across the country. Though he invited me to join him, I was reluctant to leave North Carolina. After having lived away in Guatemala, I wanted to be home. I wanted to be with my family, my friends. I loved my job. I wanted to see the bulbs I planted in the fall bloom in the spring. At the same time, I wanted a family of my own.

We were entangled. After over two years of transcontinental dating, I chose to uproot my life, toss my fate to the wind, and plant myself with him. I was filled with hope and fear as I plunged into the unknown.

I departed North Carolina in mid-September 2004 in eighty-seven-degree heat and landed in Seattle in sixty-two-degree mist. The chill in the air descended into our new home together. Before the boxes were unpacked, I sensed a change. He didn't want to share his car, his friends, his space. Days after arriving, I went for a walk, rain washing the tears off my face. Though he did not say so, I thought he did not want me there.

Shortly after this walk, I discovered I was pregnant. How would I handle being a mother in a new city with no support other than my partner, who was slowly moving away from me? I feared he would feel stuck with me. Though I wanted to have a child with him, I wanted to wait until we were settled and solid.

On an overcast October day, we went to Alki Beach in West Seattle, an area where the salty water of the Pacific is fed by the fresh water of the Cascade and Olympic watersheds, to discuss what to do. On a quiet stretch of the shore, we huddled on a driftwood log. I pragmatically laid out the options. While waiting for his response, I watched the white gulls and black crows circling each other in the gray sky. One of each hopped around a few feet away, vying for the french fries left behind by the tourists. I wondered which would win.

Though it took some time for him to compose his thoughts, Wade accepted the baby without reservation, and we decided to step into the adventure of parenthood together. At the first ultrasound appointment, where we saw the grainy image of the fetus that I nicknamed *Almita* (Little Soul), he squeezed my hand and smiled, his quiet way of saying he was happy.

At the end of my first trimester, I went to Guatemala to visit the program in Petén. I was with one of my former colleagues when I felt a quickening. My colleague pulled out a portable Doppler and said that since I had recently passed twelve weeks, we could probably now hear the fetus's heartbeat.

"Would you like to try?" she asked.

"Wow, of course!" I responded and hurriedly called Wade. She squeezed some cold gel on my belly and then placed the wand gently into the gel. As the sound of fluttering emerged from static, I held the phone to the Doppler so that we could share this first of many firsts.

I sensed he loved me and would love our baby. With me prodding him along, he often spoke to my belly—"I'm going to love you like crazy"—and then Almita would respond with hard kicks to my ribs.

"Ouch! She's definitely going to be a daddy's girl," I would tell him, to which he always responded with the wide smile I fell in love with.

For many years, the heartwood held our tree upright. Our daughter was a new branch. We bought a little house, delved into countless projects, and planted our garden. I sowed the seed of the idea of our little family traveling, living, and working in Latin America, perhaps because I thought that if we were doing what we loved with each other, we would prune the decaying limbs and new growth would sprout. The early version of us lay inside, but the layers that grew year after year made it harder to reach.

Holding on to the hope of reviving what was dying between us, I stayed at a job I hated for years to save money for our trip. Every year that passed, I thought we were a little bit closer, but in reality, we were drawing further apart. After a decade together, the heartwood rotted, and a hollow pith formed.

Still, by force of my will, our family held together, and we planned to go to Bolivia. When Wade canceled our trip and soon thereafter split apart our family without consulting the powers that be, our marriage was felled.

Was the spirit of our failed marriage left standing? Did it haunt him the way it haunted me? And yet, out of the stump of what had been carelessly cut, new life was emerging.

7

INSIDE THESE WALLS

THE *POPOL WUJ* tells a story set in the Guatemalan highlands of how humans were formed, divided into the multiple language groups by which they identified themselves, and then sent out to different parts of the world. As these groups spread, their range extended from southern Mexico to Honduras, and the population grew to upward of two million people.

Despite their vast expanse, their civilization was a society, not an empire. Though they shared a common culture in related language groups, dress, and religion, they did not share a polity. For the most part, they lived in contained city-states, most notably Chichen Itza, in what is now Yucatán, Mexico, and Tikal, in what is now Petén, Guatemala. These city-states were interconnected through trade, but each had its own government within its walls. No one ruler could conquer all. Eventually, the vast cities with their temples and palaces were abandoned, perhaps due to drought, war, overpopulation, or some combination thereof.

By the time the Spaniards arrived in the early sixteenth century, these peoples were on the other side of the height of their civilization and were living in scattered villages according to their respective ethnic and language groups. Since that time, the Spaniards had attempted to fold them into their empire, and then the Ladinos expected them to assimilate into the Central American and then Guatemala republics. They failed to homogenize the Indigenous peoples—or rather, failed to wipe out their culture. During the bloody Guatemalan Civil War from 1960 to 1996, a series of Ladino-led governments razed and burned hundreds of Indigenous villages, seized their land, and displaced and murdered hundreds of thousands of Maya.

Still, no one ruler could conquer all. The Maya now comprise half the country. Their communities have their own justice, health, and education systems. Perhaps this is the legacy of Maya city-state political organization, or maybe this is due to distrust and disorganization of central governments.

The villages around the rim of Lake Atitlán, with no road to connect them all, were somewhat self-contained, operating in a bubble separate from the outside world. The local mayors dictated the projects, such as a new soccer stadium or sewage system, and allocated government jobs to supporters.

But outside of our village, on the Cox family's television, I saw reports of political unrest across the nation. The weekly protests against corruption that Kenneth had described swelled into thousands of people marching in the streets of Guatemala City. Other graft schemes included health and environmental contracts awarded to unqualified companies that resulted in deaths and destruction. This administration was one of a long line of governments made up of crooked politicians who had enriched themselves and their friends with impunity while half the population lived in poverty.

Some pundits thought that the steps toward accountability meant that Guatemala was about to usher in its version of an Arab Spring, a flourishing of democracy uniting the nation, while others saw this latest series of scandals as part and parcel of predictable unpredictability. This pandemonium seemed a world away from our peaceful waterfront village, as if it were happening to another people in another land.

Had I successfully cloistered us in these city-states, or would the unrest seep in and affect us also?

Increasing my unease was knowing we were soon to leave the impregnability of the Cox home and family to live in San Marcos, where Lucia would be studying at a Waldorf school. An ODIM sponsor loaned us a house for a few weeks, but I needed to search for a permanent place, so we went to look during our first free Saturday.

San Marcos was a village of about 2,000 Kachiquel inhabitants. Most of the Indigenous population lived on the two hills that flanked the town. The valley in between and the area near the shore were inhabited by scores of semipermanent and transitory expatriates from Europe and North America, who operated nearly all the restaurants, hotels, and tourist-oriented services. As such, this area was known as the gringo section. The town had an unobscured view of Volcán San Pedro, calm waters, and a broad swath of low ground that foreigners could buy cheaply and clear to build their homes and businesses.

From the dock where we disembarked, we navigated the well-maintained paths within the low-lying section near the water. We saw signs and announcements in English for psychic healing, tarot card reading, rebirthing, month-long courses on the sun and the moon, Thai massage, spiritual sexual shamanism, and every form of yoga imaginable. Anything that involved the words "organic," "sustainable," "healing," or "spiritual" could be marketed.

Was this just the hippie version of the overzealous Jesus-speak that continued to strike a discordant note in my being? Was this the type of place I wanted to raise my daughter? Would this community foster the love and respect for Guatemala that I hoped she would have?

I feared not.

I had arranged to get together with Lucia's teacher, Natalia, and her son, Aniceto, just a year younger than Lucia, at one of the expat-run restaurants. A high bamboo fence and trees partitioned us off from the rest of San Marcos. We ordered *limonadas* and fruit with yogurt and granola—snacks too expensive for the locals.

Natalia was a White Ladina from Quetzaltenango, also known as Xela, the second-largest city in Guatemala. She was warm and enthusiastic about incorporating principles from a conference she had just attended into her class lessons. I nudged Lucia to describe her school in Seattle to Natalia and Aniceto.

"I finished the fourth grade last month. My school was in half English and half Spanish," Lucia proudly explained.

"Lucia, your Spanish is so good," Natalia assured her. "You will have no problem fitting in with the class. Just so you know, our school year doesn't end until November, so you will still be in the fourth grade. Actually, it is a class of third and fourth graders combined."

"What? But I was supposed to go into fifth grade in September!"

"Lucia, we decided this would be better so that it will give you a chance to catch up with them in Spanish. Also, kids are a little older when they start school here, so some of the fourth graders will be closer to your age."

Hoping to change the subject, I asked Natalia about what I had seen in the online marketing videos. They touted the school as an intercultural mix of Indigenous and international students and showed happy, healthy children weaving, playing in the forest, singing, and smiling.

"Why are there so many expat families here?"

"Some people who pass through this area think it's magical and want to stay. Some come to get away from the fast-paced life in their home countries. There are also some Ladino families that moved here to get away from the delinquency of the cities. Most of the outsider families work in tourism."

"What's the mix of kids in your class?"

"All the children are Indigenous except a boy, Emilio, from Italy. His parents work for an NGO in San Juan. Most of the expat children are in the younger grades."

"And what about you? How did you end up here?"

"After years of teaching in Xela, I became disillusioned with the traditional education system. I was also averse to raising my son in a city with so much crime. I learned about Waldorf's emphasis on the emotional development of children and wanted to give it a try."

Lucia and Aniceto engaged in an eating competition and ordered plates of food and more drinks. Though I had not brought much money, I didn't want to stop the kids from enjoying their afternoon together, so I didn't slow down their spending.

"Ay, Lucia! I'm impressed you can eat as much as Aniceto," Natalia commented. Lucia responded with a satisfied smile and a pat on her belly.

After we said our goodbyes, I told Lucia, "I had no idea we were going to spend so much money. I only have ten quetzales left. A lancha ride back to San Pedro is twenty Q, so we're going to have to walk."

"What?! How far is that? Why did you spend your money? Why did you treat them?" she demanded.

"Because it was the polite thing to do. Natalia met us on her day off," I explained and then continued, "It's not that far, maybe ten kilometers."

I thought answering her with the metric system would distract her.

"Six miles?!" she exclaimed. I should have realized that her education at ten years old was much better than mine had been.

"Well, I have enough for a tuk-tuk ride between San Pablo and San Juan, so we can break up the walk. Plus, we can use this as an opportunity to get a feel for the communities." I knew this wasn't important to Lucia, but she realized that we had no choice.

We walked up the path out of the waterfront section to the village center. Wrought iron and wood benches were occupied by chatty old men and young backpackers. A stone bridge over a brook looked like a scene lifted from one of Lucia's picture books. A group of dogs pillaged the overflowing garbage receptacles. We peeked into one of the handful of tiendas to see that it carried food products ranging from packets of chicken consommé and aguardiente for the locals to curry and boxed wine for the foreigners.

"See, we'll be able to get most of what we need here."

"You mean you'll be able to get most of what you want," Lucia replied.

"Uh, yeah, more or less."

We shortly reached San Pablo, the poorest town of the region, which does not make it onto the tourist maps even though it is larger than San Marcos. San Pablo is devoid of attractions for tourists and the money they bring. There is no town center, no market, no gathering place.

As we passed through the streets, I saw children selling peaches swarmed by flies, squatting mothers crocheting Minions hacky sacks that would be sold to tourists in Antigua, and barefooted grandmothers strolling along the main street. The packs of dogs that roamed San Marcos were absent. There is little wasted food in San Pablo and hence no garbage or extra scraps for them to eat.

We traversed the town within ten minutes and caught a tuk-tuk to San Juan. The driver dropped us off in the middle of town by a statue of the patron saint, John the Baptist. I found myself, yet again, in the middle of a political rally. There was a sea of red banners and blouses, the color of the party the people were championing.

"Mommy, is this safe? Is it okay for us to be here?" asked Lucia.

"Don't worry, honey. They're not angry or protesting. The candidates pay people to wear their parties' colors and to show their support at rallies. We have no idea who these people really want to win. Next week they could all be out in the street again wearing orange or blue for the other parties."

As we walked through the town, I noted that San Juan was about the same size as San Pablo but more developed, with public works projects such as a new football stadium, a pool, a basketball court, and a municipal *salón* (waiting or meeting room). The Catholic church anchored the sizable plaza, which was surrounded by small shops. Several brightly colored murals depicting folk tales, local history, and daily life were scattered around the town. Souvenir shops were filled with textiles and paintings from local cooperatives.

I later learned that although San Juan participated in the tourism industry, the community was intentional about its relationship with foreigners and did not want to become like San Pedro or San Marcos. Locals owned all the hotels and restaurants, creating a burgeoning middle class.

At the end of the following week, Kenneth helped us move into our temporary home in San Marcos. It had modern appliances, a luscious garden, a steep and secure wall, and a full-time groundskeeper. After sharing cramped quarters in the Cox household, we were overwhelmed by the space to spread out.

Soon after we were settled, I invited the Cox family for lunch. They politely picked at the salad I offered and looked confused by the absence of tortillas. They were amazed to see a trash can with a pedal that opened the lid and took turns playing with it, as would a child with her first jack-in-a-box. While I was grateful to have ample space to host them, I was embarrassed by the comparative extravagance we were living in.

Still, the whole family seemed content, not uncomfortable like me. They relaxed in the tranquility of the garden and enjoyed the fresh air and having no chores. Josefina walked along the winding paths and plucked vegetation samples to take home. The tranquility was soon disturbed by a passing truck blaring one of the season's catchier campaign jingles: "Jimmy Morales—*ni corrupto, ni ladrón*" (not corrupt, not a crook). Morales was a comic not-so-surreptitiously backed by the right wing. He based his platform on distinguishing himself from the corruption of the current administration.

"I am surprised to see that Morales has such support in Guatemala," I commented.

"Why?" Balvino asked.

"He has no political experience. He's only known for having a television show, right? All our recent presidents have been governors or in Congress. I can't imagine someone like him running for president in my country," I asserted, oblivious to what was happening in my country in the late summer of 2015.

At that moment, Lucia ran up to us and cried out, "Mommy! The door closed behind me when I walked out of the kitchen. I didn't know it was locked. I'm so sorry."

"Oh, no! The gardener has the only other key, and he isn't coming until tomorrow."

"Hey, the windows upstairs are open. If I could get up there, I could crawl through and then open the door."

I did not like that idea but acquiesced since there seemed to be no other choice. Balvino helped me lift Lucia onto the flimsy vinyl over the patio, and she shimmied across the awning. After she emerged out the kitchen door, the Cox family applauded.

Noting Lucia's triumphant expression, I asked, "Did you lock us out on purpose just so you could do that?"

With a grin, Lucia responded, "Can we show them the *reserva* [nature preserve] now?"

After lunch, we walked to a wooded area on the shore. This part of the lake was free from toxic runoff and inaccessible to people doing laundry. We passed a tall, wooden platform where bikini-clad tourists were sunbathing to find a spot where other locals were picnicking. Balvino and the kids donned T-shirts and shorts and plunged in for a swim.

Josefina and I sat on the rocks on the edge of the lake and dipped our feet in the clear, still waters. I pointed out the three other towns on the bay.

"San Pedro looks so small. I've never seen it this way," Josefina told me.

"What do you mean?"

"This is the first time I've ever been to San Marcos."

"Why haven't you been here before?" I thought that after years of hosting international students, most of whom had likely visited San Marcos, she would know more about the area.

"I never had a reason," she responded.

Indeed, what would compel her to leave her community? Domestic chores filled six days of her week, and church filled her Sundays. She did know Guatemala City well, she told me. When she was twelve years old, her family sent her there to live with extended family and find domestic work. After laboring for years and mastering Spanish, she eventually returned to San Pedro with a little money in her pocket. She had no reason or desire ever to leave again. Having spent time in the city as a child away from her home, Josefina was content with life inside her walls.

What would it feel like to be content with where I am, I wondered, *without the desire to seek something missing or escape from something painful?*

We leaned back on our hands, wiggled our toes in the water, took in the sun on our faces, and frittered our day away. At this moment, we were both exactly where we wanted to be.

On the weekends when I wasn't searching for a permanent place to live, I wanted to visit the villages and hike the numerous trails along the lake, discover exotic flowers and fruits, and listen to the tropical birds overhead. However, Lucia, exhausted from speaking Spanish and navigating the unfamiliar social structure of a Guatemalan school, just wanted to Skype with her friends in Seattle and research jokes to tell her father during their nightly calls.

One Saturday, I suggested a compromise—that we explore the wild, vibrant garden we had to ourselves.

"Why don't we play the game with the flowers we do at home when we walk to the library?"

For this game, we each choose a color and count the different flower varieties with that color; the one with the higher number wins.

"Oh, yeah! I pick pink!"

Of course, I thought. "I'll take yellow."

After three or four rounds, along differing paths and with differing colors, Lucia stopped to build a fairy house at the base of a large tree.

"When I was your age, I used to make dollhouse furniture out of shoeboxes," I told her.

"Then can you make a table and chairs out of these sticks? I'm going to decorate it with flowers."

"Why do I get the hard job and you get to do the fun job?" I joked.

"Because you're the mom. You're supposed to do the hard stuff."

If only I had the magic to turn scraps of nature into a home. If only I'd had the magical thinking to see that wherever I was with my daughter was already home. I had ventured to another country, yet I was ensconced within stone walls that insulated us from the rest of the world. Had I boldly ventured out as had Josefina and her ancestors, or had I fled out of fear, unable to cope with my feelings and my life? Could I emulate the autonomy and fierce independence I admired, or was I merely stacking stones, separating myself from the world?

8
FINDING MY FLOCK

BIRDS ARE REVERED by the Tz'utujil for the many benefits they bring. They are viewed as charmers of the ear, as messengers. Birds know the earth and sky well, so they can recognize and announce changes. If you watch the birds, you know what the sky will do. For example, robins and thrushes swarm in a specific pattern when rain is coming. The hoots of owls, in particular, but also the calls of other birds, can signal trouble nearby.[12]

I heard a story of a poor family that was saved by birds. The family had five sons who took turns using the one machete they could afford when they labored in the fields. So that he would not wait idly, one of the brothers snuck onto a neighbor's property to borrow a machete while the neighbor was elsewhere. At the end of the day, a bird called out to alert the brother, "The owner of the machete is nearing! Put it back before he notices it missing." The brother heeded the bird's warning and returned the machete without incident.[13]

Birds spread and solidify life. When a person's house is destroyed, she or he seeks to rebuild it in the same place—often foolishly, because what destroyed it may come back again. When a bird's home is destroyed, it flies

---

[12] Fergus, Rob and Kerry Hull. 2010. "Avian Ideology of the Tz'utujil Maya: Ethnoornithological Perspectives in the 'House of Birds.'" In *2010 Proceedings of the 9th Annual Hawaii International Conference on Social Sciences*, June 2–5.

[13] Nehemias my Tz'utujil teacher, shared the stories about birds in the preceding two paragraphs with me.

away to find another place to build its nest. Birds carry the seeds of fruits they've eaten with them, which allows new plants to sprout and helps other birds make future homes. Flycatchers stuff the roofs of thatched houses with moss, thereby adding stability and durability.

The Tz'utujil assert that bird calls not only are signals for people and other birds but also bring into existence the changes in the annual natural cycle. They say there is a type of bird that calls the wind of January, another that calls the pollen haze of March, and yet another calls the fuchsia cactus flowers in July. The appearance of hummingbirds brings an end to the dry season.[14]

So integral are birds to the Tz'utujil way of life that they think of themselves as *ajz'ikinjay* (people of birds).[15] Intricate, brightly colored bird motifs are embroidered on women's huipiles and men's pants.

On my first day at Sanjuanerita, I fretted the staff wouldn't accept me. I was replacing a young, fun American woman with excellent Spanish who had been there for four years. After two weeks of language school, I hoped I had improved enough to make my way through.

Would I be able to deliver on what they wanted from me? The staff said they wanted someone to source medicine and supplies from the US, yet I had few contacts. Kenneth wanted someone who could control the pharmacy inventory, yet I had never done that. I had never managed a clinic and, despite having a graduate degree in public health, had not worked in a direct-care medical setting since my high school candy-striper days. Though I had been honest about my experience, would they think I was a fraud?

I walked into the salón to find balloons and streamers hung from the ceiling and construction-paper cutouts spelling *Bienvenida Jan* posted on the wall. Patients who had all been waiting since before the doors opened

---

[14] See note 12.

[15] Vincent Stanzione. 2003. *Rituals of Sacrifice: Walking the Face of the Earth on the Sacred Path of the Sun.* University of New Mexico Press.

and were now seated in plastic chairs smiled curiously at me. Tulita, the receptionist, warmly greeted me at the door in Tz'utujil: "*Saquari, Jan*" ("Good morning," or literally "The sun has risen").

While Tulita fetched Kenneth, I looked around the salón, which had once been the sanctuary of a Methodist church. Several teams of volunteers from US churches had flown south to pour money and time into renovating the former church into a clinic. The dais that once supported the pastor now supported Tulita's desk and the laboratory. The walls had been painted a sunny yellow and bloomed with colorful health-education posters. A kaleidoscope of light streamed in from the remaining stained-glass windows.

When Kenneth walked into the salón, he greeted me with another big hug. He promptly handed me off to Ines, a nurse filling in as the interim administrator since my predecessor had left, to show me around the clinic and reintroduce me to the folks I'd met during the interview. She knew everything about the clinic's operations, so she was to take me under her wing to orient me.

Ines explained that the staff who worked in the mornings in Sanjuanerita also worked in the afternoons at Chuitinamit in San Pablo. She would do the tour of that clinic after lunch.

To begin the Sanjuanerita tour, we stepped onto the dais and into the laboratory, which was a small room stocked with little more than a few test strips, broken blood pressure cuffs, and a microscope that no one knew how to use. There, she introduced me to Herlinda, who had been staffing the laboratory while Ines served as the administrator. These two women seemed quite different. Ines spoke fast and fluttered about, making sharp gestures with her hands. With her small, squinty eyes and tightly coiled and clasped hair, my first impression was that she was no-nonsense. In contrast, Herlinda had a lilting laugh and swanned around the laboratory as she showed me her work. Her long, flowing curls framed her face, which featured large eyes and a broad smile. Their easy rapport was evident. They each beamed and listened attentively while the other spoke.

Rather than rushing through the rest of the clinic, we lingered in laboratory, and they told me about their jobs and how they came to ODIM. Ines began working with ODIM as a receptionist shortly after it was founded and learned about health by helping in the laboratory. Taking advantage of the scholarships ODIM offered, she studied for her technical-level nursing degree on Saturdays for several years, sacrificing precious time with her young family. When she finished her degree, she continued to work in the laboratory, helped in the pharmacy, provided family-planning methods, and counseled patients.

Herlinda had started as a part-time *promotora* with the diabetes program and, like Ines, had taken advantage of ODIM's scholarship opportunities to study nursing. The plan was that as Ines transitioned back to the laboratory upon my arrival, Herlinda would leave for her nursing-school clinical rotation in a hospital for three months.

Since Herlinda was getting busy, Ines took me to the exam room of the nurse-midwife Navichoc, who provided prenatal care and postpartum home visits as part of *Mamá y Yo Saludable* (Healthy Mommy and Me). This maternal- and child-health program focused on the first thousand days of a child's life after conception. Navichoc had cartons of eggs and nutritional supplements stacked in the corner and piles of newborn supplies on her shelves. She told me that when the rest of the interior of the clinic was painted, she had the walls in her exam room painted a deep violet so that the darkness could help her read the ultrasound. In the renovations, Navichoc left a stained-glass window uncovered, though. I wondered if she did this to help with the many prayers that must have been said in this space.

Across the hall from Navichoc's room was that of Tomás, the only male nurse. With his hair spiked with gel and his white coat flouncing behind him like a tail, he reminded me of a rooster. Unlike Ines and Herlinda, he had not finished his nursing degree. However, he had the privileged position of providing consults to patients—because he had shadowed the international medical volunteers—and the correspondingly higher salary that accompanied the additional responsibility. When we met, I expected him to crow about how he had been with ODIM since its founding and boast about his standing. However, he spoke gently, kindly.

Tulita had recently finished a social work degree with the support of ODIM's scholarships but had not been promoted from her position as a receptionist. Single and in her midtwenties, she walked with a lightness that the married women and mothers did not have. Her family owned the one shoe store in town, and fashion was quite important to her. She pointed out the women's cortes, blusas, and fajas and told me about their designs and what part of the country they represented. She said she liked to mix up styles by putting together pieces from different regions.

Dra.[16] Vacinta was from Xela and had come to this Tz'utujil village for her first job out of medical school because a family friend who lived in San Marcos suggested the area. She was clear that although she had accepted a year-long contract with ODIM, she aspired to be a surgeon in a big city, not to do primary care in an under-resourced clinic in a remote part of the country. Dra. Vacinta informed me that she might have to miss some days to go to conferences and take exams so that she could pursue her specialty. Because she wore Western clothes rather than a corte, I was surprised to learn later that Dra. Vacinta was a K'iche' woman. Her language being similar to the patients', she could communicate somewhat in Tz'utujil.

Manuela, the woman who managed the pharmacy, darted her eyes around the room and fidgeted with her hands as she explained to me that she had joined ODIM after Hurricane Stan to help distribute blankets and food. Though it appeared that she could speak Spanish as fluently as the rest of the staff, she did not answer me directly when I asked her questions but instead went through Ines to interpret from Tz'utujil to Spanish. Did she feel limited in her Spanish, or was she nervous about me?

I looked around and saw that all the education posters on the walls were in Spanish, but the only Spanish I heard was what was spoken to me. Should I have put my energy into learning Tz'utujil rather than brushing up on Spanish?

Since all the other team members had shared their ambitions with me,

---

[16] Abbreviation for *doctora* (female doctor).

I asked Manuela what she wanted. She was not pleased with commuting to San Pablo in the afternoons to substitute for Herlinda in the Chuitinamit pharmacy while Herlinda was covering for Ines. However, this arrangement would continue since Herlinda would be leaving soon for her clinical rotation. Manuela claimed that she had no interest in studying. She wanted to do her job in San Juan and nothing more.

Next, Ines escorted me to a two-story building adjacent to the clinic, also constructed by US church team volunteers. It held the dental clinic on the first floor, an administrative office on the second, and what once had been a medicinal plant garden on the roof. The dentist, Dr. Otto, was dressed in trendy glasses and a Che Guevarra T-shirt. He immediately told me that he had been born and educated in Guatemala City. Rather than live in San Juan, he resided in Santiago Atitlán, a much larger town on the southern side of the lake, where he had another part-time job in a US-run private hospital. Otto added that he depended on his assistant, Hilda, to interpret from Tz'utujil to Spanish and that he had recently traveled to Europe to visit his German girlfriend. I interpreted this self-description as an attempt to distinguish himself from the Indigenous staff.

Seated quietly in the back of the dental clinic was Hilda. She handled the dental instruments for Otto and fitted patients with their loaner hearing aids—*loaners* because the recipients had to promise that if they died, the hearing aids would be returned to the clinic for another patient to use. She supplemented her part-time hours as a promotora for the diabetes program, for which she checked patients' A1C levels, visited them at home, and helped with group education sessions.

Ines took me up the spiral staircase to the administrative office shared by Kenneth; Oscar, the accountant/business manager; and Alba, the volunteer coordinator. Oscar jumped up from behind his computer to shake my hand. He seemed charged with nervous energy, which may have been because (as I later learned) his pregnant wife was due with their first child or because he was simply the most extroverted member of the staff. From his perch, he was the ultimate insider and knew about all the operations.

Alba, still seated, glanced at me over her laptop computer screen.

Quiet and sober, she had dedicated her life to building a career rather than starting a family. Her parents once owned a hotel and restaurant on the shore that put them solidly in the middle class, which enabled her to study medicine in Xela. While she was in university, her family's property was engulfed by the rising lake water in less than a week. The total loss of their property and sole source of income left the family in dire financial straits, so she had to withdraw from her studies. She was the only staff member fluent in Tz'utujil, Spanish, and English. She served as the liaison with the volunteer teams from US churches and oversaw the diabetes program.

Hannah, an Anglophone Canadian, managed the community programs—diabetes, maternal and child health, and scholarships for children. Fluent in French after years of living in Quebec, she easily mastered Spanish. We only spoke briefly when she flew into the office to grab some materials before heading off to Chuitinamit in San Pablo, where a support group for new mothers was being held that morning.

After all the obligatory salutations, Ines escorted me to meet Kenneth in the *nido* (nest), which was what they called the roof. It was the only quiet space, at least when the *molina* (corn mill) next door was not grinding. There, Kenneth shared with me the history of ODIM. After Hurricane Stan in 2005, groups of US church volunteers and local people had gathered metaphorical twigs and twine to build a refuge for the community. Their dedication and resourcefulness inspired me.

I hoped I would fit in with my new flock. To do well at this job, I would have to observe how the staff circled each other, to listen to their calls, to heed their warnings, and to recognize their signals.

Like Western or Hellenistic astrology, Maya astrology sees energies that connect the individual, the earth, and the cosmos. In both systems, the date and location of one's birth can determine one's personality, characteristics, and even future. Whereas Western astrology has twelve signs based on constellations of stars light years away, Maya astrology has twenty *nawales*

(spirits or energies) based on the movement of the earth around the sun. Rather than being influenced by stars whose light may be reaching us long after they are dead, we are influenced by objects and beings with which we are in relationship, with which we occupy the same time and space.

Nawales are ascribed not only to people but also to all things. Everything has a spirit. Nawales are characterized by different animals, colors, cardinal directions, elements, energies, and traits, and are symbolized by hieroglyphics.

My nawal is *no'j*, represented by the woodpecker; so, like the Tz'utujil, I am also a bird person. No'j symbolizes the motion of the sky and the earth. It aims to combine the exercise of the brain and engagement of the body—knowledge and experience—into wisdom. The bird energy of no'j rises above and carefully observes, which allows it to learn. Sight from above can lead to insight within.

Characteristics ascribed to no'j include intelligence, dedication to medicine, dreaminess, bravery, and defending justice. People who are no'j are idealists and have difficulty coming down to reality. They were born to bring about changes. They are intuitive and prophets of the new way of life. Not always at ease with themselves, they can adapt to what fate has in store for them. The search for clarity and the profound mark their existence.

However, they lack the cunning to achieve their goals. Their sincerity can hurt others and be interpreted as being proud, overbearing, and arrogant. In matters of love, no'j perseveres. People who are no'j are faithful by nature, desire peaceful relationships, and give their partners a lot of space.

Would these no'j traits be borne out for me in Guatemala? While some instantly resonated with me, for others I would have to wait and see.

9

ASSEMBLING THE NEST

AS MUCH AS I cared about finding my bearings at my job, it was even more important to me that Lucia be in a good situation. I stacked twigs and sticks one by one to build a nest where she could thrive. I had brought magazines and workbooks to supplement her learning, arranged two weeks of Spanish-language study, enrolled her in a school with international students, and secured a lovely, if temporary, place to live.

I knew that if I was anxious about starting a new job, Lucia must be even more so about starting a new school. As we headed out to Escuela Caracol for her first day, she asked, "What if they don't like me? Can't you just homeschool me?"

"Sweetie, I can't homeschool you full-time and do my job. I'm sure you'll make friends soon. I'm working part-time my first week, so I'll be able to pick you up every day. Maybe we can arrange a playdate with the other kids."

It was a short walk down our street and then up a rock path to Escuela Caracol. Standing at the large wooden front door of the high bamboo fence that enclosed the campus, we had to pull a rope to ring a bell to announce our arrival.

"Doesn't this seem like something from a Harry Potter movie?" I asked.

"No, and you've never watched a Harry Potter movie," she curtly responded.

The grounds were nothing like the cement-block buildings and concrete yards I had seen in Guatemalan public schools and quite different from the large, institutional elementary school Lucia had attended in Seattle. A canopy of tall trees towered over the classrooms and other buildings that were connected by winding stone paths.

Natalia's classroom was a hexagon-shaped building filled with light and decorated with the year's art projects. On a cabinet sat a row of toothbrushes in cups and a stack of drawings yet to be hung. A case held two or three dozen children's books, which were among the few in the region. The village had no library or bookstore. Around the room were a dozen small desks and chairs painted with the children's names. Natalia pointed to an unpainted chair and desk and said, "Lucia, this will be your seat. You can paint your name and add any design you want."

Lucia and I looked around the classroom while Natalia drew on the chalkboard a hieroglyphic of the numbers and nawal representing the date according to the Maya calendar. I remarked to Lucia, "Don't you think that it is ironic that your teachers in Seattle write the date in Spanish on the board, and now that we are in a Spanish-speaking country, the teacher writes the date in Maya?"

Lucia didn't respond to my observations or Natalia's orientation. I looked at Natalia and gave an apologetic shrug. Picking up my cue, she placed her hand on Lucia's shoulder and said, "Last year, the class built a rabbit cage as an exercise in math, planning, and cooperation. Would you like to see the bunnies?"

Lucia perked up. "Oh, yes!"

When we reached the cage outside, Lucia's mood shifted even more. She let herself into the cage and chased around the black-and-white rabbits. She caught a small, quiet one hiding behind a bowl of water. Holding the little creature close to her chest, she cooed and stroked his head. Pausing to allow Lucia time, Natalia said, "We started with just a couple of rabbits last year, and then . . ."

"And then they bred like rabbits, right?"

"Exactly!" Natalia replied, and we both laughed.

We walked back to the classroom, which was already filling up with the kids. I sensed that Natalia was ready for me to leave so that she could start the day. Despite my assertions to Lucia that she would be in a good place, I was as hesitant to leave her this day as I had been on the first day of preschool.

Clutching my backpack, I said to Natalia, "I'm worried about Lucia making friends. She's not the kind of kid that jumps in and joins a group easily. Please let me know what I can do to help."

"This is a lovely group of children," she reassured me. "We will make her feel welcome."

Later that evening and every day thereafter, I tried to pry stories about school and the children out of Lucia. She said Natalia was "nice," but apart from math, she didn't understand what was discussed in class. She told me about the kids whose families owned hotels and the restaurants we frequented, a boy genius who was learning English on his own and was appointed to be the class doctor, and a girl whom Lucia was helping with reading. In the early days of starting school, whenever I asked Lucia about playing with the children, she claimed that she spent most of recess in the trees, watching the kids below, or in the bunny cage.

Helping Lucia find friends was an ongoing struggle. The girls in Lucia's class were kind, but due to differences in language and culture, she did not feel connected to them. After the Cox family came to our house for lunch, Lucia and Piñita didn't hang out again. I met an English man who owned a restaurant in San Marcos who also had a ten-year-old daughter and arranged for the girls to go horseback riding together. However, we did not see her again afterward, since the girl studied and spent most of her time with her mother in Panajachel, a large town on the other side of the lake.

I also had to find after-school care for Lucia. Kenneth permitted me to work part-time so that I could pick her up after school the first week, but after that, she would need something to do and someone to watch her until I came home. There were no programs because all the children had mothers who did not work full-time or had family at home to care for them, so I would have to find a *niñera* (nanny).

The owner of our borrowed house had put together a book of suggestions for restaurants, hikes, laundry facilities, and domestic help. Listed in the recommendations was Pedrina, a Kachiquel woman who had helped his guests with cleaning, washing, and childcare. I called Pedrina on the new *frijolito* (how Guatemalans refer to a flip phone) I had bought in San Pedro. Our call was so staticky that we could not understand each other, so she invited me to her home to talk.

She lived with her family in a compound of small, one-room buildings—some made with mud, some with cinder blocks—with an open patio in the middle. The buildings shared overlapping slabs of tin for a roof and packed dirt for a floor. Nothing hung on the walls, not even the free calendars with political propaganda that wallpapered many Guatemalan homes. A couple of other young women peeked out of doorways, toddlers whizzed by us, and an elderly woman kneeling at her backstrap loom gave us a toothless grin.

Pedrina was in her early thirties and single with no children, she told me, so she would be able to work most anytime I needed. When she came to our house to see us the next day, she plopped down on the sofa. She relayed how she had been the live-in niñera for a Canadian writer and her two young children at the house for several months.

"I can do the same for you. I can sleep downstairs, and you can sleep upstairs."

"Uh, no, that's not necessary. I wouldn't want to keep you from your family," I explained.

"Well, at least I can cook for you. Just leave money for me, and I'll do the shopping and have dinner ready when you come home."

Though it would have been nice to come home to a hot meal, I didn't want to send her home with an empty belly and dinner on the stove, nor did I want to invite her to join us. At the end of a long day in Spanish, I just wanted to come home to my child, speak English, and decompress. I did not want another person I needed to attend to in my space. Plus, the thought of having someone serving me in my house made me cringe.

Despite this, on many rainy evenings, I did send her home with an empty belly.

"Why don't you borrow my jacket and return it tomorrow? Here's a flashlight. Be careful!" I would tell her as if I were trying to be helpful, but I was actually embarrassed by my actions.

Although I wished that my alone time with Lucia was spent cuddling on the couch and sharing the wonders of the day, our nightly battles were often a variation of the following:

"Go ahead and do your workbook while I make dinner."

"Ugh! I already do math at school."

"Yeah, but since you are in a lower grade here, you need to do extra to keep up with your grade level in the States."

"I don't care! I don't want to do math. I can't do this! The workbook is too hard."

"Look, I bet you already know most of what is in that workbook since you covered much of the material in school in Seattle."

"No! I don't know any of it!"

Twenty minutes later, as I brought to the table a simple stir-fry of vegetables bought at the produce stand while rushing home, I noted the blank pages she was hovering over.

"You haven't done anything!"

"It's too hard for me. I haven't learned how to do these types of problems."

"Okay. Put it away for now and then try again after dinner while I do the dishes. How was school today?"

"Terrible!"

"Why?"

"I don't understand anything that is going on."

"Come on now, Lucia. You must understand something. You've been going to a bilingual school since kindergarten."

"Yeah, but those kids all spoke English, too. I don't have anyone to talk to. I don't have any friends."

"Well, what did you do after school today?"

"All I do after school is climb trees and read."

"Do you talk with Pedrina? Do you try to practice Spanish with her?"

"No, when we get home, she just cleans." Noting my tacit approval of Pedrina's dedication to duty, Lucia went on, "She also plays with your makeup and puts on your lotions."

"Lucia, you are just trying to tattle. I don't care if she uses my lotion. What she uses probably cost me pennies, and Pedrina will live her whole life in a village that doesn't even sell lotion."

And then the tears would flow from both of us. This was not the home environment I wanted to foment.

When Kenneth told me that the staff had arranged a party for me and Lucia at Las Cristalinas, the only restaurant on the road between San Pablo and San Juan, I first thought how my "welcome" at my last job in Seattle had been my new boss cleaning my desk before she left for her three-week vacation the next day without telling me. I also thought this would be an opportunity for us to connect with the staff and for us to get out of our grind and have fun with each other. Since the party was to be held on Lucia's early-release day at Escuela Caracol, Pedrina would have time to pick her up and have her change into the blusa and corte Josefina made before meeting us there.

At the restaurant, I sat at the opposite end of the table from Kenneth and Hannah to resist the temptation to fall into English. Dra. Vacinta and Dr. Otto had already left for their homes in the city, so I was with just the Tz'utujil staff. Sure, they wanted to pull together an event to welcome me, but I could tell they also wanted time to be together. Happy to be invited to one of the best restaurants in the area, they chatted, joked, and laughed nonstop in Tz'utujil. Apart from "thank you" and "good morning," I didn't understand a word.

I could or should have interjected with questions in Spanish, but after more than an hour waiting for Lucia and Pedrina, I was preoccupied with thoughts of what might have happened. *Were they lost, out of money, arguing, or kidnapped?* My stomach churned with dread compounded by the cyanobacteria illness from a week before. I couldn't call Pedrina because I was out of range of a cell tower.

Pedrina and Lucia finally arrived over two hours late. I jumped up to question Pedrina about the delay. She had misunderstood the pickup time. When I had informed her that school ended "*a las doce*" (at twelve) on Fridays, she thought I said "*a las dos*" (at two).

Frustrated, I reviewed the numbers one to twelve with Pedrina in Spanish, which was a second language for us both. Neither of us could distinguish between each other's pronunciation of dos and doce so I told her next time I would write down the times and draw a clock.

Oscar invited Pedrina to stay for lunch, and she eagerly accepted. She easily slipped into conversation in, as far as I could tell, a hybrid of their Tz'utujil and Kachiquel dialects. At my end of the table, I fell into English with Lucia. She was starving because she had not eaten since breakfast and mad for having to wait alone in the class with Natalia until Pedrina picked her up. I couldn't touch my food, and when no one was looking, I slipped away to throw up outside. Lucia's mood picked up after lunch when we joined the staff for games.

That evening, Lucia and I were both overwhelmed by the overstimulation of the day. I was too nauseous to cook dinner, too drained to argue about math, too tired to even tidy up the house. Instead, I pulled out the Kindle and read to Lucia in bed for hours. We turned our backs to each other and pressed our feet together, her toes curling inside mine. She did have fun running around and playing games, but this was how she really wanted to spend her time. I had been so caught up in trying to organize our lives, stacking all the pieces together, that I had not attended to what lies in between.

The twigs and sticks in a nest merely form the lattice that serves as a supporting structure. Birds affix up to five types of additional linings to actually make it a home.[17] The first type is to fill the spaces in the lattice—this can be needles, reeds, mosses, lichen, or smaller bits of twigs. Feathers and down in the second lining insulate and cushion the eggs. To provide camouflage for the eggs, there is a third type of lining that consists of concealing ornaments, such as stones, rock shards, and shells, or a fourth type that can include remnants of nests of other animals, such as squirrels and mice.

The fifth type of lining, artifacts, includes an array of shiny, eye-catching objects like glass, shards of porcelain, or metal scraps. These manufactured or natural materials are poorly suited for use in a nest and can harm the fledglings. A study of woodpecker species found that many of their young that had died in their nests had a potentially lethal shiny stone or piece of glass in their stomachs. The study's author, a Finnish man, questioned why natural selection would permit the continuation of a misguided behavior that can be harmful to a species' young. He hypothesized that the birds mistook the objects for glossy ants or other bugs. The birds wanted to give their babies something to nourish them but instead hurt them.[18]

This nest I was building with Lucia also had several linings. I was trying to stuff materials in the open space of the lattice to hold her and fill it with objects to protect her. I wanted to line our nest with soft feathers to keep her warm, yet at the same time, I added shiny objects that sickened her.

Perhaps the researcher was misguided in his focus on the mother birds' questionable behavior. Perhaps these birds construct and fortify their nests with everything they think will help their offspring. Instead of questioning natural selection or the birds' judgment, perhaps it is natural that while some of the things these mothers do will help their offspring, some things will hurt. But everything they do is out of their love for their children.

---

[17] https://web.stanford.edu/group/stanfordbirds/text/essays/Nest_Lining.html

[18] Terhivuo, Juhani. 1977. "Occurrence of strange objects in nests of the Wryneck *Jynx torquilla*." *Ornis Fennica* 54:66–72.

10

EL CAMBALACHE

NATALIA TOLD ME about *El Cambalache* (swap meet), a community center with various courses and activities directly across from Escuela Caracol. I took Lucia to a children's dance class, hopeful that she would find someone with whom to connect or at least have a good time. While she was in the studio with a dozen younger children, I waited outside on the terrace. I chatted with a couple of the other moms—Emma, a Dane who owned a hotel popular with backpackers, and Lana, a Croatian who lived off earnings from trading stocks online.

"My daughter and I are staying in a nearby house that was lent to us for a few weeks, but we have to find a permanent place to stay. I've been looking for weeks and can't find anything decent within my budget. Do you have any suggestions?"

With a chuckle, Lana said, "Well, it is high season for tourists, so there's a lot of competition. What have you seen?"

"First, we saw a round house with a waterfront view on the edge of San Pablo. It's owned by an Australian named Simon. It was too expensive and too far from the school."

"Oh, Simon! He's married to a young Kachiquel woman, and they have a side pizza delivery business," Lana commented.

"I saw a studio apartment owned by an older American man, Michael. He used to be a Mennonite carpenter and built incredible cabinetry."

"Yeah, he has a blues bar. He plays guitar there sometimes," Emma said.

"And he's also married to a young Kachiquel woman, by the way," Lana added.

"Ugh, is that a thing here?" I asked, to which they both nodded. "Then we saw a one-room house with no running water and a squat latrine. There is no way I could get my daughter to squat to shit," I said as we all started laughing.

"That's owned by the Dutch guy, Karl, right? He lives just above in a huge house," said Emma.

"And there was a French guy who showed us a series of dumpy, cobweb-covered shacks all with the same owner. I don't know how anyone could live in those houses, but they appear to have been occupied," I said, thinking about the embedded glass details, tissue paper streamers, chimes, and beads in each.

"Those must have been Clementine's properties," suggested Lana. "She splits her time between here and the States. She has a lot of junk housing that she rents to tourists trying to get by on a shoestring. The guy who showed you her properties was probably Theo. He's a teacher at *Las Piramides*."

"*Las Piramides*?" I asked. "Is that the pyramid-shaped yurts in the gringo section?"

Lana answered, "Yes, people from Europe and North America pay about one thousand dollars a month to study courses on the sun, moon, yoga, whatever."

"People pay that much to stay in a yurt in one of the poorest countries in the Western Hemisphere?" I asked incredulously.

Noting my sarcastic tone, Emma said, "We provide space at our hotel for guests to offer yoga and meditation classes and all kinds of therapies. That's how we make our real money. I think travelers benefit from bartering their knowledge."

When the class ended, the kids trickled out, and my ten-year-old, who had been dancing around the house since she could walk, moped down the stairs. Putting my arm around her, I asked, "How was it?"

"It was so babyish. We danced around with scarves."

"Wasn't it fun to be with other kids?"

"I suppose so."

"Hey, look, I met two moms of girls at your school. Let's introduce you to them."

At five years old, Emma's daughter, Amelia, was half Lucia's age and likely the target audience for the scarf dancing. I didn't see a friendship forming there. Lana's daughter, Stela, was just a year younger than Lucia. She warmly smiled at Lucia and greeted her in perfect English. Stela was in a grade below Lucia, so they had not met. I hoped they would connect.

Lana and I exchanged phone numbers, and within a couple of days, she called to invite Lucia to go swimming at a friend's pool. When she came to pick up Lucia at our temporary home, she inspected the house while Lucia finished getting ready.

"I see by the bamboo framing and adobe walls Charlie must have built this. He's the best on the lake," she commented.

"Yeah, I think so. I think he also designed the clinic in San Pablo. It has a similar style."

"I wish I could afford Charlie, but he's also the most expensive."

"Afford him for what?" I asked.

"I'll show you when we get back," she promised.

When they left, it was the first time I had been alone in my home in the month we had been in Guatemala. With Lucia gone and nothing to do, I realized how much I also missed my friends. I had no one with whom to share my fears and frustrations or even laugh over a glass of wine. Whenever I tried to talk with my friends in the States over Skype, Lucia would get between me and the computer, making even casual conversations difficult and private conversations impossible. I took advantage of the time to call every friend in the US but couldn't reach anyone. I felt even lonelier than before.

When Lana and the girls returned, I invited them inside for a snack while Lucia showered and changed.

"Now I'll show you what I was talking about," Lana said. We all walked down to the center of San Marcos to catch a tuk-tuk. "We could walk all the way up the hill, but the girls are too exhausted," she commented. Lana scoffed when the tuk-tuk driver offered to take us a few hundred meters for twenty quetzales. "The tuk-tuk drivers and the lancha pilots want to charge us two or three times what the locals pay because we're foreigners, but I won't stand for it."

"Yeah, I've noticed. I told Lucia that it's the 'gringo tax.'"

We both laughed, and the four of us piled into the tuk-tuk. We got out when the paved road ended halfway up the hill. Lana pointed at the dirt path ahead. "We have to walk the rest of the way."

On the path through the temperate rainforest, birds and butterflies circled over our heads, and critters scurried at our feet. This was the type of hike I had hoped we would be taking each weekend. Just when I thought Lucia might be reaching her limit, we came upon a clearing on a plateau.

"This is my parcel of land," Lana proudly announced. "I bought it this week. I've started clearing the land and want to build a house."

"Wow, this is amazing," I told her. "How did you buy this? Are you planning to stay in San Marcos for the long term?"

She explained that a Kachiquel friend helped her negotiate a reasonable price. She wanted to build a retreat center with an adjoining house for her and Stela. Since she'd spent most of her savings on the property, money for the construction was limited.

Stela pointed out the fuzzy caterpillars found only at this elevation, and then the girls took off to explore the area. Lana and I sat on some rocks and admired the view of the lake and town below. We sat in an easy silence, both happy that the girls were getting along.

An idea suddenly occurred to me.

"Lana, you know what you should do? Become a guru. You could wear a long, white robe, put a flower in your hair, and write some nonsense sayings on the internet. You can get a bunch of backpackers to come for weeklong spiritual retreats. In the mornings, they clear your land and build your house. You feed them lunch, and then in the afternoons, you sit with them to meditate. You can blather random drivel in Croatian and then tell them what you think they want to hear. People here pay a lot of money for that kind of stuff, right? You know, you could have like an Eastern European kibbutz."

"I like the way you think," she snickered. "And the backpackers, they would all be hot young men, right?"

"Of course! It couldn't be any other way! Hey, I'll help by being a guest speaker. I can make up crap too," I offered.

"So that you can have your pick of them," she teased.

"Why else?" I joked. "I mean, if all the gringo men our age are going after young women, why can't we go for younger men?"

Hearing our laughter, Lucia bounced down the rocks above to eavesdrop on our conversation. "What are you talking about?" she asked.

"Oh, just Lana's plans for her land," I answered.

Partially satisfied with my answer, she ran back up to Stela and continued playing. Lana and I shifted from planning our futures to sharing our pasts. Like me, she had come to Guatemala years before having a child and found it magical. Unlike me, she had come back with her husband and daughter. When her marriage fell apart, her husband left, and she stayed behind with Stela, hoping to give her the same experiences I wanted for Lucia.

I was able to share everything I had told Lourdes, but this time was different. Though we were from different countries, we were closer in age and shared a Western worldview. She understood the heartache of a broken marriage, the headache of negotiating a new life with an ex, and the fear-induced angst of solo parenting in another country.

I had gone to *El Cambalache* seeking friends for Lucia and found one for myself.

11

WHAT IS YOUR PLAN, JAN?

THOUGH LIVING IN San Marcos allowed Lucia to be close to her school, I had an hour-long commute to the clinic in San Juan. In the mornings, I traversed the quaint center of San Marcos down to the dock and greeted the shop owners sweeping their stoops and the women selling fruit from their baskets. Unlike the bus stops in Seattle, where blurry-eyed commuters are glued to their cell phones, the dock was where I made the acquaintance of expats and locals living in San Marcos, heard the town gossip, and had random conversations with a traveler or two.

Since I was trying to live within my $500-a-month salary, I begged the lancha pilot to allow me to pay the local fare, half of what foreigners were charged. If I was lucky, he would acquiesce, and if I was unlucky, he wouldn't bother stopping at San Juan and instead go directly to San Pedro and still charge me the double fare. Then I would have to take a tuk-tuk to San Juan. Every day I left my house, I was uncertain about how and when I would arrive at work.

The clinic in San Juan opened at eight o'clock in the morning, which was also the bell time at Escuela Caracol. This meant that in order to drop Lucia off at school, I would be nearly an hour late for work. I felt guilty about arriving well after the staff and patients, so I wasted no time when I showed up. I hurried into my office and quickly responded to the day's messages. I threw myself into organizing the garbage bags full of papers and the boxes of files that had accumulated for months.

After a couple of days of watching me rush around, Kenneth pulled me aside to say, "Hey, take your time to talk to folks. They need to get to know you to feel comfortable working with you."

Of course, he was right. The primary reason I was in Guatemala was for Lucia and me to get to know and love the country through our relationships with other people.

Then Kenneth added, "I want you to get this book, *The First 90 Days*, which is about how to set priorities for the first three months at work. Read it this week and make a plan for your orientation, including what you would need to succeed."

Alas, there was no way Lucia would allow me to sit at night and read a book that I wasn't reading to her. Even in Seattle, she demanded every bit of my attention after being away from me all day. But reading a book at work would make me seem even more antisocial. I needed to make a plan to find time to make a plan.

The way ODIM managed two clinics in two communities was to serve patients at Sanjuanerita in the mornings, close for two hours so that the staff could go home for lunch with their families, and then reconvene in the afternoon at Chuitinamit in San Pablo. Since I didn't have time to go all the way to San Marcos and still make it to San Pablo for the second shift, I had lunch alone in San Juan—either leftovers or a little sandwich of bread, tomato, and avocado from the tienda next door. Chuitinamit closed after the last patient served left, usually by five thirty, and I had to rush home to get to a hungry Lucia by six. Why hadn't I let Pedrina cook?

I came up with an idea that I thought would allow me a better work–life balance. At our weekly staff meeting, I suggested, "Why don't we shorten the lunch break to thirty minutes so that we could start and end the San Pablo clinic earlier? Those of us who finish early at Sanjuanerita could open Chuitinamit at one o'clock, and we could all be done by four o'clock. Wouldn't that be great if we were home earlier?"

I looked around at the stunned faces of the staff. If I had been in the

States, it would have been as if I'd asked my colleagues to cut their pay so they could work less at the end of the day.

Oscar jumped in first: "How would we be able to eat?"

Ines asked, "How would I be able to *tortear* so that my family can eat?"

Tomás added, "Since my children live with their mother, it's the only time of day I get to see them."

All the other staff concurred with a resounding "no."

Soon after starting my orientation, Ines informed me, "We have five nursing students who will be starting their practicum in the clinic next week."

"That's nice."

"What is your plan for how they will work?"

"I have to come up with a plan?" I asked with what I am sure was a dumbfounded look.

"Yes," responded Ines. "They are *bachillerato*[19] students at a school in Panajachel"—referring to the main town on the other side of the lake.

Oh, no, I thought. I would have to supervise a group of sixteen- and seventeen-year-olds on top of learning about the clinic and the rest of my job.

"Ines, I have no idea what to do," I confessed. "What do you suggest?"

"You can assign one each to Dra. Vacinta and Tomás in their exam rooms, Manuela in the pharmacy, Navichoc in prenatal care, and Herlinda in the laboratory, and then rotate them weekly for the five weeks," Ines instantly replied as if she knew the plan already.

"Sounds good," I agreed. "And also, Ines, *maltiox* [thank you, in Tz'utujill]."

---

[19] *Bachillerato* is equivalent to high school in the US.

"What were your takeaways from *The First 90 Days*?" Kenneth asked me. "What is your plan for getting started?"

Oh, God. He really does expect me to read this whole book, I silently lamented.

"Uh, talk to the staff individually to find out what they want from me and for themselves. I'd like to find something that helps me get a small win early so they will have confidence in me." That lesson was what I gleaned from the two chapters I had read.

"Well, since you've been working in finance, could you help review our tax forms? Since ODIM is a US-based organization, we have to file taxes in the States."

"Sure, I'd be happy to help." I agreed, hiding my hesitation. I was barely able to do my own taxes.

"And then you will also need to prepare the staff contracts for the next year. You need to finish them in time to send to the Ministry of Labor for approval."

"Contracts? I thought most of you have been working here for years."

"Yeah, but because of ODIM's legal status and how it pays taxes in Guatemala, we have to have detailed contracts for nationals that guarantee their benefits and rights. You can read about it in the labor code."

Even with a two-week refresher of Spanish under my belt, I didn't think I would be able to understand the nuances of Guatemalan law.

"And while you are putting together the contracts, you should do the annual evaluations of the staff."

"Even though I didn't work with them this past year?"

"It's a good way to learn about the team."

"Uh, okay. I suppose so."

"Great! Let me know by the end of this week your plan for getting all this done."

I popped into the pharmacy to ask Ines and Manuela about the three distinct lists I had found—written in differing combinations of English, Spanish, and French—of the over 200 medications ODIM kept stocked.

Unable to answer my question about which list was correct, Ines asked me, "Jan, what's your plan for getting the medicines that we need? We are out of metformin and are almost out of maybe ten other essential medicines."

"How do you know what you have or are supposed to have in the pharmacy if you don't have a good list?"

"When I dispense the medicines, I rattle the bottles to hear if they are close to empty," Manuela told me.

I knew sorting out stocking would be a big project. I followed up with the question "How do you usually get the medicines?"

Manuela shrugged and answered, "The volunteer teams bring some from the US, and we buy some in Guatemala. That's all I know."

Bewildered, I turned to Ines and asked what to do.

"We have a list of vendors in Xela that I can show you," she offered.

"Jan, what is your plan for the clinic's promotores? I need to know what to pay them for the rest of the year," Oscar asked.

Confused, I turned to Ines and asked, "The clinic has its own promotores? Aren't all the promotores with either the Healthy Mommy and Me or the diabetes programs? What do the clinic promotores even do?" I asked.

"The clinic has forty promotores that come to Sanjuanerita for *charlas* [talks] on Wednesday afternoons," Ines answered.

"But what do they do?" I continued. The promotores I'd worked with during my first job in Guatemala provided primary health care, did outreach and education, and built infrastructure projects. I was so impressed with the model that I took it back to my work in the US.

"We don't ask them to do anything. I suppose it is just good information for the promotores to have."

"I still don't understand. Why give the charlas if we don't have a plan for them to use the information, and why would they take a half day off a week to come to the charlas if we don't have a project for them to engage with?"

"They're not working. They are coming to the charlas hoping that we might start a new program and hire some of them. We do it to stay connected in case we ever have a job opening."

I would have loved to have the time and energy to help the clinic develop a vigorous outreach and education program, but this was too much. I couldn't risk going home so late regularly. If I continued the tradition of Wednesday charlas, I would be stuck in Sanjuanerita until after five and unable to catch a lancha back to San Marcos, resulting in me having to haggle for a tuk-tuk to take me all the way home.

"My plan is to finish the charlas already on the calendar and then use our Wednesday afternoons to take care of our internal business," I explained.

To close the series of charlas, I did a presentation on "*¿Qué afecta la salud?*" (What affects health?). I planned a dynamic, interactive training that I thought might challenge the direction of the clinic. Instead, it fell flat. Folks were confused and gave answers that seemed like they were missing the point.

When I started to feed them suggestions such as "nutrition," "physical activity," and "poverty," Oscar chimed in, "Oh, you mean, '*¿Qué afecta a la salud?*' You have been asking, 'What does health affect?'" I realized I had been asking the question backward and therefore did not get the answers I was seeking.

"Jan, what is your plan for getting a blood analysis machine?" Dra. Vacinta asked. "We have minimal capacity to make diagnoses without sophisticated equipment."

Upon hearing Dra. Vacinta's request, I thought this could be the easy win to give me credibility with staff. I solicited the specifications of the tests needed from the team and searched online for a solution. All the options I saw in the US were either out of our price range or had a warranty that was not transferable to Guatemala. Finding medical supply companies in Guatemala proved more difficult, and finding something we could afford proved impossible. I contacted everyone I knew in health care in the US to solicit a donation and once again came up empty handed.

"Perhaps I could find another easy win?" I suggested to Kenneth.

"Jan, what is your plan for Hilda's absence?" Otto asked, regarding his dental assistant.

"What do you mean, 'for Hilda's absence'?"

Otto looked at me with a mix of embarrassment and confusion. "She's eight months pregnant. She only has two more weeks before her maternity leave starts, so what is your plan?"

Hilda wore her corte tight, and her faja wrapped the top of her belly, so I'd had no idea she was pregnant. Noticing the stunned look on my face, he continued, "I have to have an assistant to help me with the air suction and clean the tools. Otherwise, I can't do my work, and we will have to close the dental clinic."

I turned to Ines once again, desperate for direction.

"Why don't you ask the clinic's promotores if any might be interested in a temporary job as a dental assistant?" she suggested. So, there had been an actual use for the trainings I had just canceled!

The next day, three young women presented themselves at the dental clinic for employment. Otto interviewed each and then told me he needed to observe them in action to know whether they would be comfortable with direct patient contact.

"In action with a patient?" I asked.

In the States, job applicants with no professional license or experience would never be allowed to handle patients for ethical and liability reasons, so in good conscience, I couldn't let the applicants practice on our patients.

"Okay, Otto. I suppose I am your guinea pig."

I leaned back in the dentist's chair and awkwardly greeted each applicant. One by one, I let these young women insert tools and devices into my mouth while Otto examined and cleaned my teeth. The one that did not gag me or try to suction out my lungs got the job.

It seemed like at every turn, I had to make plans. I was daunted by how much I had to learn to be minimally competent. Did I think that I would walk in and solve all their problems? No, of course not. But I did think that I would recognize and address my limitations, apart from language, sooner.

Maybe I'd misunderstood the question "What is your plan?" to be about the plans that I should make for the staff and clinic. Perhaps the question I kept hearing from staff and repeating to myself was "What is the plan for Jan?"

That I didn't know.

12

FOR OUR FAMILIES, FOR OURSELVES

TO CELEBRATE HERLINDA'S last day before leaving for her clinical rotation, I invited her and Ines to lunch at Las Cristalinas on a Friday after the San Pablo clinic closed. As we settled into our seats, we let out a nearly synchronous sigh. We each confessed that this was a rare occasion for us, to have time just to hang out, away from work and mothering. Once we ordered our large platters of food that we did not have to cook on dishes we would not have to wash, we started sharing our stories.

At sixteen years old, Herlinda had committed an *"error"* and consequently had a baby. Her son's father abandoned her and the child, but fortunately, her father was willing to assume responsibility and allowed his surname to be added to the birth certificate. I did not understand whether the grandfather was listed as the father, but I saw that she was grateful that her parents did not turn her out of the house.

When her son, Edmond, entered kindergarten, she took advantage of an opportunity with ODIM to be a diabetes health promotora. She received training on checking blood glucose levels, doing nutritional counseling, and conducting home visits. Through the scholarships that ODIM offered the staff, she started studying nursing on Saturdays. Since she had to cross the lake to Panajachel to go to school, more than an hour away by boat, she sacrificed considerable time with her son and money for travel. She continued to stay engaged in the clinic, learning everything she could about the pharmacy and laboratory. When Chuitinamit had opened in San Pablo the previous year, she was offered the part-time position of staffing the pharmacy.

After nearly three years of study and sacrifice, only a few steps remained to get her degree. First, she had to do a three-month hospital rotation, and then she had to pass an exam. To do this rotation, she needed to move to another part of the country, rent a room with another student, and pay for three meals a day. I didn't know how she would manage this. The scholarship only paid for tuition, not living expenses. Plus, the three months she would be away from work would be unpaid leave. She felt grateful that her family was willing to care for her son while she was gone and equally excited and nervous to be on her own for the first time.

"I've never spent a night away from my parents or my son since he was born, and now I'm going to share a room with two strangers. I think it will be an adjustment, but it could be fun," she added with a sly smile.

"You think?" I prodded jokingly.

"I know it will be fun," she affirmed.

"It was hard when I went away to do my nursing rotation, but my family was fine. My husband, Juan, lost his job at the bank when Frances was small," Ines shared, referring to her now eight-year-old daughter, "so he was already used to doing a lot at home."

"I didn't know that. Is he working now?"

"Sometimes he fishes, sometimes he paints houses, but most of the time he is with Frances. He takes her to school in the morning and picks her up in the afternoon so that she doesn't have to walk across town alone."

"I remember when Lucia's father lost his job soon after she was born, too, so he spent a lot of time with her when she was a baby. I think it made them closer. We lived just a few blocks from where I worked. I was able to go home every day at lunch to nurse Lucia, and he had lunch ready for me."

Ines and Herlinda looked at me incredulously.

"Uh, doesn't Juan do the same for you?" I asked Ines.

"Ay, no! He takes care of Frances, not me. I still have to wake up early in the morning and *tortear* so that we have food for the day, but we often go to my mother's house to eat."

"How have you both been able to study with kids? I can barely get my child to study for herself," I said.

"I live with all of my family, so they help," Herlinda explained.

"Yes, your parents, right?" I asked.

"Well, yes, but I mean *all* of my family. My family's home takes up about two blocks. All of my aunts, uncles, cousins, nieces, and nephews live there," she clarified. Her home was not a house; it was a compound.

"If it weren't for my mother feeding us most days, I never would have been able to study either," Ines added. "The nights were hard, though. With the money I was earning at ODIM, Juan and I could buy a new house, but it didn't have electricity. I had to pay the neighbor to allow me to run an extension cord from her house to ours so that I would have the light of one bulb to study by at night after Frances was asleep."

I wondered whether I could count how many light bulbs were in my home in Seattle.

"Oh, my God, Ines. I've never heard of such a thing. And to think I had to push myself to stay up at night to reread the same book to Lucia ten times."

I was in awe of these women. For several years, I had tossed around the idea of going to nursing school, but I did not know how I would manage motherhood with the extra hours of school and studying on top of working. They did, albeit with help.

I shared that, sadly, my family was not supportive of this move. My father was angry with me, and my sister was indifferent. My daughter did have a father who supported her from afar, but I felt like I was on my own.

Herlinda lamented, "Edmond is angry that I am going away for three months. He's afraid that I am going to have a good time without him."

"Lucia would just be afraid that I would eat something good without her," I joked. "She found an ice cream wrapper in my purse and got mad at me because I had a treat without her."

"Edmond would be furious if I had ice cream without him. That's why I'm careful to get rid of any evidence." Herlinda laughed.

"Frances doesn't care as much about me not sharing a sweet. She just does not want anyone to have my attention. When I would try to study at night, she would cry and cry. That is why I had to wait until she was asleep," Ines told us.

"Lucia is also jealous about my attention. When I try to talk to my friends at home on the computer, she insists on getting between me and the screen. I can't even have a phone conversation without her running up to hear what I'm talking about."

I recalled sitting with Ines in the cramped administrator's office we shared. On the wall hung a drawing Frances had made of her and her mother holding hands. When Lucia joined me at the clinic during one of the many Escuela Caracol closures, she made the same drawing of the two of us. I posted it on the wall by Frances's picture.

"Well, I know Frances is proud of her mother," I pronounced. "As I know Edmond will be proud of his mother." And dear God, I hoped Lucia would be proud of hers.

After our plates were cleared, I needed to hurry back to San Pablo to catch another tuk-tuk to San Marcos. Herlinda and Ines lingered behind, taking their time to finish another soda before plunging back into domestic life.

I hailed a tuk-tuk with a teenage-girl driver. Not only was she the first female driver I had seen, but she was wearing shorts, unusual even for more Westernized teens. I wondered whether her gender or her clothes were more shocking. Was she a young rebel, also pursuing her dreams? I boarded the back seat with an older, heavyset woman and a school-aged child. In the front passenger seat, holding a baby, was a man I presumed to be the cabbie's father because he was schooling her on driving.

The girl hit the gas when she should have hit the brakes and ran over bumps when she should have steered clear. *Why does the one girl driver I've had have to be a student learner?* I mentally grumbled. When we entered San Pablo, she chugged up the steep hill to the corner where passengers disembarked and where I could catch another ride to San Marcos. At the last curve, she lost control of the vehicle and swiveled onto a curb.

The man holding the baby leaped out, so the tuk-tuk lost its balancing weight. The driver's side with the teen driver, the heavyset woman, and the child tipped over and lifted the lighter passenger side with just me into the air. Propelled upward, I grabbed the back bar behind me as I saw the woman's head bang onto the ground.

Dangling from the bar, I dropped a short distance to my feet, then took a step back as a crowd appeared, drawn by the commotion and the screams. The tuk-tuk was righted, and the girl driver and her tutor had disappeared. The woman was now lying unconscious on the ground. A well-meaning man squirted a bag of water on her face. She regained consciousness enough to be helped up. Before I knew it, another tuk-tuk had swooped in to take her to the *centro de salud* (health center). Our clinic was closed for the day; our two nurses were still sipping their sodas at Las Cristalinas. I reached into the tuk-tuk and grabbed my backpack and laptop computer. There was nothing for me to do, so I decided to walk to San Marcos rather than risk another debacle.

When I arrived home, I sent Pedrina home and slipped into my room to call a friend to calm my nerves. I should have known that Lucia would be just outside with her ear pressed against the door.

"MOMMY, ARE YOU HURT?!" Lucia yelled.

"Lucia, I'm fine," I reassured her.

"Please don't be hurt!" she begged.

"No, really, there's nothing to worry about."

I thought about my earlier conversation with Ines and Herlinda. I'd said that Lucia was nosy because she was jealous of me having fun without her, and maybe that was true, but she was also anxious that something might hurt me or take me away from her.

I remember when, as a toddler, she saw me trip over the open dishwasher door and fall onto the rack and pointy utensils. Startled and scratched, I let out a yelp. Terror beset Lucia. Her face turned beet red, and she cried uncontrollably. This time, as I had done when she was a toddler, I wrapped my arms around her and tried to console her.

"It was just a little fall. Look, I'm fine."

How could I make her feel safe and secure in a world where safety and security are an illusion? How could I foster independence in her, something that came so naturally to me, in a country where being so could be perilous? How could I satisfy but not spoil her?

I wondered if Ines and Herlinda faced the same self-doubts, the same pangs of guilt, and also failed at holding back their frustrations. Were they, like me, uneasy about someone jumping off the cart and flipping the whole thing over? Had we not all three had that same experience to some degree?

Was the only option to reach inside for our valuables and continue our journey?

13

CLARA

LUCIA CLAIMED HER only respites at school were hiding in a tree or cuddling with and feeding the bunnies. She begged me for a rabbit to have at home. Since she spent much of her afternoons alone, I acquiesced so she could feel some sort of companionship. We had a cage custom built and adopted a black-and-white rabbit she named Oreo. Lucia was so enamored that she barely complained about the deep scratches from its claws. Pedrina and I spent more than a few afternoons chasing that rabbit all over the grounds after Lucia let it out of the cage.

Most days, when I returned home from work, Lucia was in a tree or upstairs reading alone if she wasn't playing with Oreo. I suggested she use her time alone to call Daddy so that we could make the most of our time together, but she always waited until I was home to call him. Perhaps she wanted to pretend that we were all together, even if it was just virtually.

After a few weeks of Lucia complaining about school, I met with Natalia to discuss what was happening. She confirmed that Lucia kept to herself quite a bit. When I asked why our invitations for playdates went unheeded and were not reciprocated, she told me that families worried about the girls being abused and so preferred for them to play with their siblings and cousins at home rather than in unknown situations at friends' houses.

At Natalia's suggestion, I organized a welcome party for Lucia and invited the girls in her class. Pedrina and I made punch together, and Pedrina purchased sweet bread at the town bakery. While we rushed around getting ready for the party, Lucia wanted to call her friends in Seattle.

About forty-five minutes before the party was to start at two o'clock, one of the girls from the class, Clara, arrived from Santa Cruz, a town about twenty minutes away by lancha. I assumed she came early because the boat schedule was unpredictable. Closer to the start time, the other girls streamed in and greeted each other with giggles. After the girls feasted on the snacks, I suggested they play outside in the garden. This gaggle of girls had been together since kindergarten and had a dynamic that Lucia did not readily fold into. Rather than joining the girls in their conversation, she climbed a tree to watch.

When the afternoon rain began, I brought the girls inside and lured Lucia out of the tree. The sugar-fueled girls started dancing about, so I cranked up the music and suggested a dance party. What I thought was plenty loud was barely audible to the girls accustomed to *BOOM, BOOM, BOOM*. Every time I turned the volume down, a girl would sneak behind me and crank it back up. My noise-sensitive child once again recoiled; it was all I could do to keep her from escaping upstairs.

Eventually, the sugar buzz wore off, and most of the girls went home independently. I invited the parents who came to pick up their kids inside for punch and snacks. One of the mothers asked Clara, "How will you get home since the last lancha passed at five?"

"What do you mean by 'How will you get home?'" I asked.

"The last lancha to Santa Clara passes San Marcos at five o'clock. Since there are no roads to Santa Cruz, the only way to get there is by boat. She will not be able to go home tonight."

"What?!"

The lingering parents all nodded. "She'll have to spend the night with you and take the first lancha in the morning," another mother told me.

This was unfathomable to me. I did not know this child; I certainly did not know her family. If Lucia had been stuck overnight in an unfamiliar place without me, she would have had a fit, as would I. Instead, Clara had a vacant look and a subtle smile. After a bit of prodding of the other parents and frantic calls to Natalia, I discovered that not only did Clara's mother not have a phone, but she didn't even know that Clara was coming to our home. Clara disappeared for days at a time without her mother knowing where she was.

While the other parents shrugged, this was unacceptable for me. I grabbed Clara and Lucia, and we ran down to the dock to see if we could catch a boat headed toward Santa Cruz. After nearly forty-five minutes of waiting, a private boat arrived, making its last drop of the day. I explained the situation to the pilot and beseeched him to take Clara home. He declined, saying he was done for the day, Santa Cruz was in the opposite direction of where he would be docking for the night, and besides, it was the girl's fault for getting in this situation.

I claimed that I was confident that the mother would be perturbed as she did not know where her daughter was. He called his headquarters for permission to give her a ride, provided I pay 300 quetzales (the tariff on a public boat would typically be 5). I pulled out all the crumpled bills and coins I had and gave him 120 quetzales, the equivalent of fifteen dollars, a good day's wage in Guatemala. This was a situation I had no problem throwing money at. He happily took the money and let the girl on board.

Watching the boat first go south to San Pedro to refuel and then backtrack north to Santa Cruz as darkness fell, my mind raced with thoughts. I could never imagine my daughter alone with a man on a lake or not knowing where she was for hours, much less days. Depending on the version of the story I'd heard from the other parents, Clara's mother was either a widow with three children or, worse, had a drunk husband, so her time was filled by working. It was fortunate that her children received scholarships to attend Escuela Caracol, where they were fed at least once a day. On good days, Clara ate one tortilla before coming to school. I also could never imagine what it was like to send your child to another town for school solely because snacks and lunch are provided.

I anguished over whether Clara made it home and was torn with guilt, wondering if I should have let her spend the night and taken her home early the next morning. *How did this situation spin out of control?* I wondered. I told myself that the panic the mother would feel outweighed the risk that something bad could happen. But all the next day, I felt ashamed. *How could I have put that little girl on a boat with a strange man when I should have given her a warm meal and a bed for the night? How could I have invited her to my grand house and not invited her into my home?*

Much to my surprise, on Monday, when I walked into the clinic in San Juan, Clara and her mother were sitting in the salón. Tulita told me that the mother was waiting for her diabetes appointment, and the girl had come to keep her company. I was relieved to see Clara safe with her mother, but I also felt judgmental that she had not taken greater care of her daughter and had kept her out of school for the day. I knelt at the mother's knees, introduced myself, and explained the situation on Saturday. She gave me a faint smile and replied with only a nod, leading me to think she couldn't speak Spanish. It was as if Saturday never happened.

Only later did I learn that Clara had accompanied her mother—a Kachiquel speaker—to interpret for her. Though the neighboring Tz'utujil and Kachiquel spoke similar languages and could understand each other, Spanish was the common language of these Maya communities, as English is often the common language of many Europeans. Since the Escuela Caracol policy was that students who missed the ringing of the school bell were not permitted in, regardless of the reason, Clara would have to cut the whole day of school in order to help her mother in the morning.

Though initially I thought the situation at the party arose from the cascading effects of an inability to communicate (Lucia with her classmates, me with Clara's mother), it may have been caused more by my failure to listen and see. I so desperately wanted to fix Lucia's homesickness and feelings of loss that I tried to fill the holes with new pets, new friends, new larks. Instead, she just wanted to talk with her father and friends back in Seattle and hide. I so urgently wanted to fix the situation with Clara that I didn't stop to ask what the girl wanted.

How could I incorporate the work I was doing at the clinic, of asking each staff person what they wanted, into my life at home rather than assuming I knew what was best? How could I see and hear what was happening around me more clearly, *más clara*?

14

BACH FLOWERS

EVEN WHILE INES had been filling in as the interim administrator, she continued to squeeze in the services she loved and lovingly provided, including *flores de Bach* (Bach flowers). Rather than queuing early, as did the other patients, women would show up in the middle of the clinic hours and tell Tulita, "I'm here for Ines." Knowing what that meant, Tulita would let Ines know that she had another flores de Bach patient. Ines would drop whatever she was doing to greet them and say, "Just a moment. Please, have a seat. Rest."

I had never heard of *flores de Bach*. However, I had seen a sign at one of the holistic healing centers in San Marcos offering the service for a hundred quetzales. I thought this must be another nostrum marketed to travelers.

Nearly a century ago, a Dr. Bach believed that illness resulted from a conflict between the purposes of the soul and one's actions. He also claimed that certain flowers have healing properties, based on their names, appearance, or other characteristics, and that dew found on flower petals retained the healing properties of that plant. He developed a homeopathic treatment of drops derived from the healing flowers' essences for mood disorders such as anxiety and depression. By "essence," he meant a drop could be so diluted that it no longer had any of the original plant, only the residual energy of the plant that was once there.

I looked at the peer-reviewed scientific literature and found no evidence that this treatment was effective.[20] Even though our clinic only charged ten quetzales for a flores de Bach consult, the same price as a general consult, I feared we might be cheating folks. I would have been open to using natural remedies provided they had evidence to back the claims, but I thought this was no better than any of the spiritual snake oil I'd seen in San Marcos.

As part of getting to know the staff, the services they provided, and whether this was a service that was at worst innocuous, I asked Ines if I could observe a flores de Bach session. Since the session would be in Tz'utujil, I would not understand what was being discussed, so there was no risk of breaking confidentiality. When a middle-aged woman came for her treatment the next day, Ines invited me to join them. We three climbed to the roof of the administrative building and settled into the mismatched lawn chairs clustered under the awning.

I knew enough Tz'utujil to greet the lady with, "Good morning. My name is Jan," and then I shut up for the rest of the hour.

Ines opened the woman's file in a manila folder, made some notes, and then seemed to invite the woman to speak. Apart from the occasional modifier in Spanish, I did not understand a word she said, but I did understand every gesture, sigh, and tear. Something had happened that had ruptured her home. She was desolate and did not know what to do. When she paused to take a breath or collect her thoughts, Ines made one or two statements and encouraged her to go on.

As this woman's anguish unfurled, I glanced around at the setting. We were on a garden rooftop with no whining children, no barking dogs, and no chores. If this woman shared the same life as most women I knew there, she lived in a multigenerational family compound shrouded by a tin roof and had innumerable demands made on her. She was likely never alone and never allowed to think only of herself. As she sat on the rooftop with a gentle breeze passing by while being truly listened to, I saw the grief

---

[20] Ernst, Edzard. 2010. "Bach flower remedies: a systematic review of randomised clinical trials." *Swiss Med Wkly* vol. 140:w13079. https://doi.org/10.4414/smw.2010.13079.

leave her body. Her tense shoulders relaxed; her knotted hands opened.

I was in counseling for more than a year after Wade left. I would hurriedly bike from work to my therapist's office in time to make a cup of anise tea and sit in stillness before she came in. Ensconced in a comfy wicker chair and sipping the tea that someone else had to remember to buy, I was able to enjoy one of the few moments where I had nothing to do and no one to accommodate. It was wonderful. Even now, when I feel stressed at home, I make a cup of that tea.

Toward the end of the hour, Ines changed her posture. She leaned forward and spoke two or three sentences plainly and directly to the woman. Then she opened the folder, scribbled some notes, and handed the woman a small vial of liquid—the drops, presumably. This woman was not here for the flores; she was here for Ines. However, bottling Ines for the patients to take home was not possible, so the drops were a talisman to remind them of the comfort she gave them. Is there anything more natural than the feeling of relief when you have shared your pain?

15

SMOKE SIGNALS

EARLY ONE SATURDAY morning, I woke hungover from the work week. I would have loved to lie in the hammock with Lucia and read all day, but chores and house hunting awaited. The laundry was piling up, and I would have to wash all our clothes by hand in the pila. I knew that if I asked Lucia to help with the laundry, she would take all day, and we'd never leave the house, so I allowed her to play in the garden while I washed.

Also, the toilet tissue was piling up in the bathroom. The sensitive plumbing required that the tissue be thrown into a wastebasket rather than the toilet. This system works fine when garbage is collected regularly. However, since the residents of San Marcos must take the trash to be collected to the town center and pay a fee, most people burn their wastepaper at home. There was a cement slab covered in ashes in the garden for that purpose.

This was a chore that Lucia was glad to help with. When we dumped the bathroom basket in the middle of the slab, the crumpled white bundles formed a pyramid. I tossed a lit match on the pile, and nothing happened.

"Mommy, can I try?" Lucia asked.

"Sure, just be careful with the matches," I cautioned. She randomly placed lit matches on the pile, only to have a few paper balls curl around their singed edges.

"Maybe we need other types of paper or some twigs to start the fire," she suggested. I ran around the house and collected used math workbooks while she gathered dry sticks from the yard. We placed them strategically on the slab and used another book of matches. Eventually, real flames emerged.

As we stood back to admire our accomplishment, I joked, "Too bad we don't have marshmallows. I wonder if they would have an earthy taste cooked over this."

"You're disgusting, Mommy," she laughed.

"You know, I heard that the Maya read messages in fire. What message do you think is in the fire now?" I turned away to see if there were other sticks we could add.

"Run!" Lucia screamed.

While the used workbooks and other refuse had folded onto themselves, the wind had lifted the toilet paper balls into the air. We had to run to prevent flaming balls of shit from dropping onto our heads.

After we doused the fire and our chores were done, it was time to look for a new place to live. I had already started inquiring in cafés and stores and with people waiting for the lancha but had one last place to see that I had found online.

I had arranged to meet Domingo on a path by the main street into town. I recognized him from his Airbnb photo, a striking man in his midforties with waves of dark curls. He was even wearing the same white linen shirt as in his photo. He greeted us with a warm smile when I said in Spanish, "Are you Domingo? I'm Juanita, the woman who contacted you about the apartment for rent."

"Why, of course," he replied in thickly French-accented English. "How could I not recognize such a lovely woman? And this must be your daughter, who looks exactly like you."

I blushed when I asked back in English, "Are you French?"

"Oh, no." He winced. "I'm from Belgium. My name is actually Dominique." He continued, "You mentioned in your message that you're running the clinic in San Pablo. Chuitinamit, right?"

"Yes, do you know it?"

"I know a lot of the locals from San Marcos go there. The clinic is really good for the people here. I'd love to learn more about what you do."

Is he flirting with me? Lucia must have thought so, because she positioned herself between us. I asked, "Since I only saw the apartment advertised at a daily or weekly rate, what monthly rent would you be willing to take?"

"Six hundred dollars, US," he replied.

I was earning just five hundred dollars a month, and I wasn't willing to dip that deep into my savings to cover rent, but since we were already there, I figured I might as well see the apartment. I followed him up a densely forested hill adjacent to the lake with Lucia tagging along.

Near the top, Dominique pointed out a small clearing with a stack of charred rocks covered in ashes. "The locals call this hill Tzankujil. They have a ritual site here they still use," he explained.

He headed down the path to show us the dwelling for rent. It had a constructed (i.e., not dirt) floor, two sidewalls, and a roof, with the hill's rocks serving as the back wall. Where a front wall would have been was an open space that overlooked the lake, allowing in the wind, rain, and wildlife. It would have been a romantic space to spend the weekend, but as a home for a school-aged child, no way. Still, I had never seen anything like it.

Walking into this space, he told me, "I'm sort of an amateur architect. I designed all the structures on my property, using the shapes of plants and stones as inspiration."

I was amazed. As I had shared with Lucia, I'd designed similar dollhouses made from shoeboxes when I was a kid, but I could not imagine building a real house like this.

"All the structures?" I asked.

"Yes, this, another couple of apartments, my house, and my workshop. I can show you all of them if you would like."

"Absolutely!"

As we descended the hill, he showed me his home and other properties, each with flowing, organic architecture and an open side facing the water. I wondered what the Kachiquel thought of Dominique cutting into their holy hill to build his homes. He concluded the tour by bringing us to his workshop.

"Come in," he invited. "I'd like to show you something else."

When I entered the circular stucco building with a pitched ceiling and large, round windows, I was instantly captivated by a smell.

"Chocolate?" I asked.

"My workshop is a chocolate laboratory," he answered. "I have a *cacao finca* [farm] in Huehuetenango." He pointed to a man in the kitchen and continued, "Kito is a chocolatier from Japan. He's helping me develop products that could be marketed overseas."

It was ironic that this land in the Tz'utujil kingdom, which was once dotted with cacao trees whose beans were the local currency, is now covered with coffee trees whose beans are grown for export. Instead of cultivating cacao in its native soil, Dominique was likely displacing another native crop in Huehuetenango and using this land to host other people who didn't belong.

Lucia spotted a sparrow that had flown into the room through one of the windows and started chasing it to shoo it out. This bird that had evolved to live in the temperate forest did not know how to find its way out of the "organic structure" Dominique had built in its home.

In this rare moment when Lucia was distracted, I could have an adult conversation with an attractive man. Dominique presented an array of artisan confections and shaved slices of chocolate for me to sample. A tall, dark, handsome man handing me slivers of chocolate in an astounding round building he designed himself? I was definitely going to drag this out.

"How long have you been in San Marcos? Do you spend a lot of time at your finca? What inspired you to take on this venture? What inspiration do you use for your architecture?"

With his thick accent, his answers were barely intelligible to me, but they were irrelevant as long as I had his attention. Meanwhile, Lucia continued flapping her arms and chasing the bird around the room.

"What flavors do you find most appealing? What do you think people like about your products? What else do you find appealing?" *Okay, Jan, don't be so obvious*, I told myself. "How do you know what will be pleasing to others? Who is the target audience? Women? If so, I'd be happy to sample more and let you know what I think." *Way too obvious.*

While we chatted, in walked a boy and a girl, around four and eight years old. He referred to the young boy as his son.

"You have young children too?" I inquired.

"Only a son. The girl is my sister-in-law." Dominique explained that he had married a young Kachiquel woman—apparently, quite young.

Bam! The sparrow hit a rafter and dropped dead, along with my hopes of being a sampler.

"Oh, no, Mommy!" Lucia called out. "I think the bird is hurt."

"Sweetie, the bird probably broke its neck when it hit the rafters. I'm sorry, but it's dead now."

As my mood shifted from curiosity to disappointment, Lucia's shifted quickly from disappointment to curiosity.

"Mommy, can we take the bird home? I want to dissect it to see what's inside. Didn't you used to dissect animals when you were a kid?" She was referring to the story I had told her about cutting open a frog that had drowned in a pool.

When it became clear to Dominique that I was not going to rent his apartment, he politely told me he had other things to do. He sent me on my way, not with samples of his fine chocolates but with a plastic bag to carry the carcass.

As we were leaving his property, we were waylaid by a wave of people dressed in orange T-shirts in a *Partido Patriota* rally. The Patriotic Party was one of Guatemala's minor right-wing political parties known for its clenched-fist emblem, the slogan *Mano Dura* (Heavy Hand), and its paramilitary activities. It was also the party of the current president, who was about to be imprisoned for corruption. I thought it best to wait behind the trees for them to pass.

Nothing indicated that this crowd might turn violent. However, given that the *Partido Patriota*'s candidate for mayor in San Marcos declared that he wanted to kick out the foreigners, I did not want the crowd to notice the two blond gringas. Though the foreigners had started businesses, employed locals, and built the town's park and my daughter's school, they also had bought the best land, their hotels and restaurants used more than their share of the water, and, as I had just learned, they carved their houses into sacred hills.

When I explained the party's platform to Lucia, she asked, "Why would they want to kick us out of San Marcos? Don't the immigrants contribute to the economy?"

"Good question, Lucia. People ask the same question about objections to immigration in our country," I replied.

When we were finally home, I bragged to Lucia, "You know, I studied biology in college and dissected other animals besides the frog I told you about. I have quite a bit of experience doing this."

At first, Lucia was eager to try. "Let's do it! Let's see what is inside."

We laid the specimen on paper on the tiled floor and searched the kitchen for the sharpest knife.

"Here, honey. Take the knife and slowly make a vertical cut down its belly," I instructed.

Apparently filled with second thoughts, Lucia squirmed. "Ew, yuck! I'm scared. I don't think I can do that."

"There's nothing to be scared of. You're the one who wanted to bring the bird home. I'm sure you can do it."

As she made two haphazard cuts into the bird's belly, she exclaimed, "Ahhh, this is freaking me out!"

"Look, you've gone this far; you might as well finish," I replied.

Tufts of tiny white feathers started flying around the house. I knew that if I didn't stop this now, I would be the one scouring the house for bits of bird. Still, this was the first thing Lucia had been excited about all week. After another cut, yellow-green innards spilled out.

"EEEWWW!!" We both screamed in disgust.

"Mommy, is this what a dissection is supposed to be? You told me that we could see the parts of the bird, and all I see are the guts."

"Actually, I never dissected a bird in school, probably because it would have been such a mess. I think we should have plucked the feathers so we could see where to cut."

"Then how can we see all the organs?" she inquired.

"I think we would have to rip it open and look for them."

"Oh, noooo! I don't want to tear up the bird. I want to be able to take it to school for show-and-tell."

"Let's wrap it up and put it in the freezer. The cold will preserve it until you can take it to school on Monday."

"What are we going to do tonight if we aren't going to dissect anymore?" she asked.

"Let's just watch a video," I suggested.

We cuddled on the couch to watch a downloaded episode of *Once Upon a Time*. The show's premise was that the vengeful Evil Queen had cast a spell to transport all the fairy-tale characters from the Enchanted Forest to a new realm of her creation. Unsatisfied by her act of revenge, she found that what she had really longed for was love and acceptance.

While Lucia was absorbed in the Evil Queen's machinations. My thoughts wandered. *I had also cast a spell to take us to another realm, but would this life in San Marcos be what I wanted? Did I even know what I wanted, or had I started this quest with earlier desires and motivations that were perhaps not fitting for me now?*

Did I want to live in expat luxury carved into a sacred hill, flutter around trying to capture the attention of a man who had already been captured by a woman twenty years younger, and hide from locals protesting my presence?

Would I be like the flaming balls of shit caught up in the wind or like the little sparrow who curiously flew into a hole only to bang its head into a rafter? Or was I like the people in the street, fighting for what they believe in, but perhaps without fully understanding those beliefs?

Or, instead, could I take more control and hence more responsibility for my future by better understanding what I sought?

16
PENA

WHILE TRAVELING IN Latin America and Spain, I occasionally heard the word *"pena"* (pain) in expressions such as *"Vale la pena"* (It's worthwhile) or *"pena de muerte"* (death penalty), but in Guatemala, this word was ubiquitous. Phrases such as *"Pase adelante sin pena"* (Go ahead without pain), *"¡Qué pena!"* (What a shame!), *"Me da pena"* (It makes me feel shame), and *"No tenga pena"* (Don't be embarrassed) peppered every conversation. Guatemalan culture seemed filled with pain and shame.

While at Chuitinamit, I got a call from a man who told me his name was Sergio and that he worked with the municipality of San Pablo. He asked if I would like their surplus amoxicillin as a donation to the pharmacy. I graciously accepted his timely offer. I was putting together a medicine order for a supplier in the States that the next volunteer team would bring. If I did not have to order this essential medicine, then I could use the funds to purchase other important—though not necessarily crucial—items on the list. Sergio promised to drop off the amoxicillin within the next few days.

After a week without hearing from him again, I called to arrange a time for me to pick it up. He didn't answer the phone. I continued to call him almost daily for a couple of weeks to no avail. I even went to the municipal building to look for the man I knew only by voice and first name. Two men standing by the reception desk told me that Sergio was gone, and no one knew when he would return. I asked whether he was gone for the day or gone from his job. They looked at me and shrugged. I thought either their Spanish comprehension was too limited to understand my question or mine was too limited to articulate what I meant. Neither reported knowing anything about the promised amoxicillin but instead gave me more shrugs and apologies.

Weeks later, only when I called from my personal phone rather than the clinic phone did he finally pick up. "Sergio, I've been trying to contact you. How can I get the amoxicillin? We are running low now and really need it."

"*Fijase* [pay attention]. *Tengo pena para decirle* [I'm ashamed to tell you], I don't have it anymore. I threw it out."

"What? Why would you do that?"

"A doctor told me that the medicine had expired recently and that it would no longer be good."

"Why didn't you call me about that? Antibiotics are still effective for several months after their expiration dates. We could have used it."

"*Fue porque me dio mucho pena*." (It was because I was too ashamed.)

"Well, now the pain is mine and the patients' at the clinic. I didn't order that medicine because you told me you had it, and now it is too late for the next group to bring it. I won't be able to order this for several more months."

"*Estoy de pena*," he pleaded.

Did he ever have the medicine? Had he expected me to offer payment and, when I didn't, offloaded the medicine on someone else? Or was what he said really the case? He didn't admit he should have called or apologized, but it seemed as if he wanted me to release him from his pain. I didn't. I merely said goodbye and ended the call, never to hear from Sergio again.

When I was reviewing staff salaries to prepare the following year's budget, I found that Manuela was being paid for her role as a diabetes promotora, even though she was performing this role while also being paid to work in the pharmacy. This double-dipping was compounded by the fact that we paid for extra help in the pharmacy since she was too busy with both roles to do either one well. I decided to move her out of this program so that patients would be better served and so that she could focus on her pharmacy responsibilities.

Because I was concerned that Manuela's Spanish was limited, I asked Ines to help me explain this to her. Ines began our meeting with Manuela in a respectful, deferential manner—using a slow, low voice, calling her "*usted*" and "*Doña*," and keeping her gaze turned downward. Speaking to Manuela in Spanish rather than Tz'utujil so that I could understand, she began, "Doña Manuela, thank you for your service to the diabetes program. You have been with the program longer than most promotores, and we appreciate your wisdom. However, we have found a little error that we must bring to your attention."

Noting Manuela's confused look, I clarified, "You are being paid two salaries, one from the clinic and one from the diabetes program, during the same hours. We cannot afford this expense, particularly when neither job is being fully done. You are going to have to stop working as a diabetes health promotora while you are working in the pharmacy."

Manuela burst into tears. "How can I possibly dispense medicine to patients after I have been removed from being their promotora? I've worked with them for years, developed a relationship with them, and now they will think lowly of me."

I asked, "When we first met about your work, why didn't you tell me you were also working as a diabetes promotora while you were in the pharmacy?"

"You only asked me about working in the pharmacy."

"But, Manuela, I hired extra help for you in the pharmacy because you couldn't keep up. I didn't know the reason was that you were spending much of the time doing another job."

"No one has said this was a problem before. I have so much pena. I will never be able to face the patients again. They will think I am terrible," she sobbed.

"Look, Manuela. This is merely to correct a budget error. It has nothing to do with your capabilities. You shouldn't feel any shame," I reasoned.

Her wailing went on so long that I grew concerned for her physically. Eventually, she calmed herself and left. We were uncertain if we were ever going to see her again.

Manuela did come back to work the next day, "*por la necesidad*" (out of necessity). She said, "Please do not make an announcement to staff or the patients. Make the change quietly, and they will see that I am not doing diabetes work."

"Doña Manuela, would you like a *despedida* [goodbye party] from the program?" Ines offered.

"No, *tengo demasiado pena* [I have too much shame]. I just want to go away."

Kenneth popped his head into my office at Chuitinamit one day to say, "Jan, we've got a problem." *A problem with me?* I wondered. "Dra. Vacinta just came to me to tell me about a situation with Tomás." *Okay, not a problem with me—a problem for me.*

"What happened?" I asked.

"Dra. Vacinta saw a patient with an infected ingrown toenail. The woman wasn't happy with Dra. Vacinta's treatment, so she went to Tulita and told her she wanted to see Tomás. Tomás did a consult with her and removed her toenail. He ripped up the medical history form that Dra. Vacinta had completed, and now she is furious."

"Has she tried to talk to him?"

"No."

"I suppose he didn't bother to talk to her before or even after he did that."

"Nope."

The next day, Kenneth and I brought Dra. Vacinta and Tomás together to discuss what had happened. Kenneth was ready to fire Tomás for insubordination, for malpractice, for being a troublemaker. I wasn't set on any particular course of action but instead wanted to understand what Tomás was thinking.

In our meeting, he proudly explained, "This lady is one of my regular patients. She doesn't speak much Spanish, so she prefers to see me because I speak Tz'utujil. She only saw the doctora because Tulita said I was busy. She came to have her toenail removed, a simple procedure, and when the doctora refused her, I told her I would attend to her needs."

Tomás stood by his action, thinking he'd done the right thing.

Dra. Vacinta retorted, "The patient is pregnant. You gave her the antibiotic cephalexin and ibuprofen, which are harmful to pregnant women. I didn't remove her toenail because I didn't want to give her oral antibiotics, so I told her to soak her toe in vinegar."

Taken aback by Dra. Vacinta's reprimand, Tomás responded, "Oh, I didn't know."

Dra. Vacinta continued to lambast Tomás for tearing up the medical record and replacing it with his own. Kenneth likewise joined in the roast.

"Wait a minute," I said, stopping the argument. "There's a pregnant woman out there who has medication that is dangerous for her baby? We have to find her *now* and stop her from taking it."

I called Tulita into the room and asked her to look up the woman's record to find what neighborhood the woman lived in and track her down.

"Tulita, please go tell this woman to stop taking the medicine now. Actually, just ask for the medicine back. You can give her this ten quetzales to pay her back for the consult. Tell her she can come back to the clinic for free if her toe swells," I instructed as I handed her money from my pocket.

Later, when I asked Tomás and Dra. Vacinta separately why they couldn't talk to each other directly about this case, they both replied, "Por pena."

I have a theory as to why pena, or shame, is so prominent in Guatemala. Shame comes from feeling like you have disappointed or hurt people whose opinions you care about. A strength of rural Guatemalan culture is the tight social networks of small villages. When material poverty is pervasive, personal security questionable, and support from the government nonexistent, all you have left is trust in a few people to support you. The fact that the country is divided into twenty-three language groups further narrows the group of people you feel have your back.

During the thirty-five-year armed conflict, the government set out to destroy the bonds that connected people in rural areas. They recruited people to spy on their neighbors and razed communities because of rumors that they supported the guerillas. They sent soldiers to unfamiliar regions of the country so they would not hold back in the torturing and killing of strangers. Today, police are still assigned to work in distant towns so that they will be "impartial."

When trust is broken, neighbors and family turn against each other, and in doing so, homes are ruined. This causes shame, pena, and admitting to it causes even more. Although I could understand the pain of a broken bond, it added another complex layer to my work. I wanted to create a "learning culture," as was the management fad in the States, but how could I do that in a culture swimming in shame?

17
TREES

ON YET ANOTHER night, when Lucia fussed because she was too exhausted to do her math workbook and I was exhausted from a long day at work, I snapped. I yelled at her for being lazy and ordered her out of the house and onto the porch until she stopped whining. Stunned, she backed away from me and wailed.

I sat in the kitchen, shaking like a leaf with anger I directed at us both. *How could I let out so much fury toward the person I love the most?* Rattled and ashamed by my bad behavior, I felt my daughter needed an explanation along with an apology.

The image that came to mind was how a tree's growth rings show not only the cycles of drought, disease, and damage but also the other versions a tree has been.

"I'm sorry I got so upset with you. It's like inside me are all the other Jans: the forty-year-old, the thirty-year-old, the twenty-two-year-old, the fourteen-year-old, so on. I am so stressed that five-year-old Jan broke through and had a tantrum. I know I need to put her back in."

"You need to put the five-year-old Jan in time-out," Lucia grumbled.

We both took some time to collect ourselves, and by the end of the evening, we were once again entwined. My apology was earnest, though my explanation was lacking. My temper was not about juvenile Jan escaping but rather about injured Jan bursting out. Lacerations that slice a tree open can reveal what lies within. Similarly, deep wounds from my childhood, scorch marks from past burns, and putridness seemed to be pouring out of me more often.

Throughout my life, whenever I was hurt, I sealed off the injured area and healed myself. I justified my method by claiming that, like trees, everyone is unique, so each person needs to find her or his own way to cope. Some people grow straight and tall, while others are twisted and knotty. Some have smooth surfaces, while others are covered in rough bark. Some lose their leaves when the weather grows harsh, while others continue to take in what light there is and grow throughout the year. What all trees have in common is that they cannot grow back their bark, their protective seal, and neither could I. We must find other ways to heal.

The Tz'utujil are a tree people as well as a bird people. The birds help spread the trees, but the trees in turn provide a home for the birds, as well as for other animals. Though trees appear solid and stationary, they are communicators as much as birds are.

According to Maya legend, the god Huracán (also called Heart of the Sky) formed the earth between the underworld, also called Xibalba, and the upper world, in the sky. The lords of death occupied the thirteen levels of Xibalba, and the gods and spirits occupied the thirteen levels of the upper world. Seeing that he'd left no space between the earth and the upper world, Huracán planted a ceiba tree that stretched its branches into the upper world and expanded its roots deep into Xibalba. The ceiba's trunk grew to separate the earth from the sky and leave space in between for all beings. The gods, spirits, and the dead can pass through the ceiba as a communication route between Xibalba, the earth's surface, and the upper world.

Groundbreaking research on the "minds of trees" has confirmed the connectedness and communication capacity of trees. Previously, trees were considered individual beings operating separately from others and depending solely on the sun over their crowns and the soil at their roots. Scientists have since discovered an intricate underground support system comprised of a web of tendrils connecting species.

Trees recognize when one in the network is deficient in nutrients and can send what it lacks. When trees are injured or dying, they send messages of resilience to the next generation of seedlings, increasing their resistance to future stresses. Through back-and-forth conversations, they increase the strength of the whole community. They also give life to an ecosystem of lichens, vines, moss, liverworts, ferns, bromeliads, and orchids that live symbiotically within them.[21]

I continued to worry about how Lucia's tree was faring. More than a year after the separation, before we moved to Guatemala, Lucia began to show anxiety, her outpouring of pain. While she loved her father, she did not want to sleep at his place; or better said, she did not want to be apart from me. She cried, sometimes for hours, just thinking about leaving my house. I'd hold her, let her know that I understood how hard this was, tell her she needed both her parents, and reassure her that I was always with her.

She insisted we talk nights and mornings, needing that extra soothing of her mother's voice to sleep. If we didn't speak at eight o'clock on the nights she was with her father, she would panic, even if she had seen me a couple of hours before. To soothe her, I would tell her that as my voice entered the telephone receiver, it carried through the wires between us and out of her phone, into her ear, caressing her. I wanted her to feel my consoling love through the lines just as I felt the consoling love of my family and friends. I feared that her anxieties were a projection of my pain. I wondered how much she was mirroring me.

She finally seemed to be doing better, and then, within a few short months, we moved to Guatemala. In Guatemala, was she being nourished at the roots? Was she growing toward the light? Or were parasites eating her away?

---

[21] Simard, S. W., K. J. Beiler, M. A. Bingham, J. R. Deslippe, L. J. Philip, and F. P. Teste. 2012. "Mycorrhizal networks: Mechanisms, ecology and modeling." *Fungal Biology Reviews* 26: 39–60.

One Saturday, I dropped off Lucia at Lana's house to play with Stela while I went running on the unpaved road on the ridge along the water. Lucia and Stela were going to pick jocote fruits from the trees around Lana's house for a school fundraiser.

While I ran, I heard insects chirping for the first time since last being in my garden in North Carolina. I never heard these teeming sounds in the dry summers and soggy rest of the year in urban Seattle. In our home in San Marcos, I was either too busy rushing between work, home, and shopping or attending Lucia to be still and listen.

When I arrived back at Lana's house, Lucia and Stela had moved on to a new project—caring for a baby hummingbird that had been pushed out of its nest. Since Lana had a reputation throughout town as an animal rescuer, the tourists who had found the fledgling on a path scooped it up and brought it to her house.

"What do people think my house is? Some sort of animal sanctuary?" Lana jokingly scoffed.

"I don't think this is what you were thinking of when you talked about building a retreat center, right?"

I sat on the couch in her living room. Just then, a chicken hopped from its perch on the windowsill to my head. "What the hell?" I shouted, and then we both burst out laughing.

We headed to her roof with large cups of tea to get away from the chickens and to see how the girls were faring. They had built a little nest with twigs and scraps of cloth and were hand-feeding the baby bird a tincture of lemon water with honey. The hummingbird, no bigger than Lucia's thumb, oscillated between fluttering its wings and taking the tincture through its beak. Lana and I gave the girls words of cautious encouragement and glanced at each other, knowing the fledgling's likely fate.

But at least for a few hours, this young bird would find a home in the branches of Stela's and Lucia's trees. Meanwhile, Lana and I squatted on the short stools on her terrace, swapped stories, and gossiped.

New tendrils were reaching out.

18

THE SUN, THE EARTH, AND THE SKY

IN MID-OCTOBER, WHEN Kenneth offered me a week off, I decided to take a trip to Petén—the region where I'd lived during my first stay in Guatemala—rather than rest at home. I wanted to introduce Lucia to old friends and show her the region that made me fall in love with the country.

Since we needed to renew our visas after three months in Guatemala, I planned a side trip to Belize, one of the few places during my time in Petén where I could go to decompress. In this English-speaking country, I was able to converse in my language, eat familiar food, and escape the grueling life of an impoverished, war-torn country.

Lucia and I planned to leave after school to start the 500-mile slog to Belize. As we walked down the gravelly path from our house to meet the shuttle, we simultaneously noticed a movement in the gray rocks.

"*Snaaaake*!!" We screamed in unison and then ran back.

How would we make a 500-mile journey if we couldn't even walk down the path out of the house? We snuck through a fence at a neighbor's house, cut through the yard, crossed another thicket, and came out onto a road that eventually led us to the shuttle.

After a twenty-two-hour expedition involving three buses, two shuttles, and a boat to arrive at Ambergris Caye off the coast of Belize, we checked into a cheap motel where I had stayed previously. We passed a hot afternoon walking barefoot along the seaweed-strewn beaches and sand-covered streets. Blending in with the other tourists, Lucia began to feel free and to relax.

Upon hearing a boy chide his little brother, "Put on your batteries! We have to go now," we laughed at this creative Spanglish. He had literally translated the Spanish expression *"Ponte la pilas"* (Hurry up!). Though English was the official language of this former British colony, the mingling of British, Garifuna, Maya, Ladino, German Mennonite, and North American cultures had created a creole language and people.

Lucia was excited to visit a real ice cream shop. However, she was dismayed when the shopkeeper wouldn't allow her to sample all the flavors as they did in Seattle. After a night of sipping fruity drinks and dining on fresh fish in a seaside restaurant, we fell exhausted into bed.

The following day, we rose early to snorkel in the coral reefs. Miles from shore, Lucia was at first hesitant to get in the water. Apart from boogie boarding in North Carolina, she had never swum in open water. Eventually, the endless blue water under the expansive sky calmed her. I fastened her life vest, secured her mask and snorkel, and held her hand as we fell off the side of the boat. Once she was in the water, she splashed around in delight and then found a comfortable dog-paddle stroke. Still holding hands, we saw fish of every color in the rainbow, eels emerge from rocks, and sea turtles gracefully swim by.

After an hour, the boat took us to another area to see sharks and rays. The captain threw raw meat in the water to lure them to us. Dozens of sharks raced to the meat with jaws open, piling on top of each other, snapping to get a taste. Lucia refused to get in the water this time. I had done this before and wasn't apprehensive about being bitten, but to assuage her fears, I stayed in the boat.

On the ride back to shore, a fisherman friend of the captain pulled up in another boat and offered us a fresh conch from his day's catch. With his knife, the captain pulled out the mollusk and cut it into pieces for the passengers. He then gifted the shell to Lucia, who gleefully accepted it. To see her excited about a new experience, to hear her laugh, and to feel the squeeze of her hand as she dared something new were all part of the dream I'd had when I first imagined living abroad with her, yet I had not seen or heard much of this from her in the previous three months.

That evening, I prepared a simple dinner in the open-air kitchen on the motel patio while Lucia showered and rested in the room. I struck up a conversation with a fellow traveler, a British man around my age, who offered me a beer. He told me about the countries he had visited on his six-month holiday and was intrigued by my life in Guatemala. Apart from my confusing signals with Dominique, it had been months since I'd had a drink and a chat with a man. *Is he flirting with me? Am I flirting with him?*

When Lucia came out and saw us talking, she headed straight for my lap. True to form, she did not want me to engage with any man. Likely sensing that we would no longer be able to carry on a conversation since a ten-year-old child was covering my face, he excused himself to go to his room.

"Lucia, why are you acting like this? I'm not going to be with this man. I'm just having a conversation with him."

"I don't want you to date anyone," she announced. "You can't love anyone but me!" And with that, she burst into sobs. I had dated a few men in Seattle, but nothing serious, and I had never introduced Lucia to any of them. Neither Lucia nor I were ready to bring another person into our lives.

"Lucia, I'm not going to promise you that I'll never be with someone again. One day I might meet a man I want to be close to, but it won't be now."

She shot me an unsatisfied look and repeated her response to most situations: "It's not fair!"

"No, it's not fair," I agreed. "Look, this isn't the situation I wanted either. I hoped we three would be a family forever. I wanted to be doing this together, but this is the way it is." It had already been two years since her father and I had separated, and I was frustrated that she was bringing up something irrelevant given our circumstance. "Why are you giving me a hard time about this now?"

"I want you to just be with Daddy."

"You know I will never love anyone like I loved Daddy, and you know why."

"Because he gave you me!"

"Exactly! What I can promise you, though, is that no one will ever take me away from you. I will always love you. You will always be the most precious of the most preciouses." I pulled Lucia into my lap and gave her a tight hug. After a moment, I asked, "Do you do the same thing to Daddy?"

"No."

"Why not?" I snapped, irritated by this double standard.

"I love Daddy, but you are my world."

"What have I said about how you, Daddy, and I are connected?" I prodded.

"I am the sun, Daddy is the earth, and you are the sky that holds us both."

"Yes, you are the sun that everything revolves around," I explained as Lucia snickered. "And I'm a bit spacey like the sky, Daddy is solid like the earth, but to me, you are my world, too."

We left the Caribbean and headed to Petén. Our first stop was a ranch with the most gallant horses I had ever seen and a guest lodge for tourists. A ranch hand named Asiel showed Lucia how to groom the horses and told her about the different breeds.

Asiel then offered to take us riding on a sprawling tract of land deep in the rainforest. Lucia was still learning the basics of horseback riding, and I can manage a simple trot down a trail, so I thought that this would be a leisurely stroll. However, when Asiel mounted his steed, he transformed from a gentle horse whisperer into a wailing jungle man, galloping full speed, a machete in one hand—slashing branches and vines overhead—and a whip in the other, permitting the mare no rest, steering her only with his knees. Lucia squealed with delight, and I clung to the saddle horn, to the mane, to everything, and prayed we wouldn't die.

Asiel brought us to a stony mound covered in *zapote* and *cojón* trees.

"This is a Maya ruin I found. The government and the archaeologists don't know about it, so it hasn't been excavated," he told us.

As we walked around the perimeter, he cautioned me not to step into a hole that was somewhat hidden by branches and leaves.

"That's the entrance," he indicated, pointing to an opening no more than two feet in diameter. Thinking of myself as an Indiana Jones wannabe, I kicked away some branches, hoping I might be able to see a staircase leading to a buried treasure. Lucia and I peered into the deep crevasse and saw dark, glistening movement.

"Is that water in the bottom of a well?" I asked Asiel.

"No, it's snakes," he answered.

"*Snaaaaaaakes*!!" Lucia and I screamed and ran down the mound back to our horses. Maybe I was like Indiana Jones, but not in the way I had hoped.

Back at the ranch, we cooled off in the pool and played mermaids, as we had done with Piñita. At dinner, when we were laughing and reminiscing about the events of the day, Lucia shifted to a sullen look.

"What's wrong, honey?" I asked.

"Well, if we were back in Seattle now, I would have been able to go on the fifth-grade trip to Camp Kirby this past weekend. All my friends got to go, and I didn't."

"Lucia. Really? This past week you snorkeled in one of the ecologically richest coral reefs in the world, fed sharks, ate fresh conch, galloped through a jungle, and explored ruins. Are you saying you would have rather gone to Camp Kirby for a weekend?"

The expression on her face said yes, but her reply was "No, you're right. This was better."

I then understood that while I was Lucia's world, I wasn't her everything. She might need (or rather, demand) my full attention, but she also needed her father and friends—her tree network.

19

TIKAL

DEEP IN THE heart of the Petén jungle is Tikal, one of the great Maya cities. Thought to have been settled as early as 800 BC, the population peaked around 800 AD at as many as 90,000 people. Even without the benefit of the wheel, some 3,000 structures were built, including the tallest pyramids in the Western Hemisphere. Two pyramid-shaped temples flanked a large plaza ringed by terraces, palaces, and ball courts. Found in one of these temples were the remains of *Ah Cacau* (Lord Chocolate), one of Tikal's eminent rulers, festooned with jade ornaments and surrounded by offerings of pottery, alabaster, seashells, and pearls from the Caribbean coast.

Dozens of stone stelae, each paired with a circular altar, stood in rows throughout the plaza and surrounding terraces. Carvings and glyphs noting important dates and deeds of Tikal's rulers still adorn many of these weathered monoliths. From atop Tikal's pyramids, ancient astronomers tracked the movements of the other visible planets.

Long before the Spaniards reached Petén, this city was abandoned and subsumed by the rainforest. The ruins were discovered in the middle of the twentieth century, when a plane flying overhead saw the apexes of these pyramids peeking out of the tree canopy. Archaeologists slowly excavating the site have theorized that the residents died or dispersed due to drought or war.

In my half dozen visits to Tikal over the years, I've seen the slow revelation of a city built over hundreds of years by people who likely had more false starts than successes. Where did all the people go? Were they aware of their ancestors' glory, or were they focused on ending their own suffering? When the final group left, did they turn around to say goodbye, or did they walk away without looking back?

In our weeklong expedition, we would also visit Las Cruces, the village where I lived during my first year in Petén. Part of me dreaded showing this place to Lucia because I had so many painful memories of that time, yet I wanted her to see the place that taught me how to withstand drought and war, where my resilience had hardened and my humanity softened.

I had lived and worked at *Casa de los Estudios* (the House of Studies), a compound owned by the Catholic Church that had changed purpose and occupants a few times in the 1980s and 1990s. First, a group of nuns created a makeshift convent at the height of the war until they fled from the escalating violence. Next, a Spanish NGO occupied the space until they ran off as well. Finally, the church allowed the US NGO I worked for to take over the property at no cost with the condition that they maintain it. By the time I came in 1999, the NGO had already been there for five years, and violence continued to afflict the region.

Around a dozen international volunteers had lived there for varying lengths of time, including the three who were there when I arrived, investing their sweat, tears, and sometimes even their blood. They had installed a water tank for the shower, built a composting latrine, renovated a small house into a clinic, and added two cabanas that flanked the main house. The property also had a salón and an outdoor kitchen, which consisted of an open woodstove and a well.

Casa de los Estudios had continually buzzed with activity when I lived there. Every Monday through Friday, twenty to thirty promotores or comadronas studied and slept in the salón while completing a new course. Those from the surrounding villages left their families and livelihoods for up to six weeks each year for four years to learn how to provide the only source of primary care their communities would have. They queued at the kitchen for every meal, which invariably included beans and tortillas, and ate communally on the picnic tables under the hot lámina roof. The niñera swept the dead leaves from the shade trees and left the children unattended to play on the front porch of the main house. On Saturdays, the Las Cruces promotores held *consultas* (consults) in the small clinic, and their patients waited in the shade on our porch. Sundays were for laundry, chores, and repairs around the property.

For this day I had arranged with Doña Marina to meet us there at 1 p.m. Lucia and I arrived on time to find that the property appeared deserted. The shutters on all the buildings were closed, and rusted lámina, dead branches, and trash covered the grounds. The once freshly whitewashed buildings were now caked in dirt and covered with mold. *Why would they let this place fall into such disrepair?* I wondered.

I suspected that the current residents were running errands in the village center and would return soon, so I suggested to Lucia that we could explore the property while waiting. We stepped onto the porch of the main house.

I told Lucia, "The children of the promotores who were in the classes would hang out on this porch. They would get up on that table to look in our windows to see what the gringos ate for breakfast."

"That's weird," Lucia commented.

"No," I corrected her. "We were weird to them." Continuing my explanation, I said, "The kids didn't have toys, so they would play with the sticks they found in the yard and chase the chickens around the patio. I would come out to entertain them by doing cartwheels and tossing them into the air."

"Like you used to do with me?"

"Yeah, until my shoulder gave out." I turned my head to look at the house behind us. "I lived in a plywood cubicle in this house. Brian's [one of the volunteers] cubicle was beside mine. We used to talk to each other over the wall where we were going to sleep at night. You know, like they do on *The Waltons*."

"Huh?" She had no idea what I was referring to.

Always surrounded by the other volunteers and Guatemalans, I was never alone back then, but I was lonely. I felt like a balloon floating up to the clouds, completely untethered, a bit lost. As I looked around at other expat volunteers, I'd note that those who seemed to thrive the most were with their partners, their families. I had gone to Guatemala still hurting from my broken engagement with Stuart. By the end of my time there, I was healed and craved a deeper connection, a kindred spirit. When I met Wade after returning to North Carolina, I thought I had finally found someone who could share this life with me.

"You know, I brought Daddy here to visit when we started dating. He stayed with me in my old room in this house." I slept with him in the same single bed where I'd spent all those hot nights ensconced in my *pabellón* (mosquito net), longing for a confidant and companion.

"What did he think of it here?" Lucia asked.

"Well, I don't think he cared much for the composting latrine. You know how he's weird about germs."

"Oh, yeah," she giggled.

"But he liked the people and thought the work was interesting." When I had observed how well he interacted with my colleagues and friends, the hope that he would want to share this life with me bloomed.

As Lucia and I walked across the littered lawn, I told her I had met Doña Marina there my first week in Guatemala.

"She was sitting here on the grass, embroidering with a toddler in her lap. I sat down beside her and asked if the boy was her grandson. She had a deep belly laugh and said, 'Oh, no, Walter is the youngest of my seventeen children.'"

"Seventeen children? How is that possible?" Lucia asked.

"I know. I was surprised too. She patted me on the knee and said, 'I'm forty-seven years old, and I have been either pregnant or nursing since I was fifteen years old, but that ends now. Walter is almost done nursing and'—she moved her hand to her fleshy arm—'I have started depo injections so I won't have any more. That's why I'm fat now,' she finished with another laugh."

"That's mean, Mommy. You shouldn't say she's fat. What are depo injections?"

"Hey, I'm just repeating what she said. Depo is short for Depo-Provera. It's a type of birth control. Anyhow, I asked how she managed with all those children. She said that she suffered a lot and wished she could have had family planning before.

"She whispered in my ear that her husband said she looked good pregnant, but she thought he just wanted to keep her tied down. He didn't know she was getting injections. He would want even more children. She went on to tell me that being a comadrona was her calling. It was a gift, a *don*. Her duty was not only to serve the women in her community but to train other comadronas. In this way she was serving women in the whole region."

"Like Navichoc does, right?"

"Yes, right." What I didn't tell Lucia was that the week after I met Doña Marina, our team received word that her eldest son had been killed. The rumor was that he was involved in a *narcotraficante* situation and was hacked to pieces with a machete. Brian and the other team members prepared to go to her house to be with her, but I was reluctant to do so. I had just met this woman. *How could I possibly intrude on such a personal, private moment?* I was told this was simply the way things were done, and we must all go.

We all got in the truck and went to Doña Marina's house in the next town over. When we showed up, she wasn't there. In a twist of fate, the daughter of the coffin maker was in labor, so Marina had to attend the birth and bring a new light into the world while the coffin maker was preparing to send her son into the next. When she returned to the house, she was desolate and exhausted. We stayed with her the entire night. There was nothing we could do, nothing to say; being present was enough. I slept, sort of, on a couple of planks. The family gave up a precious bed for the night for us.

"As I was still getting started with my new job, Brian told me that I was also going to work with another woman named Magali. Brian pointed this woman out in a photo of a group of promotores who had finished their four-year training course. She looked like she was in her early twenties. She had long, wavy hair tied back and was dressed in a lacey, wide-collared blouse and an A-line skirt like the evangelical women wear here. Brian said she was the brightest in the class and excelled at the clinical portion of the training, but she was more interested in community organizing. When I met her a few days later, she didn't look anything like the woman in the picture, nor like any of the Guatemalan women I had seen."

"Why's that?"

"She was rail thin and had her hair cropped short, which made her look severe. She was wearing a long, snug dress. She was polite but reserved with me. I could tell she was sizing me up. She was all business and pulled out her agenda to go through dates of upcoming meetings and events. I saw that she labeled the inside flap 'Lilian Magali Verdugo,' so I asked if her first name was Lilian. She said it was, but that people had been calling her Magali, which she hated because it sounds too much like 'MAGA,' the name for the Ministry of Agriculture. So, I started calling her Lilian, and then everyone else did too. After that, I had her respect."

Lucia and I walked around the back of Casa de los Estudios while I continued to tell her about Lilian. "She had recently divorced her abusive husband, which was almost unheard of. She was determined to make a better life for herself and her young son. Her son stayed with her mother in her village while she worked away. She wanted to get out and see the country.

"Marina, Lilian, and I were tasked with expanding the program to a remote set of villages recently settled after the end of the armed conflict and finding people to train as community health workers. Though this place here in Las Cruces was our initial base of operations, we established a new branch in San Benito, closer to these villages, and formed a new partnership with the San Benito parish priest, Padre Cirilo.

"Doña Marina, Lilian, and I would show up in a village, offering a bag of beans and a bag of corn for a family to host us for the night. These families had nothing, but we were never refused. Doña Marina would gently tease me about how I invariably forgot to pack sugar for her coffee on our outings, and Lilian and I teased back about how she kept us up all night with her snoring."

"You always forget to pack something," Lucia insisted. "And you snore too!"

"Ugh, I know. Anyhow, when my time in Guatemala was drawing to a close, I asked Lilian if there was anything I could teach her. I thought she might want to learn about evaluation, statistics, grant writing, or project management. Instead, she wanted to know how to drive."

"Drive? Why?" asked Lucia.

"The buses weren't reliable, so anywhere she wanted to go for work, she would have to ask me or a man for a ride. If she could drive, she would be able to do more on her own, and maybe get a better job. I realized helping a Guatemalan woman get her driver's license might be my greatest accomplishment during my time here."

"How did it go?"

"I tried to explain the basics, but my Spanish vocabulary for operating a manual transmission of a four-wheel-drive truck was limited. Since Lilian had never been in the driver's seat, she felt uncomfortable being in what she thought was the middle of the road and kept straying to the right, which meant that as a passenger, I kept drifting to the ditch. I had to tell her repeatedly to move to the left.

"Once, we were reeling down a hill. I tried to scream, 'Brakes!' in Spanish, but I forgot the word, so I yelled, 'Foot!' and prayed that she didn't press the clutch or gas. Eventually, she regained control of the car, learned to drive, and gained control of her life."

"That's funny. I bet you'll scream a lot when you teach me how to drive."

"No doubt," I sighed.

One of my most poignant memories of Lilian and Doña Marina was of our last night together before I went back to the US. The three of us held each other tightly and sobbed. Doña Marina gave me a note she had scribbled in her best educated-to-sixth-grade handwriting, saying how much she appreciated that I had been a light in the darkest night of her life, June 24, 1999. Lilian told me I had shown her that a young, single woman could have a career and independence. She thanked me for helping her finish high school and get a scholarship for college.

There were so many stories I wanted to share with Lucia, but I wondered what would be appropriate for a ten-year-old to hear. We walked back to the porch and sat on a bench. Silently, I remembered sitting in that spot and holding a little girl, maybe only two years old, whom I had found in the center of town, being cradled by her weeping mother while surrounded by onlookers. The girl was as limp as a rag doll, and her eyes had rolled back. The mother lived in one of the far-flung villages and had come to the government health center in Las Cruces to get her febrile daughter treatment. The health center confirmed the diagnosis of malaria and turned them away because they had no medicine. She was crying because she had no hope. I told her that I could get treatment for her daughter. The woman's tears cleared, and she nodded. A little bit of hope emerged. I ran home as fast as I could to get the truck from Brian so that I could give them a ride back to Casa de los Estudios. The girl got an injection, but it was too late. The mother cradled her dying daughter and sobbed. After having been elevated even slightly by hope, her fall was further. Before Brian took her back to her village, she handed me her dead child to hold so that she could use the latrine and drink some water. I wondered at what I had done.

Noticing the pensive look on my face, Lucia asked, "What's wrong, Mommy?"

Instead of telling her about the little girl, I shared a different memory.

"There was a stray cat that lived here. She ate whatever food scraps she could find. One day, I saw her gobble a lizard whole. The tail hung out the cat's mouth until it made room to swallow it down."

"Mommy, that's disgusting!"

"Hmm, I just saw the tail. Maybe it was a snake," I teased.

"Ew! Yuck!"

"Anyhow, within a couple of weeks, I caught on to why she had been so desperate for food; she was pregnant. She gave birth to a litter of kittens in a box on this porch. Brian and I stayed up to watch the births.

That momma cat was so skinny afterward, and the kittens looked tiny and fragile. I gave her powdered milk mixed with *agua pura* so that she could regain her strength."

"But, Mommy, you don't like animals."

"You're right, sort of. I don't like it when people treat animals like people and people like animals. There was something about this cat and her kittens, though. After all the death I saw during my first few months in Guatemala, I was adamant that the kittens would fare well. Every day, I would go into town and buy a couple of cans of tuna to feed the cat along with the powdered milk. One by one, the kittens died, though. I begged Brian to bury them. I couldn't bear to allow the mother to deal with it, and I certainly couldn't do it myself."

"Mommy, that's terrible," replied Lucia. "No more sad stories, okay?"

"You're right. Let's walk around some more."

We got up and went to the salón where the courses had been held. This large, empty room was once packed with stacks of chairs for the day and cots for the attendees to sleep on at night.

"Every few months, we would haul a dead pig onto the grounds so that the promotores could practice suturing."

"Gross."

"Doña Marina once told me that in her midwifery classes here, she had to explain that women have three holes between their legs and what each was for."

"Even grosser."

"Well, a few weekends each year, all the promotores and comadronas gathered here for a seminar that Lilian and I led to talk about the government's health policies. Serious days filled with political rhetoric were followed by *noches culturales* [cultural nights]. We divided into small groups to make up skits, songs, and games."

I proudly told Lucia, "I won a game here, chugging soda from a can. Soda was considered expensive and an occasional indulgence few could afford, so most Guatemalans couldn't swallow the carbonation without foaming at the mouth."

"Is that the only chugging contest you've won?" she questioned.

"Uh, let's go check out the clinic," I deflected.

After we had been there for over an hour, I assumed some emergency must have happened to call folks away and that they would not be back that day. I was writing a note when I heard a moped pull up, driven by a young man.

Marina jumped off the back of the moped and straightened her skirt.

"Ay, Juanita! I thought you might be here. The program moved to another location a few years ago, and I was afraid no one told you."

Before I had the chance to respond, she already had me in a big hug.

"I was wondering why it looked abandoned. Why did the program move?"

"The catechists and the new priest didn't want us to give out family planning. Have you heard of anything more ridiculous? How can you have a health program without family planning?" She gave me a knowing smile.

I then introduced Doña Marina to Lucia. "She was born on June 24." As I saw her smile fade, I said, "I know what that day means to you. I have told Lucia about the strong, wise, bold, and compassionate woman you are and that I hope she will become like you."

The smile returned.

"So, Doña Marina, is this young man one of your grandsons?"

"Ay, no. He's just some *patojo* [kid] I grabbed off the street to bring me to you. Let's go back to the new site." She told me where the program had moved, jumped back on the bike of the poor, unsuspecting young man whose afternoon she had taken, and said she would meet us there in a few minutes.

That afternoon, Doña Marina and I had less than two hours together before she had to return to her village. Two teenage granddaughters who lived with her were tying her down.

"Next year, when they are out of the house, so am I," she declared. Her husband had died a couple of years before, so her domestic duties were loosening.

"I'm so sorry for your loss," I told her.

"Eh." She shrugged. "It's fine." I gathered she had not been that distraught. "Actually, now I have a new lover."

Whoa, I didn't see that coming. At sixty-five, Doña Marina had been contacted by a former flame from when she was just fourteen years old. His family had moved away, and they had lost touch. He found her after fifty years apart, and they rekindled their young love.

"We met at a roadside motel. Ay, Juanita, I've never done anything like that in my life. I've only been with my husband, so I wasn't sure what to do. I did tell him that before I did anything, he would have to do a full exam. I brought my health promotor kit so I could check his vital signs and do a simple urine and blood analysis."

"Well, Marina, did he pass?"

"And then some." And I heard that deep belly laugh again as her plump fingers patted me on the knee.

After we left Las Cruces, we visited Lilian in San Benito. She had finished college and was a social worker helping battered women. She bought a prim little house in San Benito that she had paid for in full. She had an armoire full of tailored dresses but barely any kitchen supplies. Her son was living with her and was in college. The sharp angles in her face had softened over the years. She was doing well.

I invited Lilian and her ten-year-old niece to join Lucia and me for a tour of Tikal. I thought seeing this magnificent ancient city would be an unforgettable memory for Lucia. As I had hoped, the girls raced up the steps of the Jaguar Temple, pointed out the coatis (mammals the size of a large cat that are closely related to raccoons), and learned about the Maya ball game that was once played in the central courtyard. Though Lilian and I had been there several times, there was something new to see with each visit.

Lilian said, "I have a friend who works here as a guide. He makes up all kinds of stories to tell the tourists. He'll walk by a random plant and say, 'That can cure such and such.'"

"Really? Why would he do that?" I asked.

"If people are willing to pay to hear stories about weeds, that's their problem. My friend's problem is making sure he gets a good tip so he can feed his family."

I felt oddly reassured that Lilian's pragmatism was among the few things that had not changed.

Perhaps we will never know why Tikal was abandoned. Whatever written texts existed have long since been lost. The hopes and dreams, the sorrow and loss, have been buried beneath piles of stones overgrown by jungle. I like to think that the place no longer served the people who built it, so they moved on. Though I know they must have carried their sorrows with them, I hope they regrouped to find new homes, new loves, and new lives.

20
SEARCH FOR HOME

AFTER WEEKS OF searching, I had settled on the small studio apartment belonging to Michael the ex-Mennonite. It was perhaps not even a half mile from the house where we had been staying, but most of that was an uphill hike along a poorly marked forest path full of roots and stones. Since it was impossible to roll my suitcases, I had to pack them light enough to balance on my head, resulting in the need to make several trips, all of which had to be done before the sun set or the afternoon rains started.

After a few nights in Michael's studio, I knew that living there with Lucia long term would be a disaster. We were on top of each other in that one room and isolated from the town center. I feared we would fight all the time. Was this what Wade thought would happen in our relationship? That if we were alone with no outside support, we would have "trouble"?

A woman at a café told me about a Guatemalan named Heinrich who was soon leaving the country and looking for a tenant to sublet his house. She described the path to his property in the heart of the gringo quarter and told me to look for a bamboo fence with a red door and a massage sign. When I knocked, out came a thin, long-haired, bearded man, trailed by a waft of cigarette smoke. A quarter Swiss, Heinrich used his EU passport to go to California each year to trim cannabis plants. Like many semipermanent expats in San Marcos, he earned enough money in three months to survive the rest of the year in Guatemala. Raised in the city and partially university educated, he was neither the typical Guatemalan man I had met nor the typical migrant farm worker I had spent years advocating for in North Carolina.

The bamboo fence enclosed a plot of land with a furnished house, a separate structure with a washing machine (a major selling point), and a repurposed food truck with a cot where Heinrich slept and his sometime girlfriend gave massages. The property was owned by an American woman, but Heinrich had been the administrator for about a decade.

The house had a separate bedroom and an indoor bathroom, which was good. Its state was difficult to assess because the current tenant had scraps of cloth from her sewing projects strewn about, but it seemed in disrepair. Heinrich assured me of all the improvements being made: a water filter system, hot water for the shower, repairing the oven door, etc. The price was lower than the studio and the location more accessible, so I gave him the first month's rent and a sizable deposit. Again, I would have to pack the suitcases lightly and carry them on my head for repeated trips over rocks and roots to a new property.

As I should have predicted, Heinrich left for California before completing the repairs. Even worse, when it was vacant, I saw that our new home was perhaps the worst slum I had ever stepped foot in. Heavy rains had washed mud and bugs under the doors and into the house. Heinrich had let his mangy dogs roam the house freely, and so fleas attacked our ankles as soon as we entered.

When I complained to Lana, she told me to buy flea spray at the local pet store. I thought *how fitting that San Marcos, with its large expat population, has a store for animals but not a bookstore for children.* Holding my breath, I emptied out the entire can, fumigating every curtain, corner, and *colchon* (cushion). Upon further inspection of the premises, we found filth: rotten food in the oven, enough garbage to fill five bags, and goo caked on the cabinets.

Heinrich had left Ubaldo, a local man, in charge of the remaining repairs. Since Heinrich was unavailable to hear my rants, I let out my frustrations on Ubaldo and demanded that he have someone help clean the house. It was in no condition for us to live in.

"Who is going to pay for that?" he asked.

"YOU!" I demanded. "What was the deposit for if not a decent place to live?" He reluctantly had a woman come once, and then I insisted she come again to wipe the cobwebs off the windows, help me scrub the cabinets, and mop the floors.

"But she already worked eight hours," he replied.

"I don't care how long she works. I want the house to be clean," I insisted.

For hours, I scrubbed the guck off the floors, picked up the trash, and scraped the walls. Still, it was filthy. I soon learned that the roly polies on the floor did not just wash in with the mud but rather came up from under the floor, particularly in the bedroom. No foundation had been laid, and the clay floor tiles were placed directly on the ground, so there was no real barrier for the bugs. I would sweep them up every morning when we woke, when I returned home from work, and again at night before going to bed.

Lucia was less concerned with the mess and more focused on the multiple species of spiders crawling on the walls and lying in wait in their webs. She was afraid that she would be eaten in her sleep. We put up a pabellón and moved the bed away from the wall. At night, we were diligent about using the bathroom just before crawling into bed. We huddled together under the pabellón and tucked it tightly under the mattress. Neither of us dared to get up until morning.

The wall behind the stove had a burned hole, and the broken oven door was dangling. Heinrich had installed a new water heater because although he bathed outside with a rainwater tank, he knew that his potential gringo tenants would not tolerate doing so. This new heater was nonfunctioning, so to take warm showers, I heated our water in pots on the stove and then mixed the boiling water with tepid water in a tub. Lucia was disgusted by the bugs floating in the pot after I boiled the water. We would dip a bowl in the container of warm water and pour it over our heads to bathe. When the shower clogged or spiders came out of the drain, we resorted to bathing on the front porch, assuming no one could peer through the bamboo. I hoped to ameliorate the situation by tapping into her imagination.

"Let's pretend we are in a jungle and are bathing with water from a flowing stream," I suggested.

"We *are* in a jungle," she countered.

"Oh, yeah. Sort of, I guess."

After we finished bathing, she commented on the other pot of water on the stove.

"Why do you boil our drinking water if we have a filter? Didn't Heinrich charge you extra for a new filter?" she asked.

I knew from ODIM studies of samples from local homes that even filtered water had chloroforms. "The filter only removes the big stuff like the bugs and some of the bacteria, so we want what the filter leaves behind to be dead."

"That's disgusting!"

We had moved into Heinrich's house a couple of days before the end of October, so Halloween was just around the corner. Halloween was one of the biggest holidays of the year in Seattle. Our neighbors would decorate with skeletons, tombstones, and intricately carved jack-o-lanterns. Droves of trick-or-treaters went to houses that were decked out with ghoulish sound effects and dry ice rising from the ground. Wade and I would accompany Lucia around the same five blocks in our neighborhood while she ran up to the well-lit doors that were somewhat spooky but not too scary. Lucia loved getting a bag full of candy, I loved the opportunity to see the neighbors, and Wade loved watching Lucia overcome her fears.

Though the house was still a mess and I hadn't unpacked, I promised Lucia that we would do something for Halloween. After all, traditions are part of what makes a home. We were invited to a party the day before Halloween, thrown by one of the wealthy expat families who attended Escuela Caracol. I didn't bother assembling a costume for Lucia because

I thought since none of the other attendees were American, none would be dressed up. I was wrong. We arrived to find pirates, fortune tellers, and vampires filling our host's large home.

"I'm so embarrassed! Everyone here has a costume but me. I want to leave!" Lucia said.

"Look, we just got here. Stela and your other friends from school are here. Let's stay awhile."

"Those other kids are not my friends. They are all in Stela's grade," she protested. "And they all have costumes!"

"We are staying for at least an hour. Then we'll go," I promised. Despite her complaints, Lucia huddled with the other kids and played.

At the party, I heard that there would be a proper American-style Halloween event at Emma's hotel the next night. I thought this might be an opportunity to redeem the day. I also thought that since Emma had young children, it would be family friendly.

The next night, I felt like the mice assembling a dress from scraps for Cinderella to go to the ball. I suggested to Lucia that she wear her pink tutu and dress as a ballerina. I tightened my loose black tank top over her small torso, pulled her hair back into a neat bun, rouged her cheeks, and we were off to the party at Emma's hotel.

Though we lived in a densely populated section of town, there were no streetlights, so we had to find our way with a flashlight. On either side of the path were trees or high bamboo walls, so the flashlight only illuminated what was directly in front of us. I slipped on a wet stone and slid into a trench, which startled both of us. I couldn't see how to get out, so I reached for Lucia to pull me up.

The residual wind of the evening rains whistled through the narrow paths. We heard scurrying footsteps in different directions but could not see who they belonged to. When I heard barking, I was relieved that it was just the roaming pack of dogs and not ne'er-do-wells in the night. This felt scarier than any of the Halloween special effects in Seattle.

We arrived at Emma's hotel to find only a group of twenty-somethings dressed like backpackers at a bar.

"This is awful! No one is dressed up!" Lucia cried. "Let's go now!"

This time I didn't make her stay and instead let go of my hopes for a fun Halloween.

As we headed back to our house, I noted she hadn't said, "Let's go home." *Had I failed to make our new house a home? Was there any place Lucia felt comforted and safe here? Was there still time to try?*

After days of scraping and scrubbing and hours of griping to Ubaldo, Heinrich sent me an email from California that the owner wanted to sell the property, so we would have to move out at the end of the following month, December. I was convinced that he was merely tired of my complaints and wanted a less demanding tenant, miffed that I once again had to look for a place to live, and, at the same time, relieved to leave this rotting dwelling.

And so, my search for home continued.

21

FROM THE CENTER OF THE EARTH TO THE TOP OF THE SKY

ONE DAY, WHILE I was in the Chuitinamit clinic, I received a call from the Sanjuanerita clinic, saying they had received a call from someone who had been contacted by Escuela Caracol to relay a message to me. In a literal game of telephone, I heard, "The teacher says you need to go get Lucia because her father has died."

My heart sank, my throat swelled, and tears pooled in my eyes. After a moment, I realized there was no way they would know that. What had actually been said was "Lucia's teacher's father died, so you must go get her." That made more sense.

I called Pedrina to ask her to pick up Lucia, but she didn't answer. Rushing out of the clinic, I took a tuk-tuk to San Marcos and ran up the path to the school. I found Lucia sitting alone in a classroom with Natalia, despite my promise a few weeks previously to never make her wait again. The entire school had closed because the father of Diego, the teacher of the *manualidades* (crafts) class, had died. All the staff planned to go to the funeral.

What were parents supposed to do? Really, it did not matter for other families; they all had someone at home. I was the only single parent with no family to pick up Lucia.

Natalia said that the funeral would be continuing for some time and that we were welcome to attend, even if we did not know the man. I figured this would be an opportunity to experience the local culture, connect with the community, and show our respects. I rushed Lucia home and hurriedly changed her into her blusa and corte.

During my previous time in Guatemala, I had been in the vicinity of several deaths but had only been tangential to the burial of one.

I was taking a walk in Las Cruces when I came upon a crowd of onlookers. An epileptic man who made a living charging one quetzal (about fifteen cents) to draw water from a well had experienced a seizure and fallen into his customer's well. A few people had tossed ropes in the pit and shimmied down to pull the man out.

Juana, one of the promotoras, came up beside me and said, "He's going to die."

"No," I countered. It was easy for me to disagree with Juana. I disagreed with most of what she said.

I first heard about Juana when, on my first day in Las Cruces, Brian asked me, "What do you want people to call you?"

"Jan."

"Uh, no way. No one can pronounce Jan. You have to pick something in Spanish."

"Okay, then Juana."

"Not Juana. We already have a Juana, one of the promotoras. People would confuse you two. You have to pick something else."

"Then Juanita."

"Juanita it is."

I hated the name Juanita. It invoked for me the image of someone yelling, "Juanita, get yer ass back in the trailer now, ya hear?" or of a *chaparrita*, a squat woman with long braids. Though eventually I affectionately embraced the name and appropriated the irony, it certainly annoyed me for a while.

I met my near namesake, Juana, when she came to the compound for a clinic day. She smiled, showing the four gold stars in her front teeth. She crassly told me that her gold stars were her rating in her former life as a prostitute—four being the max. That was not one of the images I associated with my name.

Later, I saw her walking in the blazing sun with an umbrella, a rare luxury in our village.

"Why are you carrying a *paraguas* [umbrella, or literally 'for waters'] when there is no water," I attempted to joke.

"It's not a paraguas; it's a parasol."

"Oh, yes. Since it's summer, it's good to have something for the sun," I replied on that mid-August day.

"It's not summer; it's winter."

I attempted to educate her. "Well, actually, yes, it is summer. You see, we are north of the equator, so these days are longer. Summer is when the days are longer. Winter days are shorter, even if it is not colder."

Perhaps she never learned about the seasons in school. Maybe she never learned about north and south, about how the earth tilted toward the sun. Maybe she thought the world was upside down.

"It's not summer. It's winter" is what she said, again. *Stupid gringa* is probably what she thought.

It was easy for me to disagree with most of what Juana said, but most of what Juana said was right. In August, the sky darkens in late afternoon, and the rains pour at night; that is what *invierno* (winter) is in Guatemala.

The spectators by the well grew. The man crumpled against it was spitting out blood, a battered pulp. I looked at Juana, the veteran community health worker, for guidance. She plainly repeated, "He's going to die."

"No!" I declared again. There was no way I was going to give in to her prognosis. Too many people had already died around me. Once again, I ran home as fast as I could. I threw a mattress in the back of the truck and implored Brian to come with me to fetch the man. We drove back and loaded him in the back of the truck with his parents.

"He shouldn't go to the hospital. He's going to die," Juana repeated one last time. Brian didn't agree or disagree with Juana or me. By this point, he probably knew it was in his best interest to simply comply.

Down an unpaved road, we rode for an hour to the hospital. This man screamed in agony for the entire hour as his body was jostled. At the hospital, I escorted the parents into the emergency room with all the privilege "Jan" had carried my whole life and demanded that this man be treated properly. We left the parents at the hospital with money for food and bus fare back to Las Cruces.

On the way home, I had mixed feelings. I worried about the man, how he would fare. I was also proud of myself for intervening. *Would this be the one person I could save? Wasn't this why I was there?*

The next afternoon, I heard a truck slowly pass by the clinic compound with noise blaring. Since this was unusual, the folks working at the clinic ran out to see what was going on. I saw the epileptic man's parents in the back of the truck, grief stricken. Another man with a bullhorn was begging for donations to get their son's body out of the hospital.

Hospitals charge a significant fee to release a body, more than any typical *campesino* (rural farmer or laborer) family can afford. You only go to the hospital if you are moderately sick. If you are a little sick, it is better to endure than face the indignity and poor care you would receive. If you are very sick and might die, you don't go to the hospital because of the burden your death would be on your family. All that extra pain I had inflicted by forcing that man to go to the hospital was compounded by the pain his family now had to go through.

Juana was right. The world was upside down.

Lucia and I arrived at the Catholic church at the close of the mass, which was being conducted in Kachiquel, to find upward of fifty people, mostly men. Outside the church were a dozen women, all covering their heads with the local shawls (dark weavings covered in stripes and adorned with colorful pom-poms on the edges). They were huddled in the streets, embracing, crying.

The pallbearers hoisted the casket on their shoulders and made their way out of the church, followed by the other attendees and the village women congregating in the plaza. I scooted up to Natalia and the other Escuela Caracol teachers to ask them to explain what came next.

"Now we go bury Diego's father," Natalia told me. The men had to carry the casket up the same steep hill where Lana had her property, followed by the rest of us. People came out of their houses to join the procession as we went up the hill. Lucia was delighted to encounter two girls from her class. And I was delighted to see her playing with friends instead of spending time alone or with her bunny. The three girls held hands, laughed, and skipped along. I measured my steps to stay a comfortable distance behind the family but still close enough to Natalia and the other Spanish-speaking Ladinos who did not understand these Kachiquel customs.

After ascending for half an hour, we stopped at the deceased's house, where the women of the family had gathered, too distraught to attend the funeral. Natalia explained that women in the immediate family wait and wail at home.

The pallbearers took the casket inside so that the wife, sisters, and daughters could say their last goodbyes. As we stayed in the street, small bags of water were bought at the tienda and dispersed among the crowd. Kids ripped the corners of the bags with their teeth, downed the refreshments, and dropped the plastic bags on the streets.

Diego's father had died with dignity, and now he was having his dignified farewell. Well into his sixties, he had finished raising his family. He had recently been diagnosed with cancer, and rather than receiving treatment, he had chosen to die at home, surrounded by family. Now he was surrounded by family one last time.

When the pallbearers emerged from the house, the ever-growing crowd followed them for another half hour to the cemetery atop the hill. We waited again outside the cemetery gates while the family completed the paperwork and paid the fees to bury the body.

Once inside, we stepped over mounds of dirt and through thickets to reach the plot, which was on an incline. Dirt flew out of a hole still being dug, and sawdust floated in the air from wood that was still being cut. By now, the mourners must have numbered a few hundred. I continued to relegate myself to the back, behind the handful of Ladinos, who were in turn behind the Kachiquel community members, who showed their deference to the family in front. Clearly, we were fourth-tier guests, and I feared it was only marginally appropriate for us to be there.

I turned to say something to Lucia, but she was gone. I looked up to see her blond hair on the six-foot pile of dirt by the grave. The girls had climbed the mound to get a better view of the action below. Towering over half the village was the blond gringa child in Indigenous dress, capturing attention and generating gossip. Appalled, embarrassed, and terrified that my child would slide straight into the grave, I gave her the strongest stink eye I could muster and mouthed all the profanity I hoped no one around could understand. When she finally got my message and slithered to my side, we slipped away before any further mortifying moments could be had.

As do other Mesoamericans, Guatemalans celebrate *Día de Todos los Santos* (All Saints' Day) by making shrines to commemorate their lost loved ones and picnicking at the cemetery to commune with their spirits, who come down to visit once a year. Particular to Guatemala is an annual *Festival de Barriletes* (Kite Festival) in the departamento of Sacatepéquez, where hundreds of kites, some up to thirty feet in diameter, are flown. One legend about the origin of this festival is that about a century ago, someone told the bothersome children who were bored at the cemetery to "go fly a kite." The making and flying of kites evolved into the large *barriletes*. Another story is that the Maya created them to ward off evil spirits on the day the deceased were allowed to visit the human world. The kites were fashioned to make noise to frighten those intruders off, as well as to carry messages to heaven on behalf of those in purgatory. The loud bombas blasted before Catholic mass and the blaring music in evangelical churches may have their roots in this tradition of warding off unwanted spirits. The theory I choose to believe is that the barriletes symbolically communicate with the dead through messages hidden in the kites' layers.

Lucia and I caught a ride to the festival with one of the other Escuela Caracol families, who had no directions beyond the name of the town where the event was to be held. When we arrived, we followed people until we came to a cliff where throngs had gathered. The barriletes were being launched off the ledge, but I couldn't see them because of the crowd. After daringly indulging in roadside ceviche, we headed down a path skirting the cliff to get a better view.

One after another, progressively more massive and more elaborate barriletes were set loose from the high hill above us. The barriletes that found a fortunate gust of wind were applauded. Those that found stillness in the sky and dropped swiftly to their deaths were mourned.

To get a closer look at the kites and talk to their makers, I enticed Lucia out of the shaded observatory section and onto the field with the promise that we would search for ice cream. Over the course of a year, teams painstakingly assemble the kites using bamboo, twine, and plastic garbage bags. With tissue paper, ribbon, and glue, they cover the kites with mosaic motifs reflecting Maya history and myths or contemporary political and social issues. Each year, the barriletes increased in size and complexity. I don't know if this is simply due to advances in engineering or because their makers had more messages to send to the sky.

The ground was covered with barriletes that had not yet had their turn. Many of the symbols were lost on me, but the expressions of grief and loss I knew well. I had seen too many times the look of a mother disconsolate over the death of her child. The wounds of the past were still fresh after more than twenty years. The end of war does not mean the beginning of peace.

I thought about my own grief as a painstakingly assembled design that I, too, carried with me. *Was what I was holding on to—the loss of my marriage, the death of a dream, the fear that I was hurting my daughter by separating her from who and what she loved, and the realization that despite my good intentions, I am often wrong—serving me, or was it keeping me tethered to the past?*

Like these people, I needed to climb a hill and let my barrilete go, to either be lifted to the sky or crash to the ground. I looked across the field filled with hopes and sorrows and thought of the message I would send to the spirit in the sky:

You were dragged from the center of the earth and thrust to the sky. I am so sorry for adding to your pain; I am sorry for my arrogance. It's led me to climb a colossal hill, yet I am worried about my daughter falling into a hole. The world is upside down, and I am on the wrong side of it. The ties I've clung to, my convictions, my hubris, strangle others. Please forgive me.

22

BANDS

ONE DAY, AFTER the Sanjuanerita clinic had closed for the morning shift and the staff were headed to Chuitinamit after lunch, I stayed on in Sanjuanerita to have some quiet time to work. While I was sorting spreadsheets, I heard bustling in the salón, so I went to check it out. About twenty young pregnant women, their cortes loosened and their fajas wrapped tightly around their bellies, were arranging the chairs into a circle. I had forgotten that the salón was used in the afternoons for Mamá y Yo Saludable education and support groups.

The women were joking with each other in Tz'utujil, so I couldn't understand what they were saying. However, from the giggling, I could tell that they were happy to be there. As a cohort in Mamá y Yo Saludable, they would continue to meet weekly for the next two years. Since they were all around the same age and from the same small town, they had known each other their entire lives. Were their partners involved? Did it matter? Perhaps the women already felt enough support from each other that their partners did not need to be part of the group.

I recalled the couples' childbirth class I had attended with Wade in Seattle. The women were excited and a bit nervous. This was their time to be with other women crossing the threshold into motherhood—time to shine and be shined on. The men just seemed skittish. All but two of the couples were married, matching wedding bands clearly displayed, not counting the young woman who was with her mother because her husband was in the military and stationed elsewhere.

The couple sitting by Wade and me had no bands. The woman looked very young, and the man sported a bright-orange T-shirt with the words King County Jail Inmate emblazoned on the front, along with a circle with a diagonal line around two stick figures in a "doggie-style" position. With his longish, thinning hair and amber-tinted glasses, he was more Comic-Con than Seattle chic.

When it was time to go around the room for introductions, all the couples took turns sharing their names, how long they had tried to get pregnant, and other benign details appropriate to the occasion. They all appeared to be happily married, even the woman with her mother as her birthing partner. Then it was Comic-Con man and his partner's turn. She mumbled her name and nothing else. Her companion cleared his throat and let us all know this was not his first rodeo. He'd had another baby some years before with another woman, and, as a veteran at this, he would be able to guide this baby's momma as well. He then shared the whole birth story of baby momma number one, probably thinking it was fitting. Anger swelled inside me at him for trampling on baby momma two's moment.

The introductions concluded with the other band-less couple, Wade and me. Though I might have felt an affinity with those other nice, insured, middle-class couples, demographically we were in the same group as the pair to our left.

Unmarried, unemployed, and on public assistance was not my vision of being pregnant, but it was my reality. Wade had been married once before and was afraid to take another chance. Maybe he had qualms that I would hold him back, but from what, I didn't know.

While I lived in North Carolina and he in Seattle, we talked for hours nearly every night about what a life together would be like. I tried to convince him that the security of connection and commitment would allow him to take risks with the assurance that if he fell, I would be there to catch him. I focused so much on assuaging his fears that I neglected to question whether he could give me what I wanted.

The instructor, a tall, frail woman, shared the details of her child's difficult birth, which resulted in a scar that she felt for seven years. All of us pregnant women gasped, and the men squirmed uncomfortably in their seats.

For the remainder of the childbirth class, we reviewed what most of us had already read in books. All the while, the expert to my left interjected with pearls of wisdom. Granted, apart from the instructor, he did have more experience than anyone else.

As we disbanded at the conclusion of the class, we all agreed to keep in touch. We would share our birth stories and perhaps bring our newborns together. But in the end, no other contact occurred. We were not really connected to each other. It was, after all, just a class.

Eventually, Wade and I did exchange bands, but it was our daughter, not those rings, that bonded us. We found a rhythm of taking care of Lucia, making changes in our routine along the way as the demands of our lives changed. Years later, though we took the bands off, we were still bound together in parenthood and did our best to continue to care for Lucia.

At last, I spoke up and took action on what I felt I needed by moving to Guatemala. I had a fulfilling job that I loved. In my responsibilities of being the sole parent present, I felt grounded. I was no longer the balloon floating aimlessly. The sun warmed my face every day.

But I still felt the scar.

23

CRUSHED

"CRUSHING THEM WITH MY FINGERNAILS is the only way I can make sure they are dead," I explained to Lucia, referring to the lice I was picking off her head. "That's what Pedrina told me. Otherwise, they will jump from the ground back onto us."

"But I have to hear the snap. That's disgusting!"

"I know, but I have tried everything else," I said, referring to the thin combs, the organic lice-repellent shampoo that I had lifted from the clinic, the toxic gel from Croatia that Lana had given me, and even cutting off most of Lucia's long blond hair. Pedrina had picked the eggs and nymphs from my head until I was finally clean, but even together, we couldn't get them all off Lucia.

"It's Clara's fault! She keeps spreading them to everyone in the class. I can see them crawling around her hairline," Lucia complained.

"Look, lots of kids in the US get lice too. It's not anyone's fault," I argued back, more to convince myself. *Is it my fault for exposing her to this?* "Hold still. I need to finish up so that I can go pick up the sheets from the laundry."

The standard method to kill lice living in bedding is to wash in bleach and then dry it on the tin roof, scorching the lice with the heat. Since I couldn't climb onto our roof, my only option was to take the sheets to the laundry patronized by the tourists and pay a day's wage to machine-wash and dry them. "I'm in a rush because we need to get to San Juan soon."

My first weeklong volunteer medical team, which consisted of ten folks from a Texan church, was arriving that afternoon in San Juan. Although at this point I had a handle on our day-to-day operations, I wondered how I would fit others into the clinic routine. This group had previously volunteered with ODIM, so it could be that I was the person who needed to fit into their routine.

I needed a team just to help me prepare for this team. As the volunteer coordinator, Alba handled the logistics of the travel, lodging, and interpreters. Ines helped me create the schedule of who would staff the clinics, and Tomás ensured the needed supplies would be on hand. Tulita hand-delivered letters to all the churches, requesting they announce that the foreign doctors were coming. Oscar paid a pickup truck driver with a bullhorn to broadcast the *jornada* (special day of clinic). Manuela merely dusted the pharmacy.

In the meantime, I found a medical protocol in English for treatments of common ailments that had been provided to past visitors. I flipped through to find that many of the medications mentioned were not in our pharmacies, and worse, that this protocol was not in Spanish. I wondered whether the past teams had more interest in creating their own experience than responding to the clinics' actual needs.

The schedule was such that the volunteers and our clinic staff would not be working together most of the week. I was concerned that we would miss an opportunity for the staff to learn from the volunteers and that the volunteers, rather than the staff, would be seen as the experts and be more highly valued.

The plan was for the group to come straight from the airport to Sanjuanerita to drop off several suitcases of medicines brought from the US. I needed to go to San Juan that afternoon to lead staff in sorting through the medications, stocking the pharmacies, and setting aside a portion to take to the mountain village of Palestina, where we would be holding a one-day clinic on Wednesday. Lucia had to come with me because we would be finished too late to catch a lancha or tuk-tuk back to San Marcos and would have to spend the night in San Juan.

We walked into Sanjuanerita to see Ines and Oscar dragging a dozen large suitcases and duffle bags full of bottles and boxes of medicine and supplies into the middle of the salón while Manuela sat idly by, waiting to be told what to do. I had requested more than fifty types of medicine from the team, but I didn't know what they could bring.

After greeting the staff, I asked Ines, "Do we know what is in each bag?"

"No," Ines responded. "It looks like they randomly dumped different medicines in each bag. We don't know what is what."

"Okay, let's take the list of what we ordered and work our way down to see what they brought and how much," I suggested. Seeing that Manuela still had her head in her hands, I asked, "Manuela, would you mind helping?" She took a copy of the list and walked into the pharmacy with one of the bags to do her sorting separately while I joined Oscar and Ines in delving into the bags still in the salón.

Within moments Lucia announced, "Mommy, I'm bored." I noticed Frances, Ines's eight-year-old daughter, quietly sitting in a chair in the corner and playing games on her mother's phone. Rather than responding to Lucia, I asked Ines, "Does Frances mind coming with you to the clinic on a Sunday afternoon?"

"Oh, no. She insisted on coming. She says she misses me so much during the week. She wants to spend time with me even if it means I am working. If I give her my phone, she's fine."

"Lucia, why don't you ask Frances if she wants to play?" I suggested.

"Frances doesn't want to play with me. She's playing on the phone. Mommy, why don't you have a smartphone so I can play games?"

"Okay, why don't you help us count the boxes and bottles of medicine?"

"Do I have to?"

"If you help us, I'll count that as your math exercises for the day," I bargained.

"Deal!"

Ines, Oscar, and Manuela started sifting through the suitcases and grouping the medicines by type. Lucia sat with a clipboard, ready to note the names and numbers they called out.

"Look, the teams are spending a lot of money buying cheap luggage that they just leave here," I commented, pointing to the suitcases piled by the bodega. "Then they spend more money checking these bags at the airport and transporting them here. Wouldn't it be better to give us the money so we can buy what we need locally? It would cost less and support the local economy."

"Jan, the reason we don't want Guatemalan medicine is that it isn't as good," Oscar replied. I looked to see Ines nodding in agreement.

Oscar's comment struck the same nerve in me as did the thought that the community valued the gringo doctors more than our local staff. It bothered me that they regarded imported medicine as better than what was domestically produced.

"But how can that be? I read in the *Prensa* that there is a Central American regulatory agency that oversees quality control. Certainly there are inspections."

Ines explained, "The patients treated with Guatemalan medicine don't recuperate as well as those treated with foreign medicine."

I didn't believe that there was validity to that claim without a double-blind clinical trial, but I dropped the subject. I needed to decide, out of the 200 medicines in our formulary, not counting the different concentrations, what we would need for the Wednesday jornada in Palestina. I asked Ines for guidance, and she showed me a list of twenty medicines taken on a previous jornada.

"Of all the medicines we have, why did these make the list?" I asked.

"I don't know," she responded.

"Do you know if this is what is needed or most used?"

"I have no idea. This is what we have always done."

I looked over at Manuela to see if she could provide guidance, and she merely shrugged. I didn't want to take something just because it had been taken before if it was not needed, nor not take something that may have been needed simply because they did not have it on the past list. I thought it was essential to make a rational, data-driven decision, since most of the Palestina patients had not had a chance to see a doctor for three months and would probably not be able to see a doctor again for many more.

I used the pharmacy management system I had created to determine what had been dispensed over the past month. Since we saw an average of forty patients a day, the average amount we dispensed each week would be ample. In other words, I made this overly complicated, and the sorting of medicines took hours longer than planned.

While I was deep in my calculations, Lucia called out, "Mommy, I'm bored." I looked over and saw the frustration on Oscar's and Ines's faces from having to repeatedly spell out the names of the medicines to Lucia.

"Hey, here's some money. Why don't you and Frances go get ice cream."

Lucia took the money and left with Frances to find treats.

I finished the calculations and was quite proud of myself when I handed the list to Ines.

"Here's a new list of what to bring based on what was used in the past. This way, we should have everything we need and not too much extra."

"Jan, if you think this is better, then we will do it your way," Ines responded with no fuss.

After half an hour, Lucia and Frances returned with sticky hands and faces.

"Oh, no, the time!" I exclaimed when I looked at the clock on the wall and saw that it was already after six o'clock. "The team is waiting for me to do the orientation. I'm so sorry. I have to leave now," I apologized as I abandoned them to continue working into the night.

Lucia and I ran to the other side of town, where the team was having dinner at the home of Gilda, an adjunct member of our team who hosted meals for the volunteers. Since it was past dusk, I could not find my way. One woman I stopped to ask for directions offered to take me to Gilda's house for five quetzales. Galled by her request, I turned her down, which was probably not a good idea. The help would have been worth the seventy-five cents. After a few more wrong turns, I was able to find someone willing to guide us without a fee.

We met the team at Gilda's house nearly an hour late. They had finished dinner and looked exhausted from the red-eye they had taken the previous night. This group included three older male physicians and their wives, two female nurses, and a couple of other church folks that wanted to chip in. I was charged with presenting the clinic flow plan for the week and a community health profile, which was challenging since the clinic did not collect diagnostic statistics or have treatment protocols other than what had been written for the volunteers.

While the physicians and nurses were interested in my presentation, the rest of the team was more interested in me—the single mother with a young child.

"How old is your daughter?" "What's her name?" "Where does she go to school?" "Is she the only foreigner at school?" "Do the boys bother her?" "What does her father think of her being here?" "Is he coming to visit?" "Does she have any friends?" "Is she lonely?" "How do you manage?"

Though I didn't have all the data I wanted for my presentation, I felt somewhat prepared to discuss the clinic. However, I was utterly flummoxed about answering questions related to my personal life. I did not want to put my daughter or my life on display or be part of the entertainment of their exciting week abroad. I shut down that line of questioning and asked to be excused when my presentation was done.

Early Monday morning, I walked Lucia to the dock to catch a lancha to San Marcos.

"Pedrina is supposed to meet you at the dock and walk you to school. If she's not there, then wait for her," I instructed. I wondered what Pedrina thought of my request to meet Lucia at the dock and accompany her to school since children half her age were wandering the town on their own.

Lucia asked, "What if she doesn't show up? The last time I was late for school, they didn't let me in."

"I talked to Pedrina Friday. I tried calling her yesterday to remind her, and I'll keep calling her today."

"Why won't she call you back?"

"Because it is free to receive a call, but it costs money to place a call. Here's what you should do. Look at the time on your phone. If she is not at the dock by 8:10, run as fast as you can to school and don't talk to anyone."

When the lancha came, Lucia boarded. I took a deep breath and sent my baby across the bay with just a hope that someone would be waiting on the other side. Lucia told me later that Pedrina did not arrive on time, but she indeed managed to go to school on her own.

The Sanjuanerita salón that comfortably fit twenty-four patients on a typical day was packed with over seventy, many of whom had walked miles to see the gringo doctors. I depended entirely on Ines to tell me what to do, how the flow should be organized, and what tools and supplies should be provided to the team. I was afraid that I would be lost when she left in the afternoon for San Pablo, but I made it through. All day, I bounced between Spanish, English, and the tiny bit of Tz'utujil I had picked up while I ran from the exam rooms to interpret, the laboratory to decipher the orders, and the pharmacy to fill the prescriptions. It was chaotic but exhilarating.

The first couple of days, I came home exhausted and unable to fully engage with Lucia. I still had her do her evening math, but instead of hovering, I did the dishes and zoned out on the couch. Wednesday morning, Lucia woke complaining of a sore throat and did not want to go to school. I wasn't sure if she was really sick. Perhaps this was a result of the fumes from the latest lice medication, which had needed to be applied overnight, or maybe she was just trying to avoid school and spend time with me. I did not have the time to debate with her.

As I heated the water on the gas stove to wash out the gel, I said, "Lucia, this day is super important. I absolutely cannot miss work. I won't have any regular staff in Palestina, just the interpreters and nursing students. I have to run this whole show on my own. Swear to me that you will just sit quietly in a corner and read and do your math workbook."

"Of course, Mommy."

I should have known better. Lucia had already accompanied me to the clinic several times during Escuela Caracol's numerous closings—for the first round of the elections, for the rain, for holidays, because Diego's father died, for nearly any reason. She was not a docile child who sat quietly in the corner. If I went to a meeting or chatted with a staff member in another part of the clinic, she was off. She joked with the receptionists, teased the nursing students, inserted herself into the pharmacy, and poked around in the laboratory. When I reprimanded her and told her to leave the staff alone, she responded that they would say she was not bothering them. Of course not! I'm their boss, and they would be reticent to say anything about her to me.

I was trying so hard with such weak language to assert myself as somewhat of an authority figure in my new job, or at least as someone the staff might respect. *How could I gain the respect of staff if I could not control my own child?* At the same time, I wanted her to be comfortable, feel safe, and have a rapport with my colleagues.

As soon as we were dressed, we rushed out to the town center to catch a tuk-tuk, stopping briefly to buy a couple of tamales for breakfast. We showed up in San Pablo just in time to meet the van that would carry the team from San Juan up the hairpin curves to Palestina. I found that the clinic would be in a large salón with no electricity or running water, just an uncovered barrel of rainwater. Nothing was organized. The staff had thrown all our medicines and supplies into unmarked boxes after I left them on Sunday evening.

So that I could focus on setting up the clinic, I set Lucia up with the doctors' wives, who wanted something to do.

"Hey, sweetie," I called to her. "I want you to stay with these ladies. They are going to distribute the reading glasses they brought. Also, they happen to be retired teachers and have graciously agreed to help you with math."

"Ugh, do I have to? I want to go outside and play. Did you see the pasture by this building? There's a momma and a baby cow. It's sooooo cute!"

"You have to stay here. You cannot go outside. Now, look, everyone else is waiting for me, so I have to go."

I soon realized the staff was as disordered as the medicines and supplies. I was told that the people in Palestina are ethnically K'iche', not Tz'utujil, and spoke a different language, so the five Tz'utujil/English translators I brought could do little. Dra. Vacinta, Tomás and Ines had stayed behind in San Juan to serve in the clinic that remained open, so we had no one who fully understood medical Spanish.

Along with the American medical team, we had the nursing students who were doing rotations with ODIM, the interpreters, who muddled their way through the different dialects, and Alba, the volunteer coordinator. We rallied and set up a reception table with boxes of medical records at the door, another station to check vital signs, exam stations in the four corners, and a row of medicines and laboratory tests along the back wall. I assigned folks to their stations and rotated among them, checking in.

The clinic was rolling along within the hour, and I felt comfortable with the flow. A long line had formed before dawn. Among the people waiting were an elderly woman with facial twitching from when her drunken husband beat her, a man with debilitating back pain from carrying heavy loads of coffee down a mountain, and a child with such severe asthma that I thought she would die in the waiting area.

In the moments I had to breathe, I looked to the entrance to see Lucia distributing reading glasses and intermittently doing her workbook. When I walked over to check on how she was doing, Lucia blurted out once again, "Mommy, I'm bored. Can I go see the cows?"

"Absolutely not!" I told her. "Leave them alone! Mothers of all species are protective of their babies. Stay here and do your math."

By midday, we had seen over half the patients, though it seemed as if just as many were arriving as were leaving. Alba announced that the large lunch Gilda had packed was ready to be enjoyed outside. Though Lucia had gobbled both tamales since I had not had the chance to eat, she rushed to help herself to the spread as soon as the baskets of tostadas, vegetables, and salsas were opened. I was starving from having missed breakfast in the morning, but I waited for the American team to be served, which meant Lucia was done before I even started.

I was chatting with Alba about logistics for the week and savoring my tostada when someone screamed at me in English, "Jan, your daughter needs you!"

I ran around the corner of the clinic and saw Lucia with her red face contorted into a scream but no sound coming out. Despite my admonishment, she had petted the calf, and then the mother cow promptly threw her across the pasture with her horn. Lucia had entrance and exit holes in her shirt and a long scrape across her torso. The doctors gathered around and commented on how close the injury had come to puncturing her liver, which would have resulted in a certain slow, painful death.

Fortunately, she did not need suturing. The nearest hospital was at best half a day away: down that switchback road, then the wait for a boat, crossing the lake to Panajachel, and a tuk-tuk to Sololá to the Hospital Nacional. And half a day only because, as a gringa, I had unlimited resources for transportation.

I held Lucia's hand as one of the doctors cleaned and bandaged her wound. Despite my calculated methodology for determining which medicines to bring, I did not have the right antibiotic cream. Once Lucia was calmed and covered, I slipped away behind the building and broke down. *How could I let this happen? What am I doing to my child?* It seemed even the cow was a better mother than me. The majority of mothers in the world live with this type of fear, demanding compliance from their children because the alternative could be lethal. *Why did I expect any special security?*

Those other mothers . . . I had to run back to the clinic because there were streams of people who wanted medicine in lieu of hope. *How was I going to balance their desperation for their children with mine?*

"We will not accept any more patients who come after two o'clock," I instructed the receptionist so that I could get Lucia back to the clinic in San Pablo for the antibacterial cream. At two on the dot, more patients trickled in, yet I told the receptionist, "*Ya no más,*" no more.

"But there are two people *en camino* [en route]. They just called. What should we tell them?"

"Ya no más."

I felt unable to balance working full-time, being a single mom with no family, and navigating four languages. I couldn't even protect my child from being gored. And now I would have to abandon other sick people to make sure my child got a medication I had neglected to pack. If I had listened to Ines and packed what had been on the list from the previous jornadas, I would have someone else to blame. But instead, this, all of it, was my fault.

I barked at the Guatemalan staff and US volunteers to gather the supplies and load the van as hastily as possible. I needed to get Lucia to the clinic before an infection set in. The American doctors who had paid a significant sum to do this medical mission would have to wait until they came back the next year to linger in the community. Within the hour, we rolled out of Palestina to make the descent down to the lake. The van dropped off Lucia and me at the Chuitinamit clinic in San Pablo and then headed to San Juan.

I let myself into the clinic to plunder the pharmacy for the triple antibiotic cream. I found several different formulas of "triple," likely for different types of abrasions. None of the packages indicated which was for gorings. Lucia remained calm as I squeezed several tubes of different formulas onto a plastic bag and mixed them together into a paste. However, she started to cry when I removed her bandage to disinfect her wound. The abrasion was nearly an inch wide and extended from below her pelvis to her rib cage. *Oh, my God. What kind of situation had I put my child in?*

When I told people that Lucia and I were moving to Guatemala, I got incredulous looks and comments. I thought the people who were most judgmental about my taking Lucia to Guatemala were also judgmental about Guatemalan mothers bringing their children to the US. And maybe my assessment was correct. Still, I used this as an excuse to dismiss their criticism. Perhaps they were right.

After the wound was doused with a half dozen different antibiotics, we returned to our bug-infested house, now dark from a power outage. I would have loved to light a candle, pour a large glass of wine, and slip into a hot bath, but there was no wine nor bath, and the only candle served as my light for cooking and cleaning dinner.

A winter rainstorm pounded our tin roof that night as I lay flattened in bed, trying to comfort my daughter, crushed by the day.

24

GO IN PEACE

BY NOVEMBER, THE country was in the midst of a political frenzy as a dozen or so political parties vied for survival. The constitution dictates that if a party does not receive at least 4 percent of the vote or one congressional seat, it must dissolve. Since there are so many parties, several disband after each election cycle, and the members reshuffle to form new ones for the next election cycle. As a result, political parties are based on special interests and personalities, not platforms. They obtain votes mainly through clientelism, intimidation, and vote buying.

The election mania had reached San Juan. An array of propaganda posters with multiple party colors and emblems were plastered outside every tienda. Pickup trucks blaring campaign slogans circled the two paved roads. There were rotating rallies in the basketball court by the plaza.

At the end of the last staff meeting before election day, I asked folks whether they would be traveling to vote. Only Dra. Vacinta indicated that she would have to return to her hometown, Xela.

Voting at Lake Atitlán was more accessible than what I had seen in Petén, where voting was costly in terms of time, money, and risk. Caoba, a settlement I had worked with, housed about a dozen Q'eqchi' families displaced by the war. They had been granted the worst land imaginable—remote from any urban center, void of any infrastructure, low lying, and susceptible to floods. Four plagues (rats, frogs, mosquitos, and botflies) contaminated their water, infected their bodies, and devoured their meager crops. The only indications of modernity were the few plastic shopping bags on which the women made their tortillas.

In Caoba, the families collectively decided who they wanted for president and pooled the little money and food they had to send one man to vote. He had to walk four hours to catch the one bus that passed each day to the nearest polling station. He had to spend the night, rise early in the morning to wait in line the whole day to vote, and spend the night again. On the third day, he took the one bus back and walked the four hours home. Three days to cast one vote on behalf of a dozen families.

At Lake Atitlán, I was curious about whether the staff was worried.

"I understand that there may be road closures, protests, and violence."

A few people shifted in their seats. Tulita raised her hand as a closed fist, the symbol for the Partido Patriado, and said something in Tz'utujil, to which all the staff burst out laughing. That was the group Lucia and I had hid from when leaving Dominique's property in San Marcos. The team appeared to be having a lively discussion about politics, though I could only understand the names of the candidates and political parties.

Wanting to be part of the conversation and perhaps a little more upbeat, I interjected, "Are you optimistic about the outcome?"

Rather than answering my question, Oscar asked me, "Jan, who do you want to win, Torres or Morales?" Jimmy Morales, the right-wing TV comic, was up against Sandra Torres, the ex-wife of a former center-left president.

"Well, since I'm a foreigner, I don't want to take sides," I awkwardly answered.

Perpetually trying to smooth things over, Ines interjected, "That makes sense."

"Regardless of the outcome, I hope that your families are safe," I continued. "If you would like, we could close with a prayer."

The last time I had prayed at a staff meeting was coincidentally during the elections in Petén. A promotor from a remote village who was standing for election as *alcalde* (mayor) announced that he had received a death threat. Padre Cirilo offered that his family could stay in the parish house until the election was over. Shaken by his story, all I could offer was to pray, the same prayer that I was offering this day.

But this call for prayer was not heeded. Instead, Oscar chimed in, "What about your country?"

"What do you mean?"

"Don't you have elections soon?"

"Uh, not until next November. We are starting to pick the candidates now." I had paid little attention to US politics while in Guatemala, so it had barely registered that we were coming into primary season.

"I heard Trump said that we were like cockroaches."

"Donald Trump?" I supposed Oscar could only be talking about the billionaire star of *The Apprentice*. "Why would anyone care what he says?"

Kenneth said, "He's one of the Republican candidates."

"You must be joking," I scoffed. When I noted that Kenneth was serious, I turned to Oscar to say, "That's ridiculous. He's never going to win. He's just an obnoxious rich man who says stupid things to get attention."

"But I don't understand," Oscar continued. "I know people go north, but it's only to work. Why would he think it's to rob or rape?"

Oscar and the others were genuinely perplexed by Trump's comments. They had lived their whole lives dealing with the racism of Ladinos against Indigenous people. They were used to being judged for not wearing Western clothes, not speaking Spanish well, their customs. The racism of the Ladinos and their US and Spanish backers was rooted in wanting to take Indigenous land and their labor, not in thinking that the Indigenous wanted to take something from them. People living on this continent had regularly traveled north and south for trade and land for thousands of years, so they didn't understand being judged for doing what they had eternally done.

I knew Oscar wasn't asking me to defend this position, only to describe it. I couldn't. Why was I so willing to uncover conflict in another country and so blind to the brewing conflict in my own? I turned to Kenneth to find a way out of the hole I had dug myself into. He did not offer me a way out, but he did stop me from making it worse. Giving the same benediction at every meeting, he simply said, "Go now in peace."

25

SPIRAL

TIME IS SACRED TO THE MAYA. They believe that humans were created to honor the gods as well as the passage of time. The pre-Columbian peoples of Mesoamerica had a cyclical view of time and a multitude of calendars based on movements of the moon around Earth, Earth around the sun, and Venus's swerving dance with Earth and the sun. Somehow, a culture that had not yet invented the wheel marked time with an intricate system of interlocking wheels representing different calendar counts.

The *cholq'ij*[22] is a 260-day calendar that combines a cycle of thirteen numbered days with a cycle of twenty named days. It is thought to be based on the movements of Venus and corresponds with nine cycles of the moon and the gestational period of humans. This is the divine calendar used to determine the time of religious and ceremonial events. Each day of cholq'ij results from a set of influences of gods, energies, and numerals, whose conjunction gives rise to the spirit of the day, or nawal. The nawal is a force that alludes to the sacred aspect of everything that exists: geographical places (caves, mountains, villages), physical phenomena (wind, fire), and important objects (the hearth and the home).

The *jaab* is a 365-day solar calendar divided into eighteen months of twenty days, ending with an extra period of five days called the *wayeb'* that does not belong to a month or year. This calendar recognizes the

---

[22] This calendar is most commonly referred to as the tzolkin, a word coined by the American archaeologist William E. Gates.

changes in the earth, the increasing light that gives way to the dark that yields back to the light, the beginning and end of the rain, and the time to plant and harvest corn. After the earth has completed its 360 days, it is exhausted and given time to rest during the five-day wayeb'. Renewed, the earth starts the year again.

The calendar round is made from the overlay of the cholq'ij and jaab calendars. A given combination of these two calendars will not repeat itself until fifty-two periods of 365 days have passed. Recognizing this milestone, the Maya believe that when a person reaches fifty-two years of age, she attains the special wisdom of an elder. As I write these words at fifty-two years of age, I'm not sure I believe this.

During that time of my life, I felt like I was in overlapping cycles. In the previous five months, my quest for home had me leave the townhouse I had shared with Wade and led to the homestay with the Cox family, the large house lent by the ODIM sponsor, the tiny studio I rented from Michael, and the dump managed by Heinrich from which we were being evicted, and soon another home to be determined. These cycles were so short that I barely had time to unpack before we were uprooted and sent out to search again.

I was also beginning to repeat slightly longer cycles of finding and leaving schools for Lucia. I had known the language school would be temporary, just a couple of weeks for Lucia to get used to speaking Spanish one-on-one. However, rather than finding an idyllic, low-stress setting in Escuela Caracol where Lucia would thrive, it seemed we'd entered a cycle of trying to fit in, being disappointed, and starting the search for another new school.

I wanted Lucia to go to school with local children, but I also wanted her to have friends she could relate to. Although Natalia said Lucia was adjusting to Escuela Caracol, I questioned whether she was blossoming there. I feared Escuela Caracol wasn't the right place for her socially, academically, or emotionally.

While walking through the center of the gringo section of San Marcos, I saw three White kids gardening. I assumed they were the homeschooled children Lana had told me about. After more inquiries, I learned that this group was composed of Yuriel, whose Spanish mother was a wealthy hotelier and Irish father was part of the San Marcos "migrant farmworker" community; Haylie, whose Canadian mother was a burned-out social worker who moved here to be a massage therapist for tourists; and Taska, whose Latvian parents were semiretired.

These children of expats had either been born in Guatemala or had come as infants. They had attended Escuela Caracol and would have been in Lucia's class; however, their parents withdrew them because they felt it was not academically challenging. The parents hired two teachers and formed their own school, rotating among their houses, educating their children in English instead of Spanish for the first time. They also organized after-school enrichment activities, such as video gaming, permaculture, and swimming.

I met Haylie's and Taska's mothers (Kelly and Irka) separately at the dock, and upon hearing our frustrations with Escuela Caracol, they encouraged us to join the group. Though I knew Lucia would feel more comfortable learning in English with other expat kids, part of the drive in moving to Guatemala had been to share this place and the people with Lucia. I wanted her to embrace what I loved about it and to feel embraced back. I wanted her to be immersed in the culture, not spend all her time with expats. But I had to admit that my attempts at making this so had only resulted in her feeling isolated and dependent on me for comfort and companionship. This caused her to be increasingly needy, putting more stress on me and further isolating us both. She needed more than I could give.

Before she even met Taska, Haylie, and Yuriel, Lucia begged me to switch to the home school. Just the thought of playing with other kids who spoke English, who shared her imagination, who might understand her sense of humor was enough to entice her to join the group. Lucia had never loved school and had persistently liked the notion of being homeschooled, even though she shunned our evening math lessons.

I talked this over with Wade, laying out the pros and cons. His main concern was for Lucia to have a decent education so that she would not lag behind when we returned to the US.

I came up with an initial compromise for Lucia to join the group for an after-school art class in San Juan on her early-release day. Pedrina would accompany her to the dock to wait for the boat with the kids, who would be coming from Irka and Taska's house, about one mile away from San Marcos. From mid-October to the end of November, the kids learned painting under the tutelage of Felipe, a local artist of some renown.

Within a month, the girl who would not come down from her tree was proudly coming home with paintings she'd made and stories of exploits. The foursome would race through the seats on the lancha and crawl on the roof for the ride (which I forbade Lucia to do). She came home excited to tell me how Haylie brought baskets of fruit to sell on the dock, and Taska was nicknamed Chatara (junk food) because she bought potato chips at the tienda. Haylie and Taska also had brutal catfights, which Yuriel and Lucia were wise enough to stay clear of.

She clicked so well with these kids and was so unhappy with Escuela Caracol that I more seriously considered pulling her out and putting her in this home school. To help me decide, Irka invited me to observe the class at her home. Before the lake level had risen, Irka and her husband had built an open, modern house that could have been ripped from the pages of *Architectural Digest*. Perhaps on a variation of the Maya style, their home comprised a series of separate structures. However, rather than sharing a common center, these rooms were connected by walkways and overpasses, reminding me of a hamster's cage.

The day I visited was Nigel's turn to teach math, geography/history, and science. Nigel was a middle-aged Englishman living as a Daoist monk in the Tai Chi Tao Temple in San Marcos. The temple was a magnificent structure of bamboo and local materials resting on a hill overlooking the lake, with a clear view of two volcanoes. This religious community was supported by a Silicon Valley tech entrepreneur and by offering courses to help obtain enlightenment. For $2,000 (which a Guatemalan would be lucky to earn in a year), you could take a Kundalini yoga class lasting one moon cycle. Lodging and food were extra. Nigel worked out a deal with the temple community to leave a few hours a week in exchange for his earnings from teaching.

Irka escorted me to the class, a one-room workshop. Measurements of arcs and degrees were on the whiteboard, not the simple one-digit math in Lucia's Escuela Caracol class. The kids were talking over each other to answer Nigel's questions. When they finally understood the relationship between two concepts, their eyes widened, and they bounced with excitement.

They showed me the drawings of their invented hieroglyphics to explain their creation myths. My mind went back to Lucia's first day at Escuela Caracol when she was mocked for not precisely copying a Nordic design that Natalia had drawn on the blackboard. A love of learning, imagination, and play were the essence of what I wanted Lucia to have in her education. When I asked Nigel about the other instructor, who taught language arts, I was unimpressed that he spoke disparagingly of her. Nevertheless, I was struck by the level of student engagement, the creative assignments, and how he focused on relationships rather than operations in math.

During recess, the kids ran outside and jumped in the lake. Nigel pulled out a cigarette and told me that smoking was his only vice, but he never did it in front of the children, presumably because that would be inappropriate, though apparently smoking in their classroom was not.

"This 'project,' this 'experiment'"—as he referred to the school—"is an alternative to traditional didactic methods." He proceeded to tell me how he was "well equipped to handle the particular dynamics of these children" because, before his days as a monk, he was a psychiatric nurse. He treated adolescents with substance abuse problems. Watching this monk with a shaved head and scruffy beard dressed in a scarlet robe and sandals lean back into his chair, taking a long draw on a cigarette, I imagined him as the hard, working-class, educated Northern Englishman he once was, dressed in a black T-shirt, jeans, and Doc Martens.

In the end, primarily due to Lucia's pleading and after consulting with Wade, I decided to switch her into this home school beginning in December, immediately after the school year for Escuela Caracol ended in November.

Escuela Caracol held a closing ceremony to celebrate the transition to the next grade in the last week of school. As darkness fell, the families and staff gathered under the large *palopa*, a round hall with a pitched thatch roof, where a spiraling path of branches and needles was laid. To represent the unfinished journey of each little light, one by one, the children took a candle, walked slowly through the path, and then set their candle down at a place of their choosing while the families looked on quietly. As I watched Lucia make her way through the mandala, I thought about what she had learned from this experience and what was yet to come. *Was she more resilient or more fragile? More empathetic or more indifferent? More creative or more compliant?*

In December, the home school moved to the home of Yuriel and his Spanish mother, Pilar, whom I had yet to meet. They lived in Tzununá, the next town from San Marcos going clockwise around the lake. When we'd landed in Guatemala a few months earlier, Lucia couldn't even walk across the street by herself, and now she would be taking a boat and walking through an Indigenous village to school every day. If we timed the boat right, she would meet Haylie at the San Marcos dock, and then Taska would join them off her private dock at the next stop.

For the first day, Pilar gave me vague directions: "Take the lancha to Tzununá and look for a large white house on the hill."

Given that I had never been to Tzununá, I was not sure of the right dock. When the lancha stopped at a large white house, Lucia and I disembarked, not knowing that this was another person's home. We were trapped in the lawn of a stranger's house, surrounded by walls and water, and begged permission of the staff to let us pass through.

As we wandered down the road to Tzununá, we spotted a blond

woman in a Jeep, who, upon seeing another blond woman and child, stopped, knowing who we must be. After I confessed my confusion about the directions, she waved down a tuk-tuk and told the driver where to take us rather than offering us a ride back.

When we finally arrived, the class had already begun. The American woman teacher had been replaced by Calum, a twenty-five-year-old Scott. With pale skin, long, dark, wavy hair, two large, gold hoop earrings, and a thick brogue, he appeared more like a pirate than a teacher. I handed him a stack of children's magazines and pointed out articles that I thought would inspire essays. After chatting a bit about education theory and approach, I could tell he was a proper teacher, genuinely interested in the children's learning, and didn't think of them as mere participants in an "experiment." I wished them well, kissed Lucia goodbye, and headed to work.

The reality of the change hit Lucia abruptly. Natalia was a Guatemalan version of her American elementary school teachers—smart, sweet, but stern—who chose this career because they genuinely cared about children and their development. Now having two male teachers from the UK was jarring. They tolerated no horseplay, remarked how below standard the children were, and rebuked the parents' requests for more communication about their plans. Clearly, there were reasons for Pink Floyd's commentary on the British education system in "Another Brick in the Wall."

Calum was offended that Lucia could not understand him and accused her of being disrespectful when she asked him to repeat what he said. I explained to him that her only exposure to British accents had been from Harry Potter movies but didn't dare tell him that I needed to read the subtitles when watching *Trainspotting*.

When Lucia asked Nigel why he became a monk and then a teacher, he replied, "I've done everything in life I wanted to do, so I decided to do something I didn't want to do."

"What does that mean?" she asked me.

"It means that he's a smart-ass," I replied.

Still, there was some good. Calum was exploring writing techniques. Nigel was teaching guitar. Lucia was gaining independence, making the trek to school, and building friendships. *Would this time be different, or would disillusionment soon sink in?*

While the jaab and cholq'ij calendars continue their endlessly repeating, interlocking cycles, the Long Count is a third, parallel system that marks the time since creation began. The Maya use it to keep track of periods longer than fifty-two years, counting in units of up to 5,125 years. Though the Long Count is yet another cycle, its great length makes it essentially a linear count through nearly all of Maya history. According to this calendar, the last cycle began in 3114 BC and was completed in 2012 AD. The media erroneously described the transition into a new epoch in 2012 AD as a prediction of the end of the world. Instead, we are entering a new era.

I began to see these rotating wheels of school and home interlocking and forming a larger cycle or epoch. Certainly, this wouldn't be the end of the world, but I began to wonder if we would ever feel settled.

The Maya do not see time as repeating exactly. Time is a forward-moving cycle. We do start over, but in a new place, like a spiral, *un caracol*. Aligning the calendar round to the Long Count assures us that we will not return to where we began.

Is this an endless cycle that all are doomed to follow, or do we, if we are lucky, learn with each repetition and move forward? Would all my calendars finally sync and allow me to enter a new era?

26

CLASHES, CRASHES, AND QUAKES

WADE WAS COMING for a three-week visit in December. The first week, he would stay with us, which would be the first time we three would be in the same abode since the divorce. The second week, over Christmas, I would travel while he stayed in San Marcos with Lucia. The third week, they would travel, and the three of us would meet in Antigua before he returned to Seattle.

I was nervous about what he would think of the life I had made over the past five months—the life he had rejected. *Would he soften toward me or continue to spurn me? How would I navigate this?* We were a family, but we were not a couple. We would be standing in a dead dream. *How would I share my home with a man who did not want a home with me?*

A piece of me clung to the hope that somehow he would still want this, still want me. Maybe he would not fall in love with me again, but possibly in returning to the place where we had fallen in love and seeing me happy, he would see the woman he once loved and at least feel something.

On a Saturday afternoon, Lucia and I met Wade in the center of San Marcos, where the shuttle from Antigua dropped him off. She ran to him, and he grabbed her and gave her a huge hug. She clung to him tightly, relishing the kisses he covered her head with. He gave me a genuine but awkward smile and a spontaneous hug as well, the first in the two years since we had separated. Part of me wanted to melt into him like Lucia did, but my residual pain kept me stiff.

Flustered, I transformed into a tourist guide and began to state the obvious.

"Look, here we are at the town center." I pointed out all the landmarks in a 360-degree turn: the basketball court, the little park with the wood-and-iron benches, the man-made stream with a footbridge, the half dozen tiendas, the amphitheater, and the stone Catholic church. "Why don't you drop off your bag at the house, and then we can show you around?"

"Sounds good," he said.

We went down the paths to our house in the gringo section. Along the way, I pointed out every coffee shop, restaurant, and spiritual practice business and told him the backstories of the owners. He smiled politely and turned to talk to Lucia.

When we walked into the house, I held my breath, anxious about what he would say. Pedrina had helped me scour the house for two days to prepare for his visit. We waxed the clay floor, cleared the drains, and killed the bugs. I wanted him to be comfortable with Lucia being there, and honestly, I wanted him to be comfortable.

I continued my tour-guide banter. "Here's our place. We have a bedroom, an indoor shower, sink, and stove." I was aware that these were not luxuries worth bragging about in Seattle, but in this area of Guatemala, we were staying in a higher-end house. "You can sleep in the extra bed in the living room."

He set his bags down and made no comment about the house.

"I thought for dinner I would cook the Italian wedding soup dish you like."

I had taken the half-day trip to San Pedro that morning to buy sausages and other foods at a tienda that catered to expats, hoping he would be pleased.

"Okay."

After handing him a cold can of soda and a few moments of silence, I asked, "Are you ready to go?"

"Yeah."

Lucia and I escorted him along the steep hills that bookended the village, the handful of actual roads, and the multitude of footpaths. "There's the way to Escuela Caracol. The Tao Chi temple where Lucia's teacher Nigel lives is on that hill. Lana and Stela live down that street."

Every few minutes, we ran into people we knew from school, house hunting, restaurants, and lancha rides. We had built a community.

At dinner, we shared a box of cheap wine that calmed my nerves and opened him up. We laughed and gently teased each other. Lucia was delighted to have dinner with both her parents. Sunday morning, the pleasantness began to dissipate. Wade complained about the vermin in the space between the ceiling and the roof.

"Those are the neighbors' cats," I said.

"No, those aren't cats; they're rats. It's not safe for Lucia to live here."

I tried to defend my situation by explaining, "I looked for weeks for a place to live. San Marcos is super expensive because there are so many foreigners. This is the best house that I could afford."

"Well, you have to get the landlord to get rid of the rats."

"I've already complained so much during the six weeks that we have lived here that he's kicking me out. I have until the first week of January to move, and we will be gone for the last two weeks of December. We just have this week and the next when you'll be with Lucia on your own here. Since we won't be tied to San Marcos anymore because of the school, we're moving to San Juan."

Perhaps I was looking for pity or at least for understanding, but I found neither.

"That doesn't matter. Your landlord needs to deal with this now."

I don't think he understood that Heinrich had already found a way to deal with my complaints.

Monday morning, I suggested that Wade accompany Lucia to the home school to see how well she managed the commute to Tzununá and meet the teachers and other kids.

"You could stay all morning to observe how the class is conducted. You could also stay after and try to organize a Frisbee game with Yuriel's father."

There I was, trying to manage his relationship with Lucia again. But he wasn't going to be managed by me.

"No, I don't want to interrupt her class, and I don't want to go hang out with some guy I don't know. I'll wait for her when she's out of school."

Tuesday morning, I invited him to come to San Juan to see the town where Lucia and I would eventually be living, tour the clinic, and meet other people who were in our lives. The three of us walked down to the San Marcos dock together. Wade and I sent Lucia on the lancha headed north to Tzununá, and we boarded the lancha headed south to San Juan. Skittish about being alone with him, I shifted back into my tour-guide persona.

"That's the nature reserve where we saw these incredible apartments embedded in rock. That pink house belongs to the founder of my organization. Up that hill is San Pablo, which has the other clinic."

As before, he smiled politely and barely responded.

When we disembarked the lancha in San Juan, I continued my nonstop narration as we ascended the hill from the dock. Wade didn't comment on any of this and seemed indifferent to the townspeople's web of relationships that so intrigued me.

Our first stop was for me to drop off a suitcase as part of our impending move. We were moving to a house on Gilda's family compound where several expat volunteers had stayed previously. The cinder-block house was situated on a pile of boulders overlooking the lake. It was built like a motel with three rooms side by side, each with one door opening to a shared patio. The bathroom flanked one side of the house, and the pila where we would wash our dishes and clothes flanked the other, so we would need to go outside to use both. However, it was decent and peaceful. I planned to finish moving in early January after returning from traveling.

"Wow, this view is incredible!" I cheerfully declared, hoping Wade would agree. He nodded silently and continued to minimally respond as I babbled all the way through town to the clinic.

When we reached Sanjuanerita, I gave Wade a brief tour, including introductions to the clinic staff. We climbed the stairs to the office, where I presented Wade to Kenneth and Oscar. Oscar slipped me a sly grin, while Kenneth gave me a protective glance.

"Jan, are you coming to the party tomorrow?" Oscar asked. "I need the final number of people to make the reservation for food."

"Wade and I have a meeting with the parents and teachers at Lucia's new school in the afternoon, but if the tour is in the morning, we could go." I turned to Wade to say, "Do you want to join us? Kenneth chartered a boat for the staff and their guests to cruise around the lake. It would be a great way to see the lake. Also, you can practice Spanish and get to know the local people."

"Maybe," he replied.

We then headed up to the roof, where Kenneth had interviewed me for hours and inspired me to come, where I'd heard a woman bare her soul to Ines, where I had opened myself to all these strangers who became my friends.

"This building is only two stories tall, but you can see nearly the whole town from the roof. It's surrounded by mountains, except for the part where we're going to live, over there by the lake," I said, pointing all around.

"Looks nice."

Shifting out of tour-guide mode, I exclaimed, "I love what I'm doing here. After years of being miserable at work, I'm finally happy. My job is challenging, but in a good way, and interesting. I feel like I'm able to do exactly what they need. The people are wonderful, and they adore Lucia. When she comes to work, she pesters me. You know how she gets into everything. But the staff enjoy playing with her. I finally feel alive again."

"Good. I'm glad you like what you do. I want that for you."

"You know, those mountains surrounding us are covered in coffee trees. Since you did your master's thesis on fair trade coffee and years of advocacy, you might want to know about the coffee cooperatives. I could introduce you."

"No, that's okay. I'd rather just relax until Lucia finishes school."

Taking a deep breath, I summoned up memories from when we were dating, our long conversations about social justice and love of Latin America, and suppressed the stirring of emotions in my stomach.

"I don't have any illusions that we might be a couple," I half lied, "but maybe you could live here for a while. It would be fabulous for Lucia to have you here. You could experience all this with her. I'm sure you could get a job. In fact, I know a lot of the NGOs in the area now. I could introduce you to them too."

"No, I'm not going to leave my job or my family," he replied.

You've already left your family. I was your family is what I thought but did not say. Instead, I continued, "Wasn't this our dream? We talked about this life for years."

"It's not what I want."

"Well, what do you want for your life? Don't you have any dreams?"

"Of course I'd like to travel more, but I just want to have a good life. What I want most is for Lucia to be safe and well taken care of."

"She's learning Spanish, making new friends. It's hard, but she's doing fine."

This was going nowhere. I was either on the verge of or had already crossed the line of sounding like the groveling, desperate woman I didn't want to be. It was time to let go of the dream I had and embrace the dream I was living.

"Okay, why don't you go home, and I'll get started with work."

That night Wade declined to take the cruise with me the next day.

Wednesday morning, I made it to the dock promptly at 8 a.m., but found no boat and no staff other than Kenneth. We waited until well past nine for the rest of the team and the vessel. Eventually, a horde of staff and their families gathered. When each new person showed up, there was a cascading chain of kisses, hugs, and introductions.

When the boat finally appeared, the captain misjudged the boat's inertia and rammed into the dock. The staff squealed in amazement as a third of the planks fell into the water. Within moments, the children were catwalking on the still-standing structure to get a better look at the damage.

We would have to wait for the police, the boat's owner to be contacted, and the report to be filed. We were going to be there for a while. I had assumed that we would be back from the three-hour tour by noon, which would be plenty of time to be back in San Marcos for the meeting at Lucia's new school; I could not miss learning about the plans for this school or miss this opportunity to reassure Wade that his daughter was in a good place, even if the world was crashing around me. But it was also vital that I spend time with the staff to show that I was part of the team, so I decided to stay until the authorities came and permitted the boat to go.

Coffee was purchased from the lakeside café of the family that provided ODIM's land travel. Sandwiches brought by the mother of one of the nursing students were distributed. Staff ran up to the other travelers waiting for lanchas on the remaining portion of the dock to tell them what had happened. We posed for photographs. A visiting donor pulled out her ukulele, and we sang and danced on the roof of the boat. Up and down, from the roof to the deck to the dock, we all carefully crawled over fallen planks, chatting and chortling.

What could have been a disaster was just another day in Guatemala. I was relieved Wade was not there. Rather than yielding to the flow of the day, he would have been annoyed—or at least shown his annoyance with me.

Finally, after the police appeared and made their report, the boat set off close to noon, and I headed to San Marcos to rendezvous with Wade for the meeting at Pilar's mansion. At the last minute, Pilar changed the meeting location to a café in San Marcos, notifying us via email instead of calling, which I did not get since I did not have a smartphone. Instead, Wade and I learned about the change when we saw Irka at her private dock, heading west to San Marcos as we headed east to Tzununá. We had to disembark our lancha to join Irka in another lancha to return to San Marcos. I feared that this disorganized change in plans would tarnish Wade's impression of the home school.

We accompanied Irka to a café patronized by backpackers. There we joined Pilar, Nigel, and Calum around a small table. I politely ordered tea to compensate for taking over a table. Irka was indignant that the café did not serve beer and so went to buy one from the tienda next door and brought it back to drink in the café. Pilar and the teachers ordered nothing, indifferent to the accommodation.

Rather than waiting for Kelly, the group started the meeting by questioning whether Kelly would pull Haylie out of the home school since Haylie had missed a few days of class and no one had heard from Kelly. Irka said she had called the American school to ask whether Haylie was enrolled there for the following year. I was silent, completely taken aback by the brazen invasion of privacy.

Pilar and Irka then laid out the terms to me: the three founding parents would make all the decisions since they had a long-term commitment, and I would pay the tuition they set. They both agreed that Nigel could have a week of paid leave for his hernia surgery, and Calum could flex his schedule for a week of paid leave for a silent retreat. Even though Nigel, not Calum, was the monk, the other parents agreed that this was a perfectly reasonable request.

"I don't get a week of paid leave at my job a couple of months after starting," I asserted.

"Well, that's because you don't come from a civilized country," Nigel countered.

Nigel expounded on the goal of the "educational project to create a natural and holistic learning experience," as if he viewed our children as lab rats. When I asked him to present his curriculum, he responded, "It would develop organically and could not be constrained by a timeline." In other words, he hadn't prepared anything. However, Calum, a trained teacher, provided some cogent explanation of his education theory and how he planned to sequence introducing concepts.

More than an hour into the meeting, Kelly materialized. She had not received the last-minute email changing the location either, so she had gone all the way to Pilar's house in Tzununá. Rather than being warmly greeted with apologies for the mix-up, she was brutally accosted by Irka, Pilar, and Nigel for her plans to transfer Haylie to the American school. Kelly was silent at first and then vehemently denied the planned move.

After a couple of hours of rambling and further accusations, we adjourned. Stunned, Wade and I slipped out of the café and into the next bar down the alley. We seated ourselves on the deck by the water, ordered beers, and rehashed the meeting, both of us astounded by the absurdity.

I was anxious about Lucia being in a toxic mix, but Wade was more amenable to giving the school a chance. He was the open-minded one, not me. Being in a group of confrontational people made us appreciate how we were indeed sober and civilized toward each other. The conversation evolved from the meeting, to hopes for Lucia's education, to our own lives. Briefly, our guards lowered. We drank another beer, looked out onto the lake, and enjoyed a moment together.

Thursday, I woke with dread. This was the day that Kenneth, Oscar, and I would tell Manuela that we would not renew her contract for the following year (i.e., we were firing her). When I'd talked to Manuela about the need to have the pharmacy be more organized, she told me that she dusted regularly. When I asked her to alphabetize the medicines within categories, she got stuck after the letter "D." When I tried to explain how to calculate doses based on the patients' weight, her eyes glazed over, and she recoiled. She showed no interest in learning.

I hired Ofelia, one of the nursing students, to help me organize the pharmacy because Manuela could not do so. Ofelia was the brightest student and, I later found out, Navichoc's daughter. Ofelia's ambition was to finish nursing school and become an ultrasound technician. Though a few health-care providers on this side of the lake, including her mother, had access to an ultrasound machine, none had formal training or certification to use them. She wanted to be the first.

The interpreters who had helped in the pharmacy told me that

Manuela was advising the patients about inappropriate uses for the medications. For example, she advised patients to use salicylic acid, which is for warts, for their fever blisters on their lips. There was a lot of publicity around that time about the high rates of acetaminophen overdosing in children and high mortality due to medical error, and I was scared we would kill or at least seriously hurt someone.

Seeing the contrast between Ofelia's and Manuela's aptitudes and attitudes toward their jobs made me more frustrated with Manuela. If Manuela wasn't willing or able to learn the math and alphabet to safely dispense medicines, she had to go.

I asked Alba if she wanted Manuela back in the diabetes program. No. I asked the manager of the Mamá y Yo Saludable program if they could take her. No. The scholarship program? No. Healthy housing? No. She'd had so many emotional outbursts that no one wanted her.

Kenneth, Oscar, and I agreed that the best time to tell her was the day before we left for the two-week December break. Laying off someone the week before Christmas sounds like a callous move, and maybe it was; however, it would help her save face if she did not have to leave the clinic in front of other staff—or so I told myself.

The ritual for paying staff was for each to go to the office upstairs, check in with Kenneth about how things were going, sign a receipt with her or his name and thumbprint, and receive a month's salary in cash. Oscar agreed to stay to translate from Spanish to Tz'utujil to be sure we understood each other. We waited to call Manuela up for her turn after all the other employees had been paid. As she entered the room, Oscar looked down and fastidiously straightened the stack of five months' worth of wages that we would give her.

When she was seated, Kenneth and Oscar, sitting on either side of me, nodded at me as a cue to begin.

"Thank you for this past year of service. In the new year, we are moving to a new service model in which the clinic will be staffed by only the nurses, who will rotate through all the positions in the clinic [consult, laboratory, and pharmacy] so that they will be cross-trained to fill in for one another."

That was a long sentence. My nerves had me rambling. She looked confused, so Oscar interpreted into Tz'utujil. She still looked confused. I said the same thing in Spanish, and Oscar interpreted again, twice more.

Finally, she asked me in Spanish, puzzled, "You mean I will not work here again?"

"No," I replied.

Kenneth added, "However, in recognition of your years of service, we are offering you two months' salary in addition to the three months' salary you are receiving as your year-end bonus, even though you were already paid out your severance each year. All you have to do is sign a paper that you will not take any action against ODIM."

Oscar interpreted twice again.

Her face quivered, and I felt my heart palpate. From somewhere deep inside her began to flow a series of accusations and insults. All I could understand were the names of other clinic staff and the expression "*y Dios sabe*" (and God knows). She blamed her dismissal on staff gossip about her. I tried to assure her that this had nothing to do with anyone else and that no one else knew.

The condemnation of staff, me, Kenneth, Oscar, and the organization devolved into calumny and curses. After a while, Oscar stopped interpreting because her language was so foul. She was shaking her head back and forth and swinging her pointed finger up and down. With every downward motion, I felt jolts like she was throwing lightning at me. I was so unsettled by her accusations that I felt shivers throughout my body.

Then I realized that the feeling of the ground shifting under my feet was actually the ground shifting under my feet; we were in an earthquake. As she continued invoking God's wrath, we trembled in our chairs, the windows wobbled, the pile of money shook. Here we were in the ring of fire, in a tiny country with seven active volcanoes, yet Manuela's wrath was far more explosive. Kenneth, Oscar, and I clutched the arms of our chairs while we waited for the quake to settle.

Eventually, Manuela acquiesced, signed the paper, took the money "*por la necesidad*," and left.

I stayed behind for a few minutes with Kenneth and Oscar to process what had happened. I knew that Kenneth endorsed terminating Manuela's contract, and Oscar supported what Kenneth wanted, but it was Ines's opinion that mattered most to me.

I called Ines with the pretense of informing her that Manuela would not be at Chuitinamit that afternoon and why. I explained that I had not told her about the dismissal antecedently because I had not wanted to put her in an awkward position.

Ines merely responded, "Of course, Jan. Thank you for letting me know. I'll let Herlinda know we need help in the pharmacy today."

Rather than going to Chuitinamit to help the short-staffed clinic, I headed home, but not before I bought a beer in a corner store and chugged it down in the street to settle the tremors still in me. When I returned home after such an earth-shattering day, I found Lucia and Wade drying off after a swim in the lake.

"Daddy wouldn't jump off the cliff into the water. He was afraid he might get hurt," Lucia teased.

Wade attempted to defend himself. "Oh, come on, Lucia. That ledge is ridiculously high," he said as he popped open a cold *agua mineral* from the fridge.

My thoughts shifted from the drama in the clinic to the blithe scene I found at home. I was reminded of when Lucia was a baby, and I worked while Wade took care of her. I would come back to our apartment, stressed by the day's events, to find the two most important people in my life waiting for me. I would return to a happy home.

But those days were over, and it was clear that apart from this week, we would never be living under the same roof again. I could no longer bear staying in this house with this man because it hurt too much to see the mangled version of my dream.

Even though the agreement had been made well in advance that I would travel on my own while Wade and Lucia vacationed together during the two weeks the clinic was closed, I hadn't made any plans. Perhaps subconsciously, I had thought that we would end up staying together as a family during this time, but by the end of our week together, I understood that was not going to happen. That night, I bought a ticket to Managua, Nicaragua, for the next day.

When Chuitinamit closed at noon the following day, I rushed home to prepare for my two o'clock shuttle to Antigua. While I was hastily throwing my clothes into my backpack, I realized I had packed my passport in the suitcase I had taken to the new house in San Juan. *Damn!*

Frustrated once again with myself, I confessed my dilemma to Wade. He gave me the same bewildered look I had seen so often before, which always led me to wonder how I could be so forgetful and incompetent. I rushed back to San Juan and fortunately found Gilda at the house. I begged her to let me in the middle room to retrieve my passport. Document in hand, I raced back to San Marcos just in time to grab my backpack and say goodbye before heading out.

After a week of constant conflict, internal and external, I felt like I was once again fleeing the scene of a crash.

27

THE PUSH

FOR THE FIRST TIME IN MONTHS, I was alone in a place where I had the chance to relax and reflect. Instead, I pushed myself to go out into Antigua the evening before my flight to Managua.

As soon as I checked into Posada Merced, I walked to the plaza by the church to get enchiladas from one of the many food stands set up in the evening. I sat on a little plastic stool and watched the strangers—families indulging their children with fried plantains covered in chocolate, young lovers coyly sharing a platter of samples, and old men sipping *atole* (a traditional drink made with hot corn and masa).

So much had changed since Lucia and I had walked through this plaza on our first day in Guatemala. Even more had changed since I had been there with Wade nearly fifteen years before. And almost twenty years had passed since I'd sat in the same corner of the plaza the first time. Even then, I was pursuing what I thought was my dream, looking for refuge and hoping for some kind of connection.

Saturday afternoon, I landed in Managua, unsure what to do next. I parked myself at an airport restaurant and scanned the travel book I had just downloaded on my Kindle to map out a loose itinerary. I'd start with San Juan del Sur, a popular beach destination, and then go to León, the intellectual center of the Sandinista revolution in the 1980s. Scribbled notes in hand, I queued at the information counter at the airport behind two young Israeli men in tank tops and shorts to inquire about transportation options.

"Tell us how to go to San Juan del Sur," one asked the attendant directly in English.

"We are looking for cool waves and hot women," the other chimed in.

The attendant, a somber, middle-aged woman, sold them tickets for the last bus of the day.

"*Buenas tardes*," I greeted her.

She smiled as she replied, "*Buenas tardes. ¿Cómo le puedo servir?*" (How may I serve you?)

Not willing to tie my fate to those two men, I answered, "*Un bus a León.*"

Within hours, I was in León at the Museo de la Revolución, viewing grainy, enlarged photographs and reading yellowed newspaper clippings of a past I had once romanticized. The tour guide—a disabled Sandinista ex-combatant who slept in the back of the museum—spun a tale of revolution and the fruits of justice, equality, and the security it brought.

"We have no hunger and no delinquency. All the children are in school."

The propaganda reminded me of visiting one such museum with Wade when we snuck into Cuba on our trip to Guatemala. Confirmed leftists, we'd felt solidarity with the old men playing chess on the sidewalks and were amused by the young children playing Monopoly on the corners. Now I laughed to myself, thinking about the lies we tell ourselves—that one valiantly fought war would change everything, when in reality, battles must be fought continuously for any hope of change.

Over the next few days, I sand-boarded down the slope of an inactive volcano, leaned over the crater of an active volcano, wandered the wide colonial avenues in Granada, and cruised the tiny islands of Lake Cocibolca. Everywhere I went, I chatted with strangers, hit the highlighted spots in my guidebook, and filled my time with every attraction I could find. But no matter how I tried to occupy myself, the pain lay like a thin veil over it all.

Following my guidebook-suggested itinerary, I went to San Juan del Sur after all. Since it was Christmas Eve and nearly every room in the town had been taken, I ended up in a shared room in a youth hostel, surrounded by backpackers half my age. The two Israelis would have blended in better than me. I tried to chat with the other travelers, but their banter about who had the most stamps on their passports did not appeal to me. Instead of communion and caroling as was the Christmas Eve tradition for Lucia and me, the kids wanted to do shots and sing karaoke. I left to go on a walk to the ocean. I wanted to hear the comforting sound of water swishing on the shore, but all I could hear was the blasting, discordant music of the crowded bars that lined the beach.

After spending every moment of every day trying to occupy my mind, I could not forget about Wade, mainly because I could not forget about our daughter. This was my first Christmas without her since she had been within me, at a beach in Costa Rica. That trip I sensed Wade's growing distance. That Christmas Eve, I went alone to a church and cried, fearful of what the future would bring. This Christmas Eve, I was filled with sorrow at what the future had brought.

This misery had to stop. I could not enjoy my place in the present if I could not let go of the pain of the past.

On Christmas Day, despite the scant public transportation available, I cobbled together a series of bicycle- and horse-drawn rickshaws, taxis, buses, boats, and pickup trucks to make it to the town of Altagracia on Ometepe, an island made of two volcanoes in the middle of Lake Nicaragua. I felt I could not be in a more remote place on earth, or at least in this hemisphere.

My plan for the first day was to walk contemplatively along the shore. I boarded the island's one bus to take me to the lake. At the next stop, I looked up to see someone I knew—Michelle, an American woman who lived in San Marcos so her half-Nicaraguan son could go to Escuela Caracol. Both our jaws dropped at the surprise of finding each other. Rather than spending the day wallowing alone in my own woe, I listened to hers.

Like me, she was an emotional refugee. Over a decade before, this young city girl from the urban northeast had relocated to this remote island, bought a piece of land, and begun her new life as a homesteader. Years later and now pushing forty, her body was nearly broken from running a farm, and her heart was only partially healed. The sorrows she had fled were replaced by the new stresses of raising a child in Central America. I had intended to dedicate that day to finding myself and instead found another me.

The following day, my last full day before starting the journey back to Guatemala, I resolved to exorcise this pain that still gripped me, even if it meant forcibly ripping it out. I planned to climb the volcano on the other side of the island to reach a spectacular waterfall. There was no particular reason why; the water had no magical property. I only wanted to go because it was hard to do.

I rented a rickety, single-speed bike, packed a water bottle and about five dollars in cash, and headed out on a gravel road that hugged the perimeter of the island. When I reached the volcano hours later, I sat a few minutes and refilled my water bottle before starting the two-hour hike straight up. Along the way, I passed and was passed by groups and couples making the journey together. Only I was alone. Once I finally reached the waterfall, I cooled off in the water and chatted with fellow travelers. I could relax for a while, but I could not linger; I would need to return to my room before dark.

By the time I reached the bike, I had the beginnings of blisters on the palms of my hands. The fourteen miles back to Altagracia were definitely going to be long. Since my iPod battery had run out that morning and I now knew where I was going, I had nothing to distract my thoughts. I focused on one thing: having the strength to get home—home to Altagracia, and then home to Lucia.

As dusk settled, I reached a sign that said I still had five miles to go. A group of young guys on the roadside were leaning on their bikes and drinking liquor from glass bottles.

"*Oye, mamacita!*" one called out to me.

Oh, my lord, I thought, *the drunk Nicaraguan equivalent of the Israelis I saw last week*. I imagined that because it was dark, they couldn't see I was twice their age.

The one who had called out to me jumped on his bike and started pursuing me, yelling, "*¡Espera! ¡Te quiero!*" (Wait! I love you!) and other nonsense I couldn't understand. The others also mounted their bikes and followed their friend to egg him on. This could be bad. I firmly grabbed the handlebars with my blistering hands, stood up on the pedals, and pushed as hard as I could up one last hill. My pursuers started to fall behind and eventually gave up.

Back in my eight-dollar-a-night room, I was physically exhausted and could barely move, but inside, I was still churning. I realized that I had done to myself what I had done to Lucia. I thought that if I could stay in motion, ride the wind, I could distract myself enough to not feel the sorrow. It didn't work for Lucia, and it didn't work for me either. Instead, I had pushed myself so hard the past few years—physically, emotionally, professionally, and spiritually—that I was in danger of becoming broken before I was fifty.

The next day, I journeyed back to Antigua to meet Wade and Lucia. The three of us would be together for a day and a couple of nights until he left for the States on New Year's Day. When I met them in the central plaza, a sand-covered Lucia ran up and squeezed me hard.

"Mommy, I left your jacket on the bus. I'm so sorry. I know it's your only jacket, and now you will be cold" was the first thing she said to me.

I consoled her, saying, "Don't worry, sweetie. I lose things too. I'm just glad you made it here safely."

Shifting gears, Lucia blurted, "Mommy, guess what? Taska and her family were at the same beach as Daddy and me!"

"Oh, really?" I asked with a grin as I turned to Wade, knowing there must be a juicy story.

"Yeah, it was good that Lucia had someone to play with in the water.

However, Irka and her husband wanted Lucia to spend all her time with Taska, but I wouldn't allow that because I wanted her to spend time with me," he explained.

"Hmm, I can imagine that they would want to latch on to Lucia as a distraction for Taska. So, was Irka better behaved this time?" I asked.

"She was a total jerk. We had dinner with them at a restaurant, and she sent her pizza back three times because it wasn't prepared the way she wanted," he told me.

"Definitely not a happy person," I added, and he nodded in agreement.

The three of us walked the tourist circuit of the city. The rubble and ruins caused by past earthquakes added to the city's charm. I pointed out to Wade scenes that we had long ago photographed together and the places that I had frequented—not to convince him of the worthiness of the city but rather to fill the awkward silences. Meanwhile, Lucia relished the attention of both of her parents.

While Lucia rested in our room, I asked Wade to talk outside. I had felt a thaw between us since he had come to Guatemala, so I thought it would be a good time to discuss our unresolved financial agreement. I hoped that he would be open to hearing my point of view. I brought up all the debts I felt he owed me, described how much I had helped his family over the years, asked him to pay more child support, and suggested he chip in for the expenses I incurred from his visit to Guatemala. In other words, I sank into a scarcity mentality and threw the kitchen sink at him.

When people argue about money, it is usually about something else—what people value and want others to value. I finally confessed that the support I really wanted from him was his blessing for what I was doing. I began to sob in the street.

I didn't tell him I still wanted him; I didn't ask him to stay. It wasn't true, and it wasn't even what I wanted anymore. I cried for the loss, not for the longing. This moment of stillness and openness with him allowed me to release the pain I had been holding on to all year, or for several years perhaps. I let go of wanting Wade to be part of the dream I had thought we shared, as well as my trepidation about parenting in

Guatemala without him. I had thought I needed a helpmate, an Adam, to do this, but somehow, I had managed on my own.

The spreadsheet of credits and debits from our marriage that I kept in my head was pointless. There wasn't a pivot table I could make to analyze our relationship or a formula I could derive to solve our problems. Our account was a tale, not a tally.

He apologized for how he had treated me and left me in a mess. When the time had come for us to fly off together, he felt compelled to flee. Despite the other differences in our personalities, we both flew away as a reaction to stress. Perhaps that was what drew us together; perhaps that was what pushed us apart.

Part II

28

NAJIT

THERE IS A PLACE in the world where the sense of creation remains intact. In this place lies the magnificence of being, the essence of existing, the knowing of the purpose of life. Here, space is not given to alienation, to the path without meaning. Here, the energies that go into the infinite cosmos can be perceived. Here, we feel the energies that live in the eternal fire, in the heart of our Mother Earth.

We teach our descendants to respect everything that exists. Our grandmothers and grandfathers have known that we are not the owners of what is on the face of the earth.

Everything is a manifestation, as it was for our Great Mother (Heart of the Earth) and Great Father (Heart of the Sky). There is a natural order, and it is what governs us.

Our ancestors, the august sages, lit the sacred fire thousands of years ago, and it has never gone out. It is our light, the heat of our spirit. This is the call that keeps us united in the Heart of Heaven, the Heart of the Spirits. Sages gave us the science of the cosmos and guided us on the path of life within the creation—the spiral of creation, the turns of *Najit* (intersection of space and time) in which the manifestation of reality arises.

This knowledge is the legacy received by the first mothers and the first fathers. The consciousness of life, of reality and its connection with the cosmos, is a guide, a way to manage the influence of the energies of each day, in each person.

This cosmovision is the reason for creation. The reason for existence is to be human and to be in harmony with Mother Earth. The respect of all forms of life begins with us.[23]

Within a few days of returning to San Marcos at the beginning of the New Year, we finished our move to San Juan.

The differences between San Marcos and San Juan were noticeable. While San Marcos's economy was based on remittances from cannabis farming in California and spiritual tourism businesses owned by expats, San Juan's businesses were controlled by and more directly benefited the local people. Instead of intuitive healing, drum circles, and deep tissue massage, San Juan had women's weaving cooperatives, galleries of local artists, and simple *comedores* (diners). The streets were paved, and the water usually worked. The few foreigners who lived in town worked for NGOs or were long-term retirees. Murals illustrating the history and glorifying the Indigenous culture wallpapered the buildings.

San Juan did not want to be San Marcos, nor did it want to be San Pedro, but rather maintained its own sense of self. The community had a municipal hall and a basketball court that also served as a gathering area, but the small library was the town's treasure. It had the most books I would see anywhere in Guatemala. All the books were in Spanish, except for a small section in English. The only Tz'utujil books were language textbooks gifted to the children. The residents wanted to preserve their culture, their language, and their identity, but they also desired education and opportunities for progress. San Juan had found its own intersection of space and time.

Carrying our backpacks with the last of our possessions from San Marcos, Lucia and I arrived at our new home to find Gilda and her two daughters busily mopping the floors with bleach and cleaning the windows with newspaper. While the three women bustled about, three

---

[23] Barrios, Carlos. *Ch'umilal Wuj: Libro del destino*. (Maya' Wuj Editorial, Guatamala City) 2015.

children were swinging on the porch hammock.

"The house looks spotless! Thank you so much, Gilda!" I complimented as we walked onto the porch.

responded, "*Qué bueno*, Juanita! I'm so glad you like it."

"Who are these children?" I asked with a smile.

"Little friends who want to meet Lucia." Pointing with pursed lips to a round-faced girl sucking on a piece of candy, Gilda said, "You know Verna, my granddaughter, right?" She grabbed my arm and whispered in my ear, "Her father abandoned her and her mother, so they live here. *Pobrecita*." She called out to them, "Hey, come greet Lucia."

The kids jumped up and ran toward us while Lucia remained frozen in place. I leaned forward to ask, "What are your names, and how old are you?"

A small, skinny girl with sharp features stepped forward boldly to say, "I'm Karin, and I'm ten years old. This is my brother, Felix. He's eight years old." Pointing to a house not more than fifty feet below ours, she said, "We live there."

I replied, "Nice to meet you all," and turned to Lucia to say in English, "Come on, now. Introduce yourself."

"I'm Lucia, and I am ten years old," she said plainly.

"The same as me!" Karin said with a gaping mouth. "But you are so tall! What blue eyes you have! I love your eyes!"

"I love your hair!" Verna added, twirling her lollipop.

Uncomfortable with being noticed for her differences, Lucia began to squirm.

"Where do you go to school?" I asked.

"My brother and I go to the Catholic school in the center of town. It's called La Salle. I'm entering fifth grade, and my brother is entering second."

"Wonderful! If we were in the United States, Lucia would be in the fifth grade also."

Verna offered up, "I'm seven years old, and I'm starting first grade at Nuevo Amanecer, the evangelical school. It's on the other side of our house."

"Well, Lucia goes to school in Tzununá, but I know she would love to play with you when you all are not in school," I offered and nudged

Lucia, who simply grunted. "What do you like to do?"

Speaking for the group, Karin said, "We play on the rocks. We go down to the lake and collect shells. We explore the evangelical camp next door. Oh, and we climb trees."

At the mention of one of her favorite activities, Lucia's face lit up. However, the light quickly faded when she turned and saw that the cage I had brought earlier when I dropped off the rabbit was overturned.

"My bunny!" Lucia exclaimed and ran to the empty cage. "What happened?!"

Gilda's grip on my arm tightened as she whispered, "Ay, Juanita, the dogs." The neighbors' unleashed dogs had certainly had a snack.

"Please don't tell Lucia the dogs got to the rabbit. Just say it escaped. ¿De acuerdo?" I begged.

"De acuerdo," Gilda agreed.

"Oh, sweetie," I called out as I approached Lucia. "Gilda told me that the dogs set Oreo loose when they flipped his cage. He got away from them by running down to the rocks."

"Really?" she asked with tears in her eyes.

"Maybe the kids could help you look." Turning to Karin, I asked, "Could you please help Lucia find her rabbit?"

Karin and Felix shot off across the rocks, followed closely by Lucia, while Verna stayed behind. She pulled the lollipop out of her mouth and informed us, "I saw the dogs catch the rabbit."

"Please don't tell Lucia," I asked. "It would upset her very much."

Verna responded with a grunt that I wasn't sure was an acceptance or rejection of my plea.

Remembering that the nearby open-air market, the one place in town to buy produce, closed at noon, I asked Gilda to watch Lucia while I went to get food. There, I saw a half dozen women selling produce that was spread across a piece of cloth on the ground or on a table and a couple of men with more established stands selling dry goods. While calculating the size and cost of my week's groceries, I heard a loud call from behind.

"Jaaaaaan!" I turned to see Daniella, the mother of Emilio, the Italian boy from Lucia's Escuela Caracol class. Before I could respond, she pulled me into an embrace and gave me a big kiss on the cheek. With her thick Italianol (half-Italian and half-Spanish) accent, she asked, "What are you doing in San Juan on a Saturday?"

"Lucia and I moved here today. Heinrich evicted us. We are living by Gilda's house. I figured since Lucia was not going to study in San Marcos, there was no reason to stay there, so I decided to try San Juan instead," I explained.

"Weeelcome! Yes, I heard Lucia was studying in that home school. How are those crazy hens?"

"Hens?"

"Sí. Pilar, Irka, and Kelly are all insane. They formed that home school because they and their kids are too nuts to study anywhere else."

"That explains a lot."

"Good you are out of San Marcos. That place is nuts as well. You'll love San Juan. We've been here for five years, and I wish I never had to leave."

Daniella was a force. She'd brought her whole family, including her husband, Edoardo, and her sons, Emilio and Aldo, to Guatemala to work for Centro Maya, an NGO that serves people with disabilities.

Noticing her huge shopping bags stuffed with samples of everything at the market, I commented, "Dani, I have no idea what to do with the produce here. I can cook a few things, but in Seattle, I'd gotten used to buying dishes at the deli or going out for sushi when I'm too busy to cook."

"Jaaaaan," she laughed, "when I look at the succulent fruits and vegetables, I think of a hundred recipes I want to try."

I smiled. "Then we are definitely coming for lunch."

We said our goodbyes with more kisses. After filling my bag with my estimate of a week's groceries, I headed back to the new house. What I'd thought would be a brief visit to the market took the better part of an hour. Every few feet, I ran into ODIM staff or townspeople who went to the clinic: Tulita eating a *paleta* (popsicle) with her boyfriend on his motorcycle, Ines weighed down with bags of beans, and Alba returning from her day of studying in Panajachel. With every stop, there were more hugs, kisses, and explanations. I had a sort of movable welcoming party for the couple of blocks home.

I crossed through Gilda's patio to find her and her daughters preparing food for the next week's group.

"Where's Lucia?" I asked.

"She is playing with the kids on the rocks," she answered.

I put the food away in our mini-fridge and single cabinet and changed the bug-catching tape dangling from the kitchen ceiling's one light bulb. I then sank into the porch hammock to watch Lucia and her new friends on the adjacent property. They were scouring the coffee trees to pick the few remaining beans. In early January, the coffee harvest was ending, as were the daily afternoon downpours. The sky was clear; no rain was in sight. Every day had more light.

I looked over at the water below. At high noon, done for the day, the fishermen were pulling their small wooden skiffs onto the shingle. A lancha coasted up to the rebuilt dock, bringing tourists who wanted to shop for San Juan's renowned textiles and paintings and locals who had finished their morning shopping in Panajachel, eager to get home before the afternoon wind made the water choppy. Gilda's chickens were pecking in the grass and pooping on my freshly washed patio. Life teemed around me. The walls were gone.

This is the right place, I thought. Here, I didn't have to rush in the morning to catch a lancha that might not actually take me to San Juan, depending on the whim of the captain, who would inevitably overcharge me. I could help Lucia get ready for school, and Gilda would be here when she got home. I felt sad for her about Oreo but hoped the neighbor kids would be better companions. And I might develop a new set of friends separate from the hippie expat community in San Marcos.

I thought I might have found Najit: the sacred place where the sense of creation remains intact. This would be a chance to make another fresh start.

29

VALUES

THE NEW YEAR ALSO BROUGHT CHANGES to the clinic. Replacing Dra. Vacinta full-time was Dra. Faustina, who left her position as a hospital administrator for the Ministry of Health to join us because she had not been paid for three months. Though Faustina was taking a salary cut, she wanted to work for a solvent organization that paid on time every month.

What was important to the staff was that—though she was a Ladina—she was a longtime resident of San Pedro and showed respect for the Tz'utujil community. What was important to me was that she was supportive of my plans to enhance sustainability, improve quality, and increase efficiency.

One of my plans was to change the role of the physician from being the clinic head to supporting and building the capacity of the nursing staff. During Dra. Vacinta's many absences when she was summoned to conferences in the city, half of the patients had not been seen since only she and Tomás did consults. It did not seem right that a clinic staffed by eight people could only serve twenty-four instead of forty-eight patients in a day because one person was out.

I thought ODIM should take advantage of the investment in the nurses' education by having Ines and Herlinda, who had returned from her nursing rotation, provide consults rather than being relegated to the laboratory and pharmacy. Ines and Herlinda would improve their clinical skills by shadowing Dra. Faustina in her consults, and Tomás would learn the pharmacy and laboratory.

Tomás initially protested being pushed aside and sharing the responsibility of cleaning the medical equipment. In the end, he admitted that learning more about the tests and medicines helped his practice. Eventually, Ines and Herlinda would see patients on their own. They were proud to finally don their own lab coats and be treated with the same respect as Tomás and the doctora.

A related challenge was that the clinic had an outmoded practice model. Each patient visit started with a new medical intake form that was subsequently placed in the patient's folder. Apart from the patients participating in the diabetes program, there was no tracking of an individual's health status over time, much less the health status of the panel of patients. There was no consensus on our top diagnoses or the methods of treatment. The only clinical protocols were for the international medical volunteers, and they were in English, making it impossible for our staff to read them. As I reviewed these protocols, I saw that they called for medicines that our pharmacy didn't stock.

Ofelia, the nursing student who replaced Manuela, helped me review medical records to create a list of the top diagnoses, and I asked Dra. Faustina to develop uniform protocols for our most common diseases to standardize treatments and inform the ordering of medications.

I started weekly case-review meetings with the staff to improve clinical quality.

"What is something you found odd, interesting, or tough?" I would ask. From these weekly talks, I learned about three babies that died within days of each other, the epidemic of plantar warts among the barefooted grandmothers, the gringo who had a splinter buried deep in his thumb, chili-pepper-induced hemorrhoids, and debilitating menstrual cramps. I also learned that our staff were diagnosing and treating similar conditions differently.

In addition, I started requiring medical-volunteer teams to train staff and support them in consult rather than seeing patients on their own.

A study that had recently been released in the US found that medical error was the third leading cause of death.[24] Terrified that we would make a fatal mistake, I insisted that the volunteers' medical records be recorded in Spanish, not English, so the staff could understand them. Such a case nearly occurred with a patient of Tomás's, whom I recognized from our jornada in Palestina as the woman with a facial twitch. Since Tomás could not read in English, he didn't see that the American volunteer physician had prescribed that woman an anticonvulsant that was contraindicated by the medicine Tomás had just prescribed her. If I had not happened to notice the error and she had taken the medication Tomás prescribed, she could have died.

As I talked to the staff and observed day-to-day operations, what emerged was the need for better systems to track data, which, in turn, would drive better decision-making and staff development. No single comprehensive list of what was stocked in the pharmacy existed. Instead, there were multiple partial lists in differing combinations of English, Spanish, and French. The Chuitinamit and Sanjuanerita clinics each had their own pharmacy inventories, which were not standardized, so there could be a surplus of a medication in one and a shortage in the other. Because there was no registry of the leading diagnoses, there was no list of what should be stocked based on the frequency of use. Ofelia stepped up to help me create a pharmacy inventory system that measured what we had, what we dispensed, and what we needed so that we could plan purchases and maintain a stable stock in the two clinics.

The pharmacies and storage rooms overflowed with unnecessary gifts from US volunteer teams and discarded medicines dropped off by tourists heading home. I found bottles of contact lens solution and bags of prescription eyeglasses with large, 1980s frames, though no one had contact lenses or access to an optometrist. Meanwhile, boxes of reading glasses that could be distributed lay unopened. These boxes and bags were flanked by other boxes and bags of baseball caps, T-shirts, baby powder, and assorted combinations of vitamins and herbal supplements. In the bodega, I found a garbage bag full of XXXL medical scrubs donated by a

---

[24] Makary, Martin A. and Michael Daniel. 2016. "Medical error-the third leading cause of death in the US." *BMJ* 353: i2139.

Texas team that our petite staff would drown in. Rather than discarding them, I sent them to Centro Maya for their clients to convert into sheets to cover our bare exam tables.

To hone the focus of the whole organization, Kenneth pulled together the staff for a strategic planning meeting. It was one of those typical sessions I have done in multiple work settings where the staff talks about the organization's values, lists them on flip chart paper, consolidates the list, and then votes on the priorities with sticky dots. The three North Americans (Kenneth, Hannah, and me) converged on quality, sustainability, and effectiveness as the most important values. *Well, of course,* I thought. *Aren't these the values that inform everything I have been working toward? Aren't they what the clinic should be about?*

I took a few steps back to see where the Guatemalans stuck their dots. Overwhelmingly, they agreed their most important value was *confianza*, or "trust," followed by *humanidad* (humanity), and *respecto* (respect).

Uncertain what they meant by trust, I asked the group, "Do you want to trust in the quality of the services? In the competency of the staff?"

They unanimously replied, "No."

Alba spoke up. "Confianza means that staff would not gossip about the patients or each other."

In these small towns where families have lived together for hundreds of years, where war can break out that pits neighbor against neighbor, trust is everything. The North Americans' values were about how we worked within the organization; the Guatemalans' values for their lives were the same as for their work.

When I reviewed the previous year's budget to plan for the new year, I noted inconsistency among staff salaries. There seemed to be no rationale for why some were earning more than others. Tomás had not completed his education but was paid substantially more than the female nurses with degrees. The lack of uniformly applied standards and the fact that the less credentialed man earned more than the degreed women rubbed me the wrong way.

With input from Kenneth, Hannah, and Oscar, I created a salary scale that I felt represented the organization's values of education, service, and leadership. A specific hourly rate for each would be extrapolated to an annual wage, which would result in a raise for most staff, but a few would have a reduction. I adjusted the budget so that no one would have a salary cut, which meant that some would have to work more hours to receive the same money.

At a staff meeting, I walked through the variables, their values, and the composite score and then explained how an hourly wage could be translated into a monthly salary. Eyes shifted down, fingers wiggled, and mouths moved silently as folks calculated what the changes would be. Yes, to avoid cutting salaries, some people would have to work more hours to make the same money, but wages for the group as a whole would go up by 5 percent, meaning some people received a 10 to 15 percent increase. I thought at least those receiving raises would be thrilled. Silence.

Later, I asked Ines, "Why aren't the staff happy about their raises? Why did no one mention the disparity in salaries before now?"

What I was really wondering was *Why had no one recognized that I had righted a wrong?*

Ines replied, "Some people would prefer to do less, even if it means that they have to be paid less, so that they can spend more time with family."

To pay for these wage increases (that no one had asked for) and to compensate for a reduction in donations, I pushed to raise the price of consults. The ten-quetzal fee (about a dollar twenty-five) for a consult included lab tests and medicines. At first, I thought a modest adjustment to twelve quetzales (about twenty-five cents more) was much as the patients would accept. I sent Ofelia to do market research at all the other clinics and pharmacies in town and found that the next lowest price for a consult was thirty quetzales, which did not even include tests and medicine.

When we asked a sample of the patients what increase would be acceptable, they unanimously replied, "None." Regardless, we raised the price to twenty-five quetzales. We gave staff talking points and planned for the change to happen in a couple of months so folks would have time to get used to the idea.

Both clinics had a surge in consults before the fee increase went into effect and a significant drop in consults afterward. The diabetes patients in San Pablo, who once received their treatments for free because their community was poorer, protested to Alba that they would now have to pay a small fee for a consult and threatened to quit the program altogether.

The questions I asked Alba were "Don't they see they would be hurting themselves? Don't they understand that we are not the government? That we have to pay for the medicine?"

The question I asked myself was *When did I start to sound like a neoliberal?* In time, the San Juan clinic bounced back from the price increase, and the number of patients seen daily returned to previous levels. However, the numbers in San Pablo did not.

Were my changes motivated by values that resonated with the community? I acted out of a desire for quality, sustainability, and efficiency, but did I behave with trust, humanity, and respect? Had I treated Manuela with respect when I told her that her contract would not be renewed? By telling Ines (though not the rest of the staff), had I maintained her confianza? Was I breaking confianza now? By raising the fees so drastically, had I treated our patients with humanity?

Concepts like quality, sustainability, and effectiveness are defined and measured by SMART (specific, measurable, attainable, relevant, and timely) objectives that are used in North American project management. From the Guatemalan perspective, there was no point in measuring an uncertain future. I needed to learn that adapting to another culture isn't just about learning a new language or system or being willing to tolerate inconveniences. I needed to avoid being myopically focused, pecking at the dirt for grubs and worms, and instead call upon my no'j nature to rise above my limited viewpoint and see the clinic, the community, and the world from their eyes.

"Doctora, I need to talk to you," said a woman standing outside my office door when I arrived at Sanjuanerita early one morning. Though I'm not a physician, I didn't correct her, because I knew that "doctora" was an honorific title for the middle-aged clinic administrator. Setting her straight would be rude.

"Please come in," I said, motioning for her to take a seat.

She was visibly shaken. Her eyes were watery, and her face was flushed. "I am a good Catholic. I go to mass every week and follow the church's teachings. My family is quite Catholic too." Hearing her measured phrasing, I recognized her look; it was anger, not despair.

She paused for a moment, and I said, "Yes, go on."

"I have also been coming to Sanjuanerita for years to get injections for family planning."

"I am glad to know that the clinic has served you. How may I serve you now?" I asked, not sure where this was going.

"I come here because I thought the clinic was discreet. Yet my sister-in-law told me that she knows that I am getting injections. She says Navichoc told her. She is threatening to tell my husband. If my husband finds out, I don't know what I'll do." She began to shake.

"I understand your situation. I know that Navichoc cares a lot about her patients' privacy. As soon as she comes in, I'll talk to her."

"Yes, please," she answered and then left.

When Navichoc came in a few minutes later, I relayed what the woman had said. Navichoc emphatically denied the accusation. "I would never reveal anything about my patients."

"Of course I believe you. There must have been a misunderstanding. Someone may have seen her here and jumped to conclusions. Why don't you go talk to her now, and then the two of you can talk to the sister-in-law together?" I suggested.

Navichoc ran out, leaving her half dozen pregnant patients waiting in the salón. They could wait, but mending this rift could not.

Alba was right. Trust is everything. Without it, we have nothing.

30
NUEVO AMANECER (NEW DAWN)

ALTHOUGH IT SEEMED like our new situation was working out fine, every evening I came home holding my breath, hoping that the day had gone well. I paid Gilda to keep an eye on Lucia after school while she played with the kids. Still, I was apprehensive about her commuting all the way to Tzununá and back.

One Friday afternoon, Lucia stormed home with her guitar and book bag filled with all her papers and swore she would never go back to the home school. Nigel had whacked her on the head with a pencil for daydreaming. Over the weekend, since Nigel did not have a phone, I wrote to him that "apart from a couple of toddler scuffles, she has never been hit. Ever. If this did happen, I have two requests. First, please don't strike her. You can tap her desk, ask her to do jumping jacks, or do anything else to get her attention. Second, would you please talk to her privately about this? I want this situation to work for her, but I also want her to be in a safe and secure place."

He concurred with her account and assured me that it would not happen again. I was willing to take into consideration his own probable severe British education, accept his apology, and then hope that he would, as Wade said, "meditate on that shit." Finally, I coaxed Lucia to return the following Monday, saying that Nigel had promised to apologize. It turned out that Nigel's apology was to say, "I'm sorry I did *this* to you" as he whacked her with a pencil again.

While the kids were snacking in the kitchen during recess, he told them that he had to shower. The girls bombarded Yuriel with questions. "Has he asked your mother?" "Whose towel is he going to use?" "Where is your mother?" "Why does he need a shower now?" Nigel disrobed in the bathroom and then popped his naked, towel-less torso out the door to ask Yuriel, the ten-year-old boy, to come in to show him how to turn on the hot water.

We quit that night.

The cycle of looking for a school began again. The two private schools in town were Nuevo Amanecer (New Dawn), the evangelical school behind our house that Verna attended, and La Salle, the Catholic school that Karin and Felix attended up the hill beside the church. With either option, now that Lucia would be studying in the same town where I was working, I could be home for lunch to have a midday check-in.

Asking around at the clinic, I heard that both schools were good and that Catholics went to the evangelical school and vice versa. Lucia wanted to go to the Catholic school because Karin went there and had told her that it had less bullying than the evangelical school. I argued that kids are kids and there would be bullying everywhere. I chose Nuevo Amanecer because Navichoc's and Ines's daughters studied there, so there would be *conocidos* (known people), and it was directly behind our house. After worrying so much about her taking the lancha alone to Tzununá, a school three minutes away felt safer.

Wade was initially reluctant with this choice, mainly because he assumed they would teach her that he was going to hell for being a nonbeliever. I reassured him that this would merely be a cross-cultural experience for her, a different view of God, an opportunity to continue to improve her Spanish, and another taste of real Guatemala. I assumed that with Lucia being the only foreigner, there would not be the division between gringos and Guatemalans as in San Marcos. She would be in the fold. I hoped.

I checked out the school during preregistration in late January, the day before school began. Unlike other buildings in this Indigenous village, Nuevo Amanecer was painted blue and white, the colors of the Guatemalan flag—a nod to supporting the government, I presumed. US evangelicals had backed right-wing governments in Guatemala, so I surmised that this school, funded by US evangelical churches, had the same politics.

The campus had two parts: a bigger, somewhat newer cinder-block building with large windows opening onto the courtyard that housed the older primary grades during the morning and the middle school classes in the afternoon, and a smaller, older set of buildings with narrow slat windows clustered together that housed the administrative offices, kindergarten, and younger grades. The barren schoolyard was enclosed by a chain-link fence and had a few broken 1970s-era swings and slides cast in a corner. This was not going to be like Escuela Caracol, with the winding stone paths, trees, and bunny cages.

The director was a jittery pastor who spouted lots of Jesus-speak, such as "*Que Dios le bendiga*" (May God bless you) about a dozen times. I asked him point blank, "Do you hit children?" because I had heard that corporal punishment was common in Guatemalan schools.

"Oh, no, we are Christians," he assured me.

I enrolled her in sixth grade, though in the States she would be halfway through fifth grade. Since Escuela Caracol had been too easy academically, I thought moving her up a grade would be more appropriate.

I dropped Lucia off the next morning at the new school year assembly. As we walked in, everyone turned to stare. We sat in the back and listened to the director bless the students, the school, the teachers, etc. After I connected her with her *maestra* (teacher), Judit, I left because I needed to meet a group of volunteers at the clinic. Lucia later told me that the director advised against cliques and peer pressure. He explained that just because someone is rich or has nice clothes doesn't mean she or he is better than others. All the children and teachers turned to stare at her again. So much for just falling into the fold.

That afternoon, I arrived early to pick her up so that I could reintroduce myself to Judit and check in about how the day went. As I stood listening outside the classroom, I heard the teacher say, "There are two stories of how the world was made. The true story of creation is in the Bible. The other is the scientific theory, which says a big bang formed the world, and then came the monkeys, and then people came from monkeys."

I thought Wade would die if he heard this right now.

The assigned homework was to research the "scientific theory" in groups at the small town library or at the internet café, since those were the only two public places with access to the internet, and prepare a presentation for the next day. As the kids poured out of class, I suggested that the girls in Lucia's group come to our house because we had a computer *and* internet access. Amazed looks spread across their faces. After lunch, three sweet twelve-year-old girls showed up on our front porch.

I busied myself in the bedroom while the girls huddled around my laptop on the patio. A while later, I stepped out, eager to hear their presentations. They each talked about how scientists think a star exploded and made the other stars, the planets, our world, then the plants and animals and that people came from monkeys who lost their tails. They chuckled at the thought of rotten monkey tails piled somewhere in the forest.

I shared with them that I used to be a scientist whose work was related to these theories, and then I told them a different story. "The world is eternally changing. Creation happens every day. The language you speak in San Juan, Tz'utujil, and the language of San Marcos, Kachiquel, are derived from the same language: proto-Mayan. Our skin color differs depending on how far from the sun our ancestors lived. Everything changes, and everything is related. Scientists do not think humans came from monkeys, because monkeys have evolved as much as we have. Rather, scientists think we have common ancestors. Here, let me show you."

I sifted through the internet's depictions of *Australopithecus* and various other extinct hominids.

"See. Is that a monkey?"

"Oh, no," the girls commented nearly in unison.

"Or a human?"

"Not that either."

"This is a drawing of what scientists think both monkeys and people evolved from. Everything changes, and everything is related."

Stepping back into the bedroom as they revised their presentation on the porch, I smiled to myself, thinking that I would love to be a fly on the wall in that class the next day. I contemplated how the creation debate in the US had spilled into this faraway part of the world. While the evangelical Nuevo Amanecer supported the Judeo-Christian myth, they were silent on their own culture's origin story.

In the sixteenth century, part of the Spaniards' plan to subdue the Indigenous peoples in the Americas was to bring Catholic clergy to convert them to Christianity. The Spaniards destroyed nearly all the Indigenous codices. Notwithstanding, some priests and monks studied their languages and transcribed hieroglyphic writings into Latin script to teach Christian concepts in a form that the people would understand. These multilingual priests and monks developed such an interest in registering the history, describing the genealogy, and documenting rituals that the Spanish crown prohibited the writing and publication of Indigenous history and traditions for fear of keeping the old culture alive.

Among the chroniclers during this time, an anonymous K'iche' or Kachiquel person or people relayed their history to an unidentified Spanish cleric, who wrote it down in Kachiquel, using a Latin script. The manuscript now known as the *Popol Wuj* clandestinely passed through hands for two centuries. Since then, numerous translations have been made of the "original." There is no definitive version of the *Popol Wuj* and no definitive Maya origin story. Each group has its own collection of stories from its own perspective. Like creation itself, the story of creation evolved.

The summary below is my loose English translation of an updated Spanish version of the original Spanish translation of Kachiquel written in Latin script by an unknown clergyman, based on what he likely understood from early Kachiquel speakers in the early seventeenth century.[25] It is not the only myth nor the only version of this myth. Like all venerable lore, the meaning lies in the broader themes, not the literal account.

In the beginning, the face of the earth had not yet appeared. There was only the infinite sky, the expansive sea, the dark silence. All was languid; all was at rest. The Maker and the Molder had the qualities of divine will, formative force, and the infinite empty space from which sprouts all the universes. The Maker and the Molder were with other female/male pairs of gods—Quetzal Serpent and Sovereign, Xmucane and Xpiyacoc (the Great Mother and the Great Father), and Heart of the Earth and Heart of the Sky. They were in the water, wrapped in quetzal feathers.

Then came the word. The gods assembled in the night and talked. They discussed and deliberated until they united their words and their thoughts. They planned for beings to appear who would speak the gods' names and keep their calendar for their glory and grandeur.

The land was set apart within the waters. Out of the sea emerged the mountains, like the carapace of crabs. They formed the valleys and rivers. They put forth cypress groves and pine forests.

They created the animals, giving each a name, a dwelling, and a function. The deer would live along the streams, sleep on the straw in the ravines, and tend the grass. The birds and lions would guard the mountains, and the snakes would care for the vines. Nevertheless, when the Maker and the Molder ordered the animals to honor the gods, they responded with their shrieks, howls, and growls. Offended, the Maker and Molder condemned the animals to be hunted and their flesh sacrificed.

The Maker and the Molder told the other gods, "Make another attempt to create beings that would honor us," so the gods decided to

---

[25] Anonymous. 2013. *Popol Vuh: Versión actualizada de Agustín Estrada Monroy, basada en los textos quiche y castellano.* Editores Mexicanos Unidos, México City, Mexico.

form humans out of mud. The bland mud men appeared crushed and crouching, watery and weak. They could not move their heads, see, or reproduce. They could speak but had no understanding.

"These are worse than the animals," complained the Maker and the Molder, as the mud men dissolved back into the earth.

The Maker and the Molder summoned the soothsayers Xmucane and Xpiyacoc to consult. Together they discussed how they would decide how to make the next beings.

"Cast lots with grains of corn and seeds of the tzite fruit," the gods told Xmucane and Xpiyacoc. They read the tzite and the corn to say that the next attempt should be made from wood. The Maker and the Molder built men from sticks and women from twine. These new manikins could speak, walk, and have children and thus multiplied on the earth. However, their legs were weak, their arms had no blood, and their faces appeared to be masks. With no heart or understanding, they could not praise the gods.

Once again, the gods destroyed them, this time more violently. They called the vultures to take out their eyes, bats to cut their heads, and jaguars to disfigure them and grind their bones. Even the chickens, the dogs, the rocks, and the stones took their revenge on the failed manikins. The remnants of these beings that eluded destruction became the monkeys who wander the mountains, which is why monkeys resemble humans.

The Maker and the Molder called Sovereign and Quetzal Serpent to say, "Now the dawn draws near, and we must finish perfection, the evolution of all we have made." They all came together in the night to discuss, debate, and deliberate from what material to make human flesh.

From the paradise Paxil came white and yellow ears of corn brought by the mountain cat, the coyote, the parrot, and the crow. The Maker and the Molder employed the white and yellow corn to be the food of human flesh. Xmucane ground the corn and made drinks that fattened the four men Sovereign and Quetzal Serpent had made from corn. After humans were made, the sun began its walk across the face of the earth, bringing the first dawn.

Gifted with erudition, they examined the sky and the earth. No obstacle was in their way; they saw everything. The Maker asked them, "How are you? Can you hear? Can you see? Can you walk and talk?" The Maker added, "Prove that you can see all."

The new men responded, "Truly, we give thanks for creating us. You gave us a mouth and face so we could speak and hear. We can walk and have pleasure. We know what is distant and what is near, what is large and what is small, what is the sky, and what is the earth."

The gods were threatened by the intelligence of these people.

"We need to debase them a bit. It is not good that we can see ourselves in them. Why did we make them equal to us?"

In response, the Heart of the Sky put mist in their eyes to tarnish their vision so that they could only see near—what was evident and apparent. Then the gods made four women from corn to partner with the four men and sent them off in pairs in the four directions.

The remainder of the *Popol Wuj* describes how these people became the first ancestors of the K'iche' and the family and community lines of the K'iche' people, including the related Tz'utujil.

What a completely different way of envisioning creation than the story told in Genesis. Creation was a collaborative effort of many gods and forces, full of false starts, confrontations, consultations, and adjustments. The beginning of the text describes the space-time continuum that gave birth to multiple universes. Could the Maya have understood singularity, the big bang, and the multiverse long before Einstein and Hawking?

The animals were a first attempt to make beings that would honor the gods. Humans were not created for a separate purpose from the animals or as caretakers who would have dominion. The current version of humanity was made after a series of drafts, long after creation began. Monkeys "evolved" from the third draft of humans. Could the Maya have understood evolution hundreds or even thousands of years before Darwin?

If that was the case, and if Maya learning exceeded anything in Europe at the time of the conquest and was at least equivalent to or more advanced than the ancient civilizations of the East, how could this school funded by US evangelicals purport to have the authority to teach anything? For that matter, how could my clinic, also funded by US Protestants, dare teach anything? What hubris to think I could or should explain to these girls what their ancestors knew long before mine. I also wondered, apart from teaching foreign myths about the beginnings of the world, how my culture had impacted the people and culture here.

In the *Popol Wuj*, the humans were endowed with such wisdom that the gods were jealous. There was no original sin. They may have put mist in their eyes, but not dust in their brains. Nothing separates us from the gods, from nature, from each other. If this one version of their cosmovision is representative of the others, it is understandable that the Maya would not easily relinquish it—that the Spaniards would have to resort to the most brutal force to compel the Maya to embrace a single, omnipotent god that damned them.

But have they?

The school may have been painted to show its alliance with the government, but "nuevo amanecer" refers to the Maya creation story. The Maya believe that they were created to honor the calendar. The movements of the sun, the earth, and the moon affect every aspect of life. The new day isn't just a passive passing of time. It is a sacred act of the sun being born again after resting overnight from the labor of walking across the sky to give light. Every day has its own energy: its nawal. Every day is a gift.

I was wrong in telling Wade that Lucia would learn about a different vision of God. It was I who learned.

31
HAPPY HOME

FALLOUT FROM QUITTING the home school was to be expected. Pilar called me the next day, furious. After I explained the shower situation, she said I was "a crazy, uptight gringa" and would have nothing to do with us after that.

In contrast, Irka continued to encourage a friendship between Taska and Lucia. Though Taska was like a feral princess living in a castle, I also supported this friendship, since Taska was one of the few girls with whom Lucia could easily communicate. So, when Lucia was invited to spend the night with Taska the following weekend, I agreed.

I set her out on the lancha early Saturday morning with a hug and a kiss. If Lucia was going to enjoy being a kid away from the watchful eye of her mother, then I was going to have a break from being a mother and enjoy being a woman. But how? Go on a long hike or kayak across the lake without listening to whining? Drink wine at an expat bar in San Pedro and meet an attractive backpacker? Take a lancha to explore one of the villages on the lake? At least watch a non-kid movie?

When I reached my porch at the top of the rocks, I was struck by the silence in the small space of our house. There were no complaints of boredom, chores, or homework; no sounds of laughter, dancing, or crying; no one to read to, play a game with, or cook for. I settled into the hammock and wrapped it around me like a shroud, with no one to hold or to be held by.

I lay there and let the sounds, sights, and smells pass over me. Lanchas intermittently rode up to the dock, and passengers scurried to get on and off. The fishermen in their small wooden boats repeatedly cast their nets until they were content with the measly catch of the day. Karin and Felix played on the rocks until their mother called them in for Karin to help with the fire. The aroma of Gilda's slow-cooking dish of garbanzos and brown sugar wafted over to my porch, and her chickens pecked at a nearby patch of grass. By afternoon, the only sounds coming up from the lake were the waves breaking on the shore, and the only sights were the clouds drifting across the sky, shifting their shape, and moving on.

I had read that a psychological experiment found that people would rather experience electrical shocks than be alone with their own thoughts. Not me. I relished dwelling in the primordial stew of my mind. Like the water coming and going, my thoughts oscillated between stillness and reflections of my joys and failures as a mother, daughter, wife, worker, and friend.

Stirred only by hunger, I rose to forage in the kitchen and was surprised to see the time. Now late in the afternoon, the market had been closed for hours; I had missed my window to buy food. Just as well. I made a pot of popcorn on the two-burner gas stove and sank back into the hammock to watch the sunset. The remaining evening hours I spent writing friends in the States, putting those thoughts to virtual paper.

By morning, I was anxious for Lucia to come home. I was worried, but more than that, I missed her. I greeted her at the dock with a bigger hug and kiss than I had given the day before.

"How was it?" I asked. "Did you have fun?"

"I'm so tired. Taska kept me up until two in the morning watching movies," she moaned as she handed me her backpack. She linked arms with me as a sign that she wanted me to help her walk up the hill. There would be no climbing the rocks today.

"Wow, that's really late. What did you do before then?"

"Mommy, you won't believe it. Taska smoked cigarettes she made from weeds in the yard. She wanted me to smoke with her, but I wouldn't."

"I'm glad to hear that you wouldn't smoke that."

"Ugh, of course not. She also jumped out of a tree on top of me, and she pushed me into the lake."

"What did her parents say?"

"They ignored us the whole time. I heard them fighting, but since they were speaking Latvian, I couldn't understand what they were talking about."

"I'm sure that is hard for Taska. Did you all eat dinner together?"

"No. They have a woman who does nothing but cook. She made dinner for just Taska and me. I guess her parents ate later. They have another woman who does nothing but clean. I wish we were rich and could live in a big house with servants."

"Lucia, we have all the space we need. I know it would be easier if we had help, but I'm trying to live within our means."

"But washing the clothes in the pila, boiling water, and scrubbing all the dishes is such a pain."

"And when was the last time you did any of that? I'm the one who does all the work."

"I'm going to take a nap," she remarked with a sly grin as she snuck into the bedroom.

"Rascal," I joked back. "So, I'm guessing you don't want another sleepover at Taska's house?"

"No, I'd rather play with Karin."

Irka made several invitations for Lucia to come back, but neither Lucia nor I wanted a repeat of that weekend.

"Why doesn't Taska come to our house instead? We would love to host her in San Juan," I suggested to Irka.

"San Juan is so far. Can't Lucia take a lancha to here? Maybe you could bring her."

"You know, Irka, it's the same distance from there to here as from here to there."

When Irka finally acquiesced and Taska finally came to our house, she bounced around the porch and in and out of our three rooms.

"Your house is very Guatemalan," she noted, which I interpreted as "very simple and small." "What are we going to do today?" She seemed perplexed that we did not have a widescreen TV.

"I thought we would go to the clinic so I can show you some of the equipment and tests we have in the laboratory. We could also get ice cream and hike up the *cerro* [hill]," I suggested.

On our walk across town to the clinic, Lucia and I held hands as usual, and Taska kept running off. She peeked into the window of a house to see a parrot we heard caw, jumped a fence to check out a construction site, and scaled the walls of the soccer stadium to watch the practice.

At Sanjuanerita, she disappeared onto the roof as I adjusted the microscope. Afraid that she might do something dangerous or destructive, I cut our visit short and told the girls we would head home. After we made a stop to get *chocobananos*, Taska urged Lucia to run back to the house with her. I wondered whether Taska was full of boundless energy or simply wanted to distance herself from me.

At home, I pulled out the spirograph set and suggested Lucia and Taska try out the new colored pens we had gotten from the *papelería*. Taska gave me an odd look and told Lucia she wanted to crawl on the rocks. Eventually, the girls crashed from their chocobanano sugar high and went to sleep early in the one bedroom. In the middle room, which we used as storage, I lay on the yoga mat and a towel on the concrete floor, my makeshift bed for the night.

I wondered and worried for naught about what we could do the next day. The following morning, Taska wanted to go home early. As soon as we saw her off at the dock, Lucia told me about Taska's predicament.

"She wanted to leave because we don't have a TV, and she's not used to a parent being around all the time."

"Really? Is that what she said?"

"Well, she asked me if we always do things together. I told her yeah. We play games. We go on hikes. We read at night. We buy things at the tienda. We cook. We do art projects. I help make packages of vitamins for the clinic."

"That sounds about right."

"When I asked her what she does with her mom, she said, 'Nothing. She moved out.'"

"Oh, no. That's terrible!"

"She said her mom was having an affair with Calum."

"The teacher?! That must be hard for Taska. Do you think that was why her parents were fighting when you were at their house?"

"Maybe. I've never heard people fight like that. You and Daddy never fought that way, did you? I only hear the two of you talk about boring stuff like taxes and schedules."

"Well, Daddy and I did and still do argue about some things, but we respect each other. We share the most important thing in the world."

"*Meeeee!*"

"That's right. And we both know that we have to work together to take care of you."

While I washed the dishes in the pila, Lucia spread her art supplies on the table and began drawing.

"Do you want to see if Karin would like to play this afternoon?" I suggested as I finished scrubbing the last pot that had been soaking.

"Yeah, but I want to finish my picture first."

I walked over to the table to see her filling in the last details. At the top of the page were Mommy and Lucia holding hands, and alongside she had written, WHERE MY FAMILY IS, HOME IS. Below was a grand house accompanied by the words A BIG HOME DOESN'T MEAN A HAPPY FAMILY.

I thought that if this was all she learned from her time in Guatemala, then maybe this had been worthwhile.

32

WEAVING

AT THE WEEKLY staff meeting, Kenneth announced that we would all have to paint Sanjuanerita the following weekend. "The building is looking shabby. Let's spruce it up."

Since Guatemalan labor law allows for a forty-eight-hour work week, it was within the organization's rights to require staff to work on a Saturday or Sunday.

"We'll make it fun," Kenneth promised the team. "We'll provide lunch and snacks. You can bring your families to help."

He passed around a brochure with paint samples for staff to vote on the color to be used. Since the American volunteers had done most of the renovations and painting inside the clinic, having the team paint the outside would be a contribution by the community.

"Once we're done, we'll have a new mural painted in the local style so that folks can see that we are here for them."

"I'm sorry, but I have plans this weekend. I can't help," I told Kenneth and the staff.

Since I didn't have a Guatemalan contract, I knew that he couldn't force me to oblige, but I felt guilty for using my status as a foreigner to get out of what the local staff was compelled to do. Kenneth looked at me incredulously. Surely he expected me to be there to validate him as he asked others to give up a weekend day, especially after he had backed my projects.

"One of Lucia's friends is coming over, so we'll be busy."

Though what I said about Stela's visit was true, I was too embarrassed to tell him the real reason. I couldn't manage my work and personal life simultaneously. What with Lucia being thrown by a cow and banned from the clinic for bothering the staff, I feared that if she were involved in the project, she might mix colors to her own liking, press handprints on the wall, throw a bucket of paint at someone, or worse. If I went without her and left her with Gilda, she would be upset that I wasn't spending enough time with her.

Once home, I found Gilda in her courtyard, assembling her loom.

"Gilda, I didn't know you weave. Do you work with one of the *cooperativas*?" I asked.

"I used to, but not anymore. It was too much hassle. They are so picky about what they will take. Now we sell to the ODIM groups that eat here." She pointed to a table that displayed stacks of blouses, fajas, huipiles, and table coverings. "The groups have to pass by to get to the dining table, so sometimes they see something they like and buy it."

"Gilda, these are exquisite. You and your daughters did all this?"

"Sí, gracias. Along with hosting groups, this is how our family eats. My husband, Gaspar, lost his job a few years ago. Now that we are in our fifties and are old, there are no other jobs for us."

I looked over to see Gaspar lounging on the landing outside the door. His shirt was pulled up, and he was rubbing his belly. I wondered when he had last looked for a job.

"If you would like, I could teach Lucia how to weave now. I was about to go get Verna and start teaching her."

"That would be wonderful. Yes, thank you. I'll call Verna for you and get Lucia." I proceeded down the little path to our house to find Lucia, Karin, and Verna taking turns hanging from a tree. "Hey, Verna," I called out, "your grandmother wants to teach you to weave now. Lucia, you're going to join her and learn too."

Karin looked momentarily disappointed to be left out of the invitation but said she needed to go home to build a fire to start dinner.

Weaving is associated with women's power to create and procreate. Humans are woven, and cloth is born. Women in San Juan practice weaving as they always had throughout ancient Mesoamerica. They handpluck the cotton seeds, tear apart the fibers with a comb, whorl the fibers into thread, color these threads with the pigments of the plants from the mountain, and lay these threads around a warping board.

The traditional backstrap loom is assembled from a warping board with a loose set of thirteen sticks, each of which embodies one of the thirteen *ixoq ajaw* (female nawales). The sticks are inserted into holes around the board's perimeter and used to configure the warp yarns into a form that can assemble the loom. Sections of the board are named after human body parts, such as the head, the heart, and the buttocks. The cloth on the loom is referred to as a child. The rope that attaches the loom to the support post is called the umbilical cord. And the tree or post that secures the rope and uppermost portion of the loom is called the mother tree.

When a woman sits down to weave, she is bound to the ancient, deified tree at the center of existence via her woven progeny. The loom is fed thread in the weaving process, and the back-and-forth motion of the weaver's hips simulates childbirth. Slowly, the bare bones of the loom give way to cloth, to a living entity, to a child.[26]

Gilda tied one end of a long palm leaf to a post; the other end she handed to Verna and told her to hold it taut. She showed the girls how to slide coarse threads through the warps with a stick. As I watched her mix in orange with blue and magenta in the leaves, I thought about how Gilda was able to construct and combine the disparate strands of her life. Like her weaving, she pieced together working random jobs, being the matriarch of an extended family, and serving as an elder in her church.

The power to make something valuable from virtually nothing, to be able to intertwine disparate threads to create a whole cloth, to embed symbols and meaning in a thing of beauty, to pass on the knowledge from her grandmothers to her granddaughter—that was what I saw Gilda doing in her life, and that was what I wanted to do with my life.

---

[26] Prechtel, Martin and Robert S. Carlsen. 1988. "Weaving and cosmos among the Tz'utujil Maya of Guatemala." *Res: Anthropology and Aesthetics* 15:122–132.

But Gilda wasn't doing this on her own. Her daughters aided her with her enterprise. Even Gaspar and Verna helped prepare for the teams. The ladies from church regularly stopped by to assist her in attending to the shrine that she hosted for a town saint. For that matter, Daniella, whom I also admired, had her husband help her. Maybe it was so hard for me because I was trying to do everything on my own.

I thought again about the Maya creation story from the *Popol Wuj*. The gods did not forge ahead alone. They either worked or came in pairs. Each act, each version of humans came out of consultation. *If the gods cannot manage on their own, how can we? How can I?* I wondered.

In the *Popol Wuj*, harmony through collaboration rather than perfection through individual actualization is the project of life. According to the Christian tradition in which I was raised, the ideal is to be like Jesus, the one perfect person. No one can come close to that; we all fall short.

I had let go of the idea of having a partner to share this journey with me. Now I needed to let go of insisting on doing the journey on my own, no matter the cost to my wallet or my pride.

Over the next few weeks, I reached out for more help than I ever had. I paid Gilda to feed Lucia lunch once a week so that I wouldn't have to rush home after weekly staff meetings. Though her supervision of Lucia was scant, the money was for the help she gave me in navigating life in San Juan, such as how to pay my electric bill, where to buy local eggs, who to call for gas, what the bus schedule was, and when the water would be shut off. (A truck periodically drove by to announce water stoppages in Tz'utujil, which thankfully Gilda interpreted.)

I hired Gilda's daughter Jessica to clean the house, wash the clothes, and scrub the poop from Gilda's ninety chickens off the porch. I had *tambores* (containers) of purified water delivered so I wouldn't spend evenings boiling and filtering water. I arranged for Lucia to go horseback riding on Sunday mornings with Stela and Taska while I had coffee with Lana. I turned to Navichoc for advice about raising a preteen girl. I hired Ofelia to tutor Lucia in math and Tz'utujil. I bought a shiny red bicycle from Navichoc's husband to commute to San Pablo. I pushed Lucia to take on more responsibility for buying food at the stores and the market. I asked Daniella to help foster a friendship between Lucia and Emilio. I pleaded with Ines and the rest of the clinic staff to be honest with me and with each other without fear of retribution when they questioned one of my policies or decisions. I petitioned Kenneth for a free afternoon a week to have time to myself and study Tz'utujil.

As I continued to let go of the notion that I needed to be independent and take care of everything myself to be good and to do good, I opened space to wonder if there was another purpose to life—to my life, at least. In the *Popol Wuj*, the gods and spirits created humans to praise them, but also to recognize the calendar, the passing of time, the harmony in all things. Perhaps instead of striving for the unattainable—creating a perfect life—we are made to be woven into the rest of creation. Can we fold in with others, allow ourselves to be a thread in the fabric, and not carry the whole load ourselves? Could it be that after nearly half a century in the Christian tradition, I had finally found grace in another?

33

FLOATING

THREE MONTHS AFTER our October excursion to Belize, it was time to renew our visas again. Despite Lana's urging that I simply pay someone to take our passports and bribe the border agent to stamp them—"It's what everyone in San Marcos does"—I opted to make the three-day trek to Mexico. Handing our American passports to someone who made their living from circumventing the immigration system sounded too risky. Plus, I wanted another opportunity to show Lucia more of the country.

After a two-hour bus ride, we stopped in Xela at a crowded bus depot, a huge lot where buses randomly parked in any empty space. Stepping out of the bus, we could taste the black smoke billowing from diesel engines. Over the din of blasting horns, the drivers' assistants called out their buses' destinations for potential passengers. Passengers rushed about with small sacks of personal possessions and large baskets of goods for sale. We emerged from the chaos of the bus depot and into the chaos of the market, packed with people and produce, where we found a grubby toilet and an equally grubby food stand.

"I want one of those," Lucia said, pointing at an empanada. After three bites, she threw it down, saying, "This is disgusting!"

"Let's just get some fruit. Look, there are so many more varieties here than at the lake," I suggested as I pointed at the stands filled with the produce of Guatemala's most fertile agricultural region, including eggplant-colored star apples, star-shaped carambola, granadilla, hot-pink pitaya, and *paternas*, which look like bean pods.

Within minutes of arriving at our Airbnb, she vomited in the bathroom. There was no way to know whether it was the empanada, the bus, the dirty toilet, something else, or everything combined.

While she rested, I ran down to a nearby restaurant to buy some soup and to a pharmacy for *suero* (oral rehydration therapy) if she couldn't keep the soup down. I considered chucking the trip to Mexico and taking a private car back to the lake, but we had to renew our visas that week. Instead, I called a physician friend for advice and monitored Lucia closely. That night and the next day, I force-fed her fluids, held her hair while she vomited, held her hand while she had diarrhea, and read to her every waking moment in between.

After two days, she had recuperated enough to journey through another combination of crowded buses and confusing depots to the Suchiate River, marking the southwestern border between Guatemala and Mexico.

The last time I had crossed the Suchiate River to renew my visa was when I was living in Petén. Las Cruces, the village where I lived, is on the route for drug smugglers, human traffickers, tourists, and folks who just want to go to Mexico. On a tight budget at the time, I didn't want to pay the high price for a tourist shuttle to the border, so I asked the folks in Las Cruces how they traveled to Mexico. I took a bus that transferred to a van to a pickup truck and then to a lancha to cross the river.

All the Guatemalans had scurried out of the lancha and scattered when we reached Mexican soil. I alone walked up to the border control station to have my passport stamped. On my return trip, I brought a large box of medicine and supplies that I acquired in Mexico. On the shuttle portion of the return, the Guatemalan police stopped the vehicle to inspect the passengers' papers and baggage. I was scared that this would be one of those horrific *detenes* (detainments) that I had heard about where passengers are robbed, assaulted, or worse by the police. As the only foreigner and the only woman on the shuttle, there was no way I could fade into the background of the dozen passengers. And with a box full of "drugs" for which I had no papers, I could be accused of being a smuggler and could land in jail.

Instead, the police checked all the passengers' IDs, including mine, and looked in the Guatemalans' backpacks but did not touch my box or look in my bag. Did they not care what I might be bringing into the country? Did they not see me as a threat?

Once again at the Suchiate River, though this time much further south and with Lucia, I prepared for an encounter with border control. We walked into an empty Guatemalan border control office where I explained to Lucia, "We just have to show our passports, pay a little fee, and get a stamp here. Then we walk across the bridge over the river and do the same at the Mexican office on the other side."

As I had predicted, the functionary processed our exit in a matter of minutes. We stopped to gaze at the river on the walk over the bridge. Rafts made of tires, ropes, and air-filled jugs overloaded with people, packages, and plastic containers were floating below. I pointed out to Lucia, "Look, those people are trying to go from one country to another."

"Why would they do that?"

"Maybe they're looking for a better life, maybe they are visiting family, maybe they're shopping, maybe they want cheap gas."

"I mean, why would they cross that way? Those rafts look like they are going to fall apart, and I know most people here can't swim," Lucia said. "Why not walk across the bridge like we are doing?"

"I don't know much about the Mexican and Guatemalan immigration systems, but maybe their governments require certain permissions they can't get. Since we happen to be born in the US, and the US is a big and powerful country that influences other countries' immigration systems, all we have to do is show our passports."

"But it's not like that at home, right? The US doesn't let people from here in. Is that why Pablo was deported to Mexico?" Lucia asked, referring to Wade's brother-in-law, a Mexican national who had been deported three times despite having an American wife and four American children.

"I'm not sure about Guatemala, but I know that the US pressures Mexico to stop people from passing through who are likely on their way to the US. The US only lets in people from certain countries, or who have certain permissions that either cost so much money that most people can't afford it or would require many years of waiting."

"Are they on those rafts because it is cheaper? We only had to pay ten dollars to cross the border."

"I doubt it is cheaper. They have to pay someone to get them across. Money is involved, certainly. These systems wouldn't be set up this way if someone wasn't making money. Unfortunately, it's those people floating in the water who pay the price."

During our night in Hidalgo City, Mexico, we went to a large department store where I splurged on items not available in our village—bath towels, a can opener, a knife, hair conditioner. It cost me nearly three days' wages. Simple household essentials were out of reach for most people in our village. Even if they could afford to make the trip to Mexico and pay the relatively enormous price, they would not have permission to cross the border. No wonder we saw people holding piles of boxes on the rafts. I could simply fit these items in my backpack and walk back across the border the next day, no questions asked.

How often have I been able to pass through with no questions asked because of where I am from and what I look like? I could give Lucia rehearsed answers about why Mexicans and Guatemalans faced barriers traveling between their countries and to our country, but I faltered in explaining why we were in Guatemala. All I could tell her was that we were there for the experience, for her to see what life was like in another part of the world, for her to see what I loved.

For too long, I had felt like I was clinging to a makeshift raft, hoping to stay afloat. Now I had put Lucia on this raft and was paddling as hard as I could to get to the other side. But the other side of what? Was I paddling to something I wanted or away from something I dreaded?

34

HEART OF THE EARTH, HEART OF THE SKY

LUCIA BURST INTO TEARS when she came home from Nuevo Amanecer one afternoon. I picked her up, held her like a baby, and carried her to the hammock where I embraced her, rocked her, and let her release the pains of the day.

"Maestra Judit is mean. She yells at the students, and they don't listen to her. The kids don't pay any attention. They just joke around. The boys constantly tease me, and the girls gossip about me," she cried.

"I'm sorry. You are probably so different for them. I don't think they've ever been to school with a foreigner. I'm sure once they get to know you, it'll be better."

"I hate it. They don't want to get to know me. Can't I go to La Salle instead? At least there I will be with Karin."

"Sweetie, it has only been a few days. Why don't you give it some time?"

I hung one leg out of the hammock to rock us slowly, a trick I'd learned to soothe her when she was a baby. I held her tight until the sound of her sobs was replaced by the gentle lapping of the lake.

Though I repeatedly tried to reassure her, I was constantly worried about how she was faring in school. I made up excuses to stop by her classroom to check on her. She forgot her lunch; she needed break money to buy snacks; she left a notebook behind. The top half of the outward-facing classroom wall was windows, so I would crouch at the wall and hand her lunch, money, notebook, or whatever through the window. Having the crazy gringa mother stalking her at school probably did not help her fit in, but I needed to know how she was doing, to make some sort of contact.

Another day, Lucia came home particularly annoyed.

"In our faith education class, Maestra Judit gave a talk about the family. She said that the role of men is to work, earn money to support the family, and rule the household, and the role of women is to spend the money to run the household and care for the children."

"Hmph, what did you think of that?" I asked.

"I told her that my mother works, so she said that was because my father can't get a job. I let her know that my father does have a job. And also, my parents both cook, clean, and take care of me."

"Oh, and how did that go over?"

"She said that is because I'm an *extranjera*." I noted that Judit used the Spanish word for a foreigner that was like the word for strange, *extraño*.

"Look, they have probably never met a foreign child. The fact that Daddy and I are divorced and that we still take care of you together probably seems odd to them."

"But Maestra Judit has a job. I don't understand why she said that."

"You're right. You know, every woman we know here works and supports her family, right? Look at Gilda, all the women at the clinic, even Karin's mom. All these weaving cooperatives, art galleries, and comedores are run by women. I don't know where she gets that idea either."

Within days, Lucia came home crying yet again. A boy in her class was harassing her, hurting her, more than the usual teasing. He was a heavy older boy that had repeated a grade or two. She had a red mark on her arm from where he had hit her. Filled with anger, I stormed to the school and confronted Maestra Judit. When I told her about the boy, she acknowledged, "Yes, he is abusive, even to me. His mother is on her own because his father is a police officer stationed in another part of the country, so he has no discipline. He's unruly. The school has threatened to expel him."

"Threatened to expel? That's it?"

Seeing that we were not getting anywhere, I went straight to the director. When I told him a boy in the class had hurt Lucia, he responded, "I never saw that. No way that could have happened here. We are Christians."

"Well, she came home with red marks on her arm, so I know she was hit."

"Then how do you know it happened at the school? It must have happened between school and home."

"We live right by the school. Who else is going to hit her? Gilda? My daughter told me what happened, and I believe her." I then went on to describe the boy.

"Oh, yeah, him. He's a miscreant. We've threatened to expel him." Again, "threatened."

"So, what are you going to do about it?"

"We can move her into another class."

"Don't you have only one sixth-grade class?"

"Yes, we can put her in the fifth grade but give her sixth-grade work."

Then I blew up. "Why would you punish the victim? Why don't you punish the perpetrator? The first thing I asked you when we came to this school was if you hit children. Though you said no, you let other children hit children. What else would you expect when you teach that men are over women?"

His only reply was "God bless you," basically his way of saying, "Goodbye and get out."

"No, God has cursed me by putting you in my daughter's life. I entrusted you with my most valued treasure, and you defiled my trust."

So, that was the last day of Nuevo Amanecer. The next day, I enrolled her in La Salle, and the day after that, I went to demand my money back. I argued that since we were withdrawing because they could not protect her, they should refund the tuition. He said he wouldn't refund my money because it was already spent. The school had to paint the buildings and pay the teachers. I was furious, feeling I had been taken advantage of for being a foreigner.

The torment of Nuevo Amanecer continued after she left. As soon as she turned onto the path to Gilda's house, she would be accosted by a group of boys waiting by Nuevo Amanecer who would yell at her. She tried running past them, ignoring them, and even yelling back, but they harassed her each day as she went by. When she finally told me this, I decided to see for myself. I followed her home about a hundred feet behind. I saw the boys yelling, "Fuck you, gringa," at her, and then as soon as they saw me, they scattered.

I continued straight to the director's office again to report his brutish students and demand that he take action about these threats. Though my mind was racing, I calmly—or so I thought—told him that his "good Christian boys were threatening to rape my young daughter." Though that was not an exact translation of what they were saying, the intensity of the language, the mob mentality of the group, and the hostility felt that way to me. I told him that if he did not stop this behavior, I would report them to the police.

In hindsight, making this threat could have turned out very badly. The director might have made an accusation against me to the police. However, my instinct was to use whatever position of power and influence I had to stop the menace to my daughter. Fortunately, my gamble worked; those boys never bothered her again.

While at the time I was furious with that mealy-mouthed director, the passive teacher, and those aggressive boys, I later wondered to what degree their attitudes and behaviors were a backlash against 500 years of oppression by the Spaniards, then Criollos, then Ladinos and North Americans and/or an appropriation of their oppressors' views on women. Though anti-foreigner sentiment was not part of the open political discourse in San Juan as it was in San Marcos, I knew it was sanctimonious to expect my blue-eyed, blond daughter to be accepted by people who had not been accepted by people who look like us.

Regarding their views on women, Nehemias, my Tz'utujil teacher, told me that the Spanish conquerors brought misogyny to Mesoamerica. So I thought perhaps we were seeing something that had been imposed or at least influenced by an outside culture.

The *Popol Wuj* portrays male and female gods and characters at work in creation. The male gods formed the earth, the mountains, the valley, and the forest. They also made men out of mud who could not think and were washed away. The female gods fashioned beings that would reproduce themselves, think, honor the calendar, and praise the gods.

The Maya believe that the life cycles of all plants, animals, and humans are joined together under the Great Mother, Heart of the Earth, and the Great Father, Heart of the Sky. Women are not valued just for the reproduction of men but also for their role in all of creation. Male and female forces combined are needed to maintain balance in society and the cosmos.

The *Popol Wuj* includes many anecdotes of the trickster Hero Twins, brothers Hunahpu and Xbalanque, who are thought to represent a male/female pair. In ancient artwork, the older twin, Hunahpu, is depicted as the larger brother, right handed and masculine, and the sun and antlers are his symbols. The younger twin, Xbalanque, is smaller, left handed, and often associated with the moon and rabbits, which are considered feminine.[27] The Maya concept of "feminine" does not include the passivity associated with feminine in the West. It is noteworthy that Xbalanque is the one who moves the story along and acts on his own to save his brother when Hunahpu is debilitated.[28]

---

[27] Maestri, Nicoletta. "Hunahpu and Xbalanque — The Maya Hero Twins." ThoughtCo. https://www.thoughtco.com/hunahpu-xbalanque-maya-hero-twins-171590 (accessed March 25, 2023).

[28] Gillespie, Susan D. Gendering the Hero Twins in the Popol Vuh. Gendering the Hero Twins in the Popol Vuh. In Género y Arqueologia en Mesoamérica: Homenaje a Rosemary A. Joyce, ed. by María J. Rodríguez-Shadow and Susan Kellogg, pp. 139-151. Mexico City: Centro de Estudios de Antropología de la Mujer. 2013

In contrast, the early Christian (i.e., Catholic) missionaries, as well as my childhood church, taught that there is one God, that this God is male, that only men can represent him on earth, and that woman was created to serve man and was responsible for man's fall. Even when I was a child, this did not resonate with me. I saw women and men as equal partners in creation, tending to the garden. Adam and Eve both knew what they were doing when they chose knowledge over life and ate the forbidden fruit. Not until I was older did I realize that many in my culture do not share my understanding.

Based on what I heard from Nehemias and what I read in the *Popol Wuj*, I wanted to believe that in Guatemala, a country with one of the highest femicide rates in the world, there was once a mythical Maya matriarchy, a time when women enjoyed equal standing with men. I studied piles of books and articles written by anthropologists to see if that was indeed the case.

I learned that there may have been a time when Maya society was kin-based, as was the case for many ancient peoples. When the Maya lived in extended family groups of fifty or one hundred people, their relationships may have been defined through links with the mother. Even then, males and females had differentiated roles. Women raised domestic animals, prepared meals, wove, assisted in rituals, and cared for children. Likely because they spent most of their short adult lives pregnant or nursing, their duties were closer to home. Because men were not bound by children, they could roam to hunt, tend the outfields, and trade with other groups.

Their roles were complementary; each was equally needed and perhaps equally valued. The concept of gender had fluidity. Gender was what you did, not who you were. Male and female qualities existed in everything, even in men and women themselves. Sexuality was also fluid. Men had sex with other men, at least until they were married. Male and female couples were expected to be monogamous so that the lineage of their children would be known, not because women were considered to be men's property.

Though women were the connection between clans and were revered for their ability to create life during a time of high infant mortality, if equality meant that they had equal access to wealth (as granted through inheritance) and equal control over their bodies (by being able to choose their own marriages), they were not. As Maya society transformed from scattered bands into villages and then cities, men's power grew. Men could become long-distance traders, warriors, political leaders, ritualists, and marriage negotiators—roles that gave them access to wealth and power, creating a hierarchical as well as a complementary pattern of gender relationships. Rather than being linked to a common matriarch, people began to identify their bond to each other by a particular city or political unit, usually led by a man; ties to the state became more important than ties to the family.[29]

Because of the belief that male and female energies are and need to be in all things, male leaders began to appropriate what was considered female. The male priests' costumes evolved into a combination of men's and women's clothing. They added female names to their own and even cut their genitals to emulate menstruation. As opposed to the West, where acting like a woman is degrading for a man, in the classic Maya period, acting like a woman was a means of subverting her power. Myths developed about men stealing women's weaving as a way to steal their power.[30] Even in the story told in the *Popol Wuj*, women lost their power and presence. In the beginning of the codex, women and men were named together and shared power, but by the end of the story, the only women mentioned are the nameless wives of the K'iche' lords.

Reflecting on what I have read about the Maya and on my life with Wade, I wonder how I would have defined gender roles in my marriage. I thought there was a time when we complemented each other. I went back to work after Lucia was born, and he stayed at home with her. I came up with the big picture, and he handled the details. I connected our household to the outside world, and he kept it well stocked. I told Lucia

---

[29] Joyce, Rosemary A. 2000. *Gender and Power in Prehispanic Mesoamerica.* University of Texas Press.

[30] Mazariegos, Oswaldo Chinchilla. 2010. "Of Birds and Insects: The Hummingbird Myth in Ancient Mesoamerica." Ancient Mesoamerica 21:45–61;"

many times that Daddy was the earth, Mommy was the sky, and she was the sun that illuminated us both. Was I wrong about that? Should he have been the Heart of the Sky and I have been the Heart of the Earth, or was our relationship what was wrong? Should I have been more "passive," as he once told me? Should I have stayed grounded while I let him roam? Was my floating, my forward motion, a constant contrast to his stillness? Had I lost my power somewhere along the way?

In the sixteenth century, Maya women likely had many of the same joys and struggles as did European women: birthing, caring for, and losing children; being married off to men who may have taken off for another place; making the materials around them into practical works of art. Maya men were likely similar to European men in that they held political posts, used their gods to justify their actions, and battled other peoples they then took as prisoners. Despite the similarities, I saw no record that they used rape as a weapon like the Europeans and then the Ladinos, Criollos, and North Americans did, to terrorize the people they conquered and destroy the embodiment of their culture, women—to stab the Heart of the Earth.

Notwithstanding centuries of subjugation, it is the women who run San Juan. Women's labor, particularly the weaving cooperatives, drive an economy in which few men own the fields where they work. The churches, clinics, and schools were all operated by women when I was there, even if a man was the official head. Women have seemingly continued to be the creative connectors all along.

Gilda invited Lucia and me to attend a competition in the municipal basketball court to select the town princess for San Juan. Having been a princess herself when she was young, she explained what this meant. Young women dress in traje típica, act out scenes from local legends through dance, and demonstrate their oratory skills in Tz'utujil. The winner competes with over one hundred princesses of other Indigenous villages to be the Rabin Ajaw (the daughter of the king, in Q'eqchi').

The Rabin Ajaw holds an office in the Guatemalan government for one year; although she represents Indigenous people at cultural festivals, she has no power. While the Indigenous men in San Juan try to fit into Ladino culture by abandoning their traje típica except for special occasions, practicing Spanish over Tz'utujil, and participating in politics, they expect the women to continue to embody their traditional culture.

The men cannot reach for the sky if the women are not the ground that holds them up.

35

THE LONG COUNT

LUCIA AND I HAD BEEN ANTICIPATING lunch at Daniella's house, both for the food and the fellowship. On the day of our invitation, her husband, Edoardo, and her older son, Aldo, were running errands in Panajachel, so it would be just the moms and younger kids.

Since there were no addresses or street names in town, I was worried about once again wandering about in search of someone's domicile.

"We live on the other side of the road that comes up from the dock. All you have to do is pass through, take the path after Felipe's art studio, and go through a grove of coffee trees," Daniella assured me. Though that sounded simple, I wondered if we would be attacked by dogs or have to bribe someone to show us the way.

Once on the path, Lucia and I spent a good amount of time circling in the copse of trees, always returning to where we started. The shrubby trees on every side, stripped of their cherries that were being processed into coffee, were indistinguishable to me.

"Let's focus on the trail and not get distracted by the trees," Lucia suggested. "The part that is the most worn down is probably the way."

"That's very astute of you," I commented. "Why don't you lead?"

Daniella moved to Mexico in the 1990s to work with Indigenous communities as a response to her calling to bring people with disabilities out of the shadows so that they can have productive, dignified lives. Thereafter, she alternated between pursuing her vocation in Central America and earning money for herself, seeking funds for her projects, and spending time with her friends and family in Italy. During one of her stays in Italy, she met Edoardo, who quickly became enamored with her. She took him to Mexico to introduce him to her passions. Edoardo adored her and was willing to make her dream his own, so they spent the next decade and a half oscillating between continents. I envied the life they had built together.

At this point, they had been in Guatemala for close to five years, working for *Alma de Colores* (Spirit of Colors), a Centro Maya project to incorporate people with disabilities into the labor force. They started with a sewing and crafts workshop that made everything from bags to computer cases to jewelry from recycled materials. The oversized-scrubs-turned-sheets for our clinic were made by a one-armed woman with Centro Maya.

Daniella and Edoardo went to Italy with suitcases of goods from the workshop to sell every year. By wit and by will, they also launched a vegetarian restaurant—rare in a country that viewed meat as a luxury—that employed people with disabilities. Daniella organized the menus, staff, and facility, and Edoardo administered the grants that funded her ideas and launched a side bakery business.

They made the restaurant a community gathering place and a space to learn about people with disabilities. Daniella was fluent in two signing languages, making the events accessible to the hearing impaired. They hosted movie nights with films that featured people with disabilities as people with agency.

As soon as we entered Daniella's home, she greeted us both with a big kiss and hug. Even Emilio, who was at her side, gave me a kiss but just said hello to Lucia.

"We have been busy packing."

"Are you moving?"

"Unfortunately, yes! We have been burglarized three times in the past six months. That's enough! I think because the house is surrounded by trees, the thieves think no one can see. But I saw this one!"

Lucia asked, "What happened?"

"The entrance for the main part of the house does not have a door, so anyone can walk in. Even though we lock the individual rooms, a burglar can still come and take whatever he wants from the kitchen."

"Sometimes, we might leave something valuable like a music player or shoes in the kitchen, and then it is gone," Emilio added. I thought about the times that Lucia and I left items on our front porch. Anyone who could climb the rocks could take whatever we had lying around.

"Well, the other day, I was in the shower over there," she said, pointing with her lips to a small cinder-block structure near the house. "When I entered the house, I heard someone rustling in the back room. I grabbed the metal door, slammed it shut, and locked it from outside."

"Dani, you trapped him inside?"

"Like the bug that he was."

"What did you do next? Don't tell me you were still wrapped in your towel."

"Indeed I was. I grabbed a pot and pan and started clanging them together so the women would come. The neighbor women heard me and brought their pots and pans to clang as well."

"Why would they do that?"

"So that the police would come," she said matter-of-factly.

Of course, I thought. *There is no 911 here*. There is no phone book or online directory, and no one would know the police's phone number offhand, and even if they did, it would cost money to make a call. Plus, Daniella's phone was probably locked in the room with the burglar.

"Did the burglar try to escape? Did you hear him banging around?" I had an image of a trapped cat trying to claw its way out of a box.

"No, not at all. He was quiet until the police came and dragged him away. Poor soul."

"Why do you say that? Don't you think he was the same person that stole from you all those times?"

"I know he was. I just wanted him to stop the theft, but now he is being tortured by the police. His mother came and asked me to write a letter on his behalf."

"So, if the thief was caught, why are you moving?"

"I'm sure he has already told his friends about us, and others will just try to do the same thing. Hopefully, since we will be leaving in August, this will be our last move."

"You're leaving in August?" I asked, disappointed that our new friendship would end in a few months.

"I'm afraid so. Edoardo, Aldo, and Emilio are done with Guatemala, so we are moving back to Italy. I promised them that once the restaurant was up and running and the staff could manage it on their own, we would leave."

"I'm so tired of moving," Emilio complained. "The next will be our sixth house in five years."

"Really?" I asked, raising my eyebrows as I looked at Lucia. We were not the only ones who were constantly moving.

"When we arrived, we stayed with the family of our director until we got our own place. Our first house was too small; we were cramped with four people in two rooms. We moved to a bigger house by the church, but the bell that rang every hour drove us nuts," Daniella explained.

"Then we were by a bar," Emilio added. "Men would get drunk and then start singing late at night."

"And then we came here thinking we would have peace and quiet," Daniella said with a big sigh.

"Some peace and quiet with all that clanging you're doing, right?" I joked. The seriousness fell off both Emilio and Daniella's faces, and we all laughed.

When the food was served, Lucia and I feasted on vegetable cakes, braised greens with fresh herbs, and Italian cheeses. Daniella and Emilio exchanged glances of pleasant surprise as we raved about the food.

"Just in case you were wondering, my mom does not cook like this," Lucia commented.

"Oh, come on," Daniella said in my defense. "Your mother must make something you like. What is your favorite dish that she prepares?"

"Popcorn," Lucia answered.

I shrugged and quickly changed the subject. "Dani, did I mention that Lucia has started at La Salle?"

"The evangelical school didn't last long, eh?" She smirked.

"Uh, well, it's been hard to find the right situation for Lucia."

"It was hard for us too. Aldo went to school at Escuela Caracol through sixth grade and wasn't prepared when he started *básico* [middle school] in Panajachel. That school is in English, which he didn't speak, so I had to hire tutors to teach him."

"But is he getting a good education now?"

"Not really. The administration is disorganized, and the teacher turnover is constant. There's no standard curriculum. The teachers are from all over the English-speaking world and teach in whatever way subjects are taught in their home countries."

"That must be tough."

"Indeed. In May, I am sending him back to Italy to be tutored all summer to get into a decent *lycée* [French for high school] in September. At this point in his education, he should be fluent in French and Latin, and instead, he hasn't even had a basic education in Italian."

Since youth in Italy are tracked for college or trades early in their education, her family had a lot riding on whether this summer tutoring would work for Aldo.

"But what about for Emilio? He must have enjoyed starting out at Escuela Caracol?"

"He didn't start there. I didn't want to send my five-year-old by lancha to school every day, so I enrolled him at La Salle."

"Emilio went to La Salle?" I asked, surprised.

"Yes, but just for a couple of months. He was the only foreigner there, and the children teased him all the time, so I pulled him out."

"What did you do? Put him in public school?" I couldn't imagine that proudly atheist Daniella would consider Nuevo Amanecer since it was an evangelical school.

"Ay no, Edoardo and I homeschooled him for a year. We had to take turns going to work and being at home."

With a twinge of envy, I said, "Well, I'm sure it was a big help having Edoardo do that with you. He gave up everything in Italy to support you in your dreams."

"Edoardo? He didn't give up anything. He was just working part-time as a yoga teacher. Here he has a job that means a lot to him. Plus, he was already coming to Central America almost as often as I was. He was supporting the Zapatistas too. That's how we met. This is what he wanted all along. We just happened to want the same thing. In fact, when we go back to Italy, he is going to help with fundraising for the program here."

I had been wrong about Daniella's marriage. She and her husband had started out and had stayed in step. They each made sacrifices for the other, but they never had to sacrifice who they were. I slowly began to see that being able to be my authentic self with someone was what I had really longed for.

Like me, Daniella was also spinning her wheels, searching for home and school, bouncing between countries and projects, but what was the Long Count against which she measured them? The grand arc of her life seemed to be in balancing her sense of purpose and the practical needs of her family. She knew when to call for help and when to retreat. She knew when it was time to end an era.

36

EL DON

DURING PRE-COLUMBIAN TIMES, priests consulted the cholq'ij calendar to ascertain newborns' nawales. Based on the date of birth, priests could prognosticate future careers, good days and bad, possibilities for marriage, and character traits. Now that there are few practicing Maya priests, the comadronas have taken a form of this power.

The comadrona and sometimes the mother can see in the newborn whether she or he has a *don* (gift). A don isn't a talent like music or math but rather a call to a sacred duty, such as a priest, a healer, or an artist who relays spiritual messages through her craft. The call to be a comadrona is the most revered don because it exists close to life and death. The comadrona or mother can never tell anyone the don they see. It must remain a secret until the child discovers it for herself through dreams.

Navichoc became a comadrona because she received the call to help other women not suffer as she had. On the Christmas Eve her father found out she was seven months pregnant at age seventeen, he beat her severely and mercilessly because she had shamed the family. He broke her nose, punched her repeatedly in the stomach, and locked her in a room.

That night, her bloody and broken body went into labor. She was terrified, having no idea what to do. She pulled up her corte and looked into the mirror hanging on the wall to see the baby's head crowning. Alone on a bed not much better than a manger, she gave birth, or as is said in Spanish, *dio a luz*—brought light into the world. Her mother let her out of the room only to have her father throw her out of the house with her newborn baby girl. She stumbled to the home of the baby's father, and they eventually built a life together.

Twenty years and two more bright and beautiful daughters later, Navichoc was one of the most respected members of the community. Though technically she was employed with ODIM, she was on her own mission. She leveraged every resource possible of any passing volunteer or NGO working on maternal health and had a stockpile of birthing supplies in her home. She organized two concurrent courses for local comadronas in her house. When not working a full-time job with Mamá y Yo Saludable, doing her side gig delivering babies, or raising three daughters, she supported another NGO in opening a *casa materna*, or birthing center, in San Juan.

Ofelia, Navichoc's middle daughter, inherited her mother's *don* and was her mother's assistant at the births she attended. At only sixteen years old, she was top of her class in one of the midwifery courses Navichoc hosted. She was also studying for a high school–level nursing degree, somewhat equivalent to a medical assistant in the US, and was among the nursing students doing clinical rotations with ODIM soon after I started.

When I tasked the nursing students with doing a pharmacy inventory project that involved a lot of dreary data crunching, she was the only one who embraced the project and wanted to learn more about Excel. After the students' five-week rotation ended, I gave her a part-time job to finish the pharmacy project. When Manuela backed away from learning how to calculate dosages, Ofelia stepped forward. On her own, she researched medication prices and efficacy to make more efficient requests. I trusted her abilities so much that I sent her in my place to Guatemala City to negotiate donations with a US NGO.

As much as Ofelia received the don of being a healer, she was a gift herself. When Kenneth handed her the first month's pay, she promptly gave the whole stack of bills to her ailing father, who could not afford his medical treatment. She impressed me so much that when I was searching for a tutor for Lucia, I recruited her. I furnished her with a bundle of fifth-grade math workbooks and said they could work on any math topic for one hour and then spend their second hour on other school projects.

I came late home from work one day to find Lucia and Ofelia sprawled out on the patio with tissue paper, glue, glitter, and markers. Lucia was excited to explain the latest homework creation, a poster of a tree with descriptions of its nourishments and fruits. Ofelia and Lucia spent hours wadding up bits of tissue paper to make the tree's roots, trunk, and leaves. They scribbled FRIENDS, BOOKS, FAMILY, PLAY in the roots. They wrote little notes about Lucia's qualities to hide in the fruit. I felt guilty for keeping Ofelia late, so I insisted that she go home for dinner and leave the mess for Lucia to clean, but she asked if she could stay until the tree was complete. Gazing at those two covered in glue and glitter, I was relieved that Lucia would rather engage in building a tree than escape by climbing one.

I asked Navichoc if she would show Lucia and me her gift as a comadrona. Though she agreed to allow me to accompany her for a birth when the timing was right, she said Lucia was too young and instead offered to take her on a postpartum home visit. Postpartum home visits were the fourth pillar of the Mamá y Yo Saludable program, after prenatal care, support groups, and nutritional supplements.

On the designated day for a home visit, Navichoc took us down an alley in a section of town I had not seen. The family's home was a rented room with only one window, one bed, one table, and one chair. The mother lay in the bed with her head wrapped in what looked to me like a torn sheet to help with the migraine resulting from the birth the previous day. Navichoc crawled onto the bed to examine mother and child while Lucia and I shared the one chair. Navichoc first unwrapped the baby, who was swaddled in torn sheets and looked like a mummy. Little arms and legs squirmed, and a strong pair of lungs let out a loud cry. Navichoc went through the program's protocol to check his responses. He was healthy. She handed the baby to Lucia to hold while she examined the mother. Lucia cooed at the newborn cradled in her arms.

The mother, though, was not fine. She had hemorrhaged during the delivery, but Navichoc was able to stop the bleeding with a shot of oxytocin. Navichoc knew what to do only because she pressed every NGO that came through town to teach her. And in her determination to learn, she saved this woman and child.

She unwrapped the mother's corte and did a vigorous abdominal massage to help the uterus contract. The woman likely needed a blood transfusion, but there was no blood source on this side of the lake. Navichoc was not willing to use another precious dose of oxytocin if the woman was not currently bleeding. The massage would have to be sufficient. After Navichoc was finished with her exam and care protocol, we left.

A week or so later, Navichoc ran into Sanjuanerita late. Her hair hung loose, wet, and unbrushed. She went straight to her exam room without greeting anyone. Sensing something was wrong, I asked her what had happened. As tears began to pour, she cried out, "I lost my first baby."

She explained that she had been called late in the evening to attend a difficult birth. The baby was born with the umbilical cord wrapped around his neck. Navichoc was able to navigate the delivery, but the baby needed oxygen. Since the family had means, they were able to acquire a truck in the middle of the night and rush the woman to a private birthing center in San Pedro. This clinic had no oxygen. The baby was losing the little color he had left. Navichoc tried every trick she had been taught, and nothing worked. After hours of fighting fate, the baby died.

"It's not fair," Navichoc sobbed. "All the baby needed was oxygen. The clinic should have had it. We should have it. Why does a woman have to go to another town for help? Why can't we have a simple thing like air? In twenty years as a comadrona, I have never lost a child. Why now? This is so wrong," she continued to cry. I gently twisted her hair, pulled it up, and secured it with a clip and then embraced her. I tried to reassure her about her skills as a comadrona, but I could not console her about the lack of medical resources.

Navichoc had a gift, and the Sanjuanerita clinic was full of donated gifts. Still, these gifts were not enough to save this baby. The Ministry of Health, and even private clinics, lacked essential supplies because the president and vice president had a cheating scheme with customs officials. They diverted the importers' tariffs to their pockets and directed their goods, including medicine and medical supplies, to the private hands of their friends. Though they were jailed, the whole country had to pay for their crimes.

Though the corruption schemes may not be so brazen in my country, resources are as unequally distributed—the rich have access to health care, and the poor have substandard care, if any. If babies are a gift from God, why should their lives depend upon the charity of others?

I was in awe of what women like Doña Marina, Navichoc, and Ofelia could do with so little. It was because they were gifted, I told myself. It was their magic.

But no. Thinking of what these women were doing as a gift put their power in the hands of their creators rather than in the hands of these creative women. Their abilities arose from their compassion and determination, not from a numen.

37

SOMEWHERE IN THE MIDDLE

"WE HAVE TO GO to the tienda tonight!" Lucia exclaimed as she ran around the corner to the house after school.

Relieved that she seemed excited rather than distraught about her day, I replied, "Really? What's going on? Do you have a school project?"

"Evelyn and I have a secret," she informed me. "It's Adela's birthday tomorrow, and we are going to have a surprise for her. We made her a card and are going to buy her a present. Can we go to the tienda tonight? *Please?*"

Despite the hassle with the enrollment, getting the supplies, and the questionable constant closings, La Salle was the best school situation for Lucia thus far. Her new friends Adela and Evelyn were the daughters of families I knew around town. Adela's mother was Navichoc's sister, also a comadrona, and the former head of the city's office of women's affairs. Evelyn's parents owned a large boarding house where Dra. Vacinta had lived.

"Can I leave some money for you to go with Ofelia to the papelería?" I suggested. "Maybe she can help you make a present for Evelyn."

"I'd rather go with you, Mommy. I've got other homework to do with Ofelia."

"Of course, sweetie." I gestured for her to crawl into the hammock with me. "What else went on today?"

"Maestra Elvira said I'm the best math student in the class. She had me explain how to do the problems on the blackboard."

"Hmm, so all those nights we've spent doing math workbook have paid off, right?" I teased. "You're only ten, but you are in class with twelve-year-olds, and you are helping them with math. That's marvelous!"

"Well, since I'm terrible in my other subjects, I'm glad I'm good in at least one thing. Since my Spanish isn't good, people think I'm stupid."

"I don't think that's the case."

"Yes, it is! The lady who sold me a chocolate-covered mango during recess thought that I couldn't count change, but I set her straight. I let her know that if she didn't pay me the one quetzal back, I would never buy from her again. I also let her know that I would tell everyone she cheated me."

I was both proud that Lucia could stick up for herself and mortified that she had learned intimidation tactics from me.

"Maybe you should stay away from the chocolate-covered mangos and the other snacks the ladies sell during break," I suggested. "You've been getting sick more often. Why don't we make popcorn for you to take? You could take the rice cakes we got from the last group that came down, or I could cut fruit at home."

"Mom [not 'Mommy'], the kids think our food is weird. I get teased enough for looking different. If I eat our weird food in front of them, they'll tease me even more."

"Fine," I acquiesced. "I'll agree with you about the food, but I don't agree that math is the only thing you are good at. There must be another subject."

"Okay, *educación física*. I'm good at basketball."

As we laughed and rocked in the hammock, Leticia (the director of Centro Maya) and her son Felipe popped up from around the corner, holding a box of chocolates and a giant balloon. Confused by their appearance, I jumped up from the hammock with Lucia to greet them.

"Hola. What a pleasant surprise to see you."

With a forceful shove to her son's back, Leticia said, "Felipe is here to apologize."

"For what?" I asked as Lucia rolled her eyes and crossed her arms.

"Felipe told me that he punched Lucia in class. We teach him that boys should never hit girls, so he should know that what he did was wrong." She proceeded to force an apology out of her son, and Lucia perfunctorily accepted. After a few more minutes of polite but awkward conversation, they left.

"Why didn't you tell me about what happened with Felipe today?" I asked.

"He didn't hit me hard. Compared to what I experience every day, it didn't seem like a big deal. And anyhow, Felipe is harassed by the boys much more than me. They are always trying to make him cry."

Without my knowing the details, it was evident that Felipe had a developmental disability. Likely, he was brutally teased and, in turn, teased Lucia. I was impressed by her measured response.

"I know school is hard for you, but as you can see, it is harder for Felipe, and it always will be. There will always be things you are better at and things you are worse at than other kids. There will always be people who have more and people who have less than you. There will always be something that bothers you and something to be grateful for. We have to find our place in the middle of all that where we can find peace."

"Well, what about you? Have you found peace?"

After a long pause, I replied, "I'm halfway there."

Hannah and I met with ODIM's founder, Gillian, to learn the organization's history for a grant we were writing. Gillian wove the story of ODIM's founding with her own life story.

As a social worker in Texas, she was widowed in early middle age, with three children to raise. Her network, including her church, stepped up to get her family through this sudden and painful life change. A few years later, she began going with her church on annual mission trips to Guatemala.

Her Spanish was weak, and she was not trained as a health-care provider, so she felt what she could do was limited. Still, for fifteen years, she continued the yearly visits and slowly developed relationships with people in Guatemala, through whom she learned about the country.

Eventually, she remarried to a man who also had ties to Guatemala, and together they moved to Lake Atitlán in the early 2000s. Though the marriage did not last, her commitment to Guatemala did.

When Hurricane Stan devastated the region in 2005, she tapped into the church network that had supported her during her own storm. She and the other Texas church folk distributed blankets, food, and medicine, and rebuilt homes. As the immediate crisis response turned to long-term development, she formed a nonprofit organization. She was in her late fifties when she started ODIM and served as the director for nearly a decade. The year before I came, she retired, and Kenneth joined as the new director.

I was amazed at how she had recovered from a blow far greater than mine and started a bold venture in later life. Even after retirement, she was involved in projects in San Pablo, where she had a home and an extensive social network that crisscrossed the lake.

"Now, as they say in Tz'utujil, I'm in my seventy-fifth year," Gillian explained, smiling, the wrinkles around her bright-blue eyes turning up. "I mean, I'm actually only seventy-four years old, but in Tz'utujil, they talk about the year you are in, not the year you finished."

"I guess that means I am in my twenty-fifth year," Hannah added.

Apart from a few months in Australia after university, this was the first time Hannah had lived far away from home. She had moved to San Marcos with her partner when he took a job there. When she got a job with ODIM, a whole new field of health and community development opened up to her. She threw herself into learning about diabetes and maternal and child health.

She formed a close bond—"like sisters," she said—with Alba and other staff. These friendships sustained her when the daily hassles and harassment seemed overwhelming. Like me, she battled with the lancha pilot and tuk-tuk drivers who overcharged her, but unlike me, at least since I had entered middle age, she also suffered catcallers. Their home had been robbed so many times that they eventually gave up living in San Marcos and moved into another small house on Gilda's property.

With her long blond hair and complete dedication to her work, she reminded me of myself at her age. Around the same time in my life, I had followed Stuart to Mexico, where he was pursuing his graduate research. I studied Spanish in the mornings and in the afternoons went to every meeting or seminar on health I could find in the newspaper. Through acquaintances, I eventually got a job in public health and absorbed everything I could like a sponge. And also like Hannah, I had to deal with harassment every time I walked outside. Once, I had Stuart follow me down the street to witness the predatory wolf whistles so he would understand what I had to deal with. A couple of years after that relationship ended, I moved to Petén, Guatemala, where I formed a bond with Lilian and Doña Marina that has lasted twenty years.

In what was my fiftieth year, I had settled somewhere in the middle of Hannah and Gillian's experiences. With twenty-five years of experience and a previous tour under my belt, it wasn't as challenging as when I was young. As a mature woman, men no longer accosted me. Though annoyed by the price gouging, I had plenty of savings and didn't have to count every quetzal I spent.

What was challenging for me was parenting in another country. Unlike Gillian, I had not waited until my child was grown to set out on this venture. I wasn't in a place where I could spend my days dabbling in new projects or socializing with friends. Yet there we were: three women at different stages of our lives, drawn together by a shared purpose.

Like Guatemala, and even like Gillian, I had already weathered the storms, recovered from a disaster, and was in long-term development. True, but was this who I wanted to be? Was this how I wanted my life to be?

I had been measuring the grand arcs of my life all wrong. I had been looking at the stars in the sky and seeing constellations that did not serve me. Marking the pivotal moments of my life by the heartbreaks I had experienced from Stuart, my ex-fiancé, and then Wade, my ex-husband, had me centered on tragedy. Did I want this to be how I defined my life?

If I instead focused not on the destruction but on the demiurgic forces that have come from me, how would I measure the milestones?

What would comprise the eras of my new Long Count? First, the time as a young woman with a growing desire to do good in the world through her career; then, as a middle-aged mother of a spirited girl; and finally, as, well, who knows what I will become.

Halfway through my adult life, I was halfway through raising my daughter, halfway through this second era.

I was in the middle of it.

38

HIDDEN TREASURES

AS PER OUR SUNDAY routine, I took Lucia to the stables in San Pedro, which were run by a man named Moises, so she could go horseback riding with Stela, Taska, and Moises's twelve-year-old daughter, Yenifer, while Lana and I had coffee and two hours of uninterrupted gossip. The girls, followed by Moises, explored the trails along the base of Volcán San Pedro through forest and coffee fields. It was the highlight of Lucia's week.

Among my Sunday-morning errands before meeting Lana was to buy fresh greens. Along the perimeter of the lake, concealed behind a fence and between hotels, was a plot of land where Geronimo, the proprietor and sole worker, grew organic chard, kale, lettuce, basil, and many other varieties of vegetables and herbs that he sold to the restaurants and passersby.

Geronimo tended his garden six and a half days a week. I caught him as he was putting away his gardening tools before he departed for his weekly visit with his family a couple of hours away. As usual, I requested a twenty-quetzal ($2.50) mix of whatever was ripe and handed him a canvas bag to fill.

While Geronimo darted up and down the rows, selecting the most mature vegetables and clipping the broadest leaves, I sat on a crate in his hut, which was made of four wood posts and a lamina slab as a roof. The ground was littered with clothes, razors, a few dishes. *This must be where he slept all week*, I thought. He did not leave his field on the edge of town unattended at night because he would be robbed.

I knew about this spot, preserved from tourism redevelopment, because Hannah had pointed it out when we had a meeting in San Pedro.

I wondered how long this parcel that nourished Geronimo's family, my family, and others would be preserved. How long would he be willing to sleep in this hut before taking the one-time cash payment for his land and giving up?

I then went to meet Lana and the girls at our regular spot down the road—one of the businesses that cater to tourists, with a pool and restaurant that on Sundays served Southern US–style barbeque complete with all the fixings. Usually, Lana and I would catch up and chat with other expats while the girls swam after their hot and dusty ride. This Sunday, I waited nearly an hour for Lana and the girls. I was beginning to worry when Lana stormed up, followed by sullen-looking Lucia and Stela, not from the direction of the stable but from the direction of the trail.

"What happened? Where's Taska?" I asked.

"Taska and Irka still are looking for their dog," Lana huffed.

"Huh?"

"Taska brought her dog, this huge German shepherd, with her when we went riding. The dog got spooked and ran away. We called and called for it, but it wouldn't come back," Stela explained.

"When we came back to the stable without the dog, Irka was there waiting on us. She made us go back to look for the dog," Lucia continued. "We went all along the trails around the volcano calling out for the dog—in English, Spanish, and Latvian."

"It's ridiculous. The side of that volcano is huge. How are we supposed to search the whole area?" Lana asserted. "Why would anyone bring a dog horseback riding, and why is it our responsibility to help her search? We had enough, so we left."

"And that's not all the trouble Taska got into," Stela added.

Wanting to fill in the juicy details, Lucia interjected, "When we were giving the horses a break, Taska went to the edge of a cliff. She was balancing on a rock and then slipped and fell off and over the cliff."

Stela finished, "She grabbed some weeds, so she didn't tumble down. Moises and Yenifer had to help her up."

Lana rolled her eyes while I asked with surprise, "Is she alright?"

"From that, yeah," Stela said.

"She also got stepped on by her horse," Lucia continued.

"Huh?" I again asked.

"She tried to get on the horse the wrong way, and then it stepped on her and tore off her sandal. She had to spend the rest of the ride with one shoe." Apparently, the girls liked to gossip as much as the mothers.

"Well, apart from all that, did you have fun?" I asked.

"Mommy! You won't believe it. We went on a new trail and found an abandoned building where they used to process coffee. It has the old railroad tracks and train cars that used to carry the coffee beans away. We went in to explore the building and played on the equipment," Lucia said. Noting my disapproving look, she added, "Taska insisted." And to further justify, she said, "Yenifer was with us. She had been there before."

"It was fun until we startled the bats, and they chased us out!" Stela interrupted.

I thought, *Hmm, bats equal rabies, rusty equipment equals tetanus, abandoned buildings equals nefarious dealings, Taska equals trouble, and dogs, well, they are all half-demon to me.* Nevertheless, this was the kind of escapade I wanted Lucia to have. Four girls on horseback freely exploring the coffee fields and forests on the side of a volcano was an experience that I could have only imagined in a novel, and far different from playing tag or practicing handstands with her friends in our front yard.

After we stuffed ourselves with pulled pork, coleslaw, and mac and cheese, the girls jumped in the pool, and Lana told me about her week. She was battling with her ex-husband in Croatia over child support. The risky online-trading venture was not yielding enough money to make ends meet. The title for the land she bought a few months ago was in dispute. She was worried about what to do for Stela's school once she finished sixth grade at Escuela Caracol. She and her Guatemalan on-again, off-again boyfriend had different visions for their relationship.

She had come to San Marcos to recapture the magic that she had felt when she first visited as a young woman. This was probably not what she had imagined.

After lunch, Lucia and I made a few more stops in San Pedro to buy Mexican paletas and a pirated download of the second Star Wars trilogy. Despite Lucia's usual protest that we take a tuk-tuk home, I insisted we walk. There was no rush, and besides, we might see other people we knew on the way and could stop for a chat.

When we arrived home, Lucia scooted down the rocks to play with Karin and Felix, the other part of her near-daily routine. The kids crawled further down to the little beach by the lake, where they collected empty mollusk shells—hidden treasures that they found on the shore. They came back up to our porch with armfuls of their spoils. Verna heard the joyful ruckus and ran down from Gilda's to join them. They used Lucia's fingernail polish to paint colorful designs on the shells and lined them on our porch to dry.

With Lucia occupied, I ventured out for my own exploring. I climbed and crossed the dock and went another fifty feet or so to gaze at the moored wooden boats that carried the fishermen I watched from my porch in the mornings. Every day, they canvassed this stretch of water with their nets in search of a depleting stock of fish. In the market, I occasionally saw a few tiny, bony fish, the surplus of their catch. How could there be anything left to find here?

Past the dock, I came across a large wooden house with a well-manicured lawn. On the bit of pasture by the side of the house, a mare nuzzled her foal, which the guardian told me was only four days old.

I thought that Lucia would love to see this. Though dusk was close, I asked him to please wait for me to return with my daughter. I couldn't imagine anything else that would have torn her away from the comfort of home after a long day. When I brought her to the pasture, Lucia was delighted to see the baby horse.

The foal wobbled toward us on her knobby legs. After the horrific experience of petting the offspring of another animal, I warned Lucia not to touch him, but the guardian assured us that the mother was securely tied and encouraged Lucia to pet him. We both ran our hands down the softest fur I had ever felt. Lucia wrapped her arms around his neck and giggled with glee to pose for pictures.

We are all looking for something that we may or may not find. Along the way, we may uncover other hidden treasures that are better than what we wanted, or we may lose the desire to search for something elusive.

39

ROGELIO

ALBA POPPED BY my house one morning to ask me to interpret for her father, Rogelio. He was to speak to a visiting group of US volunteers from a Tennessee church about the armed conflict in Guatemala. I was disinclined to do so because it would be during one of my rare free afternoons, and I assumed that she could do this herself since she spoke fluent English. However, I wanted to repay Alba for all the help she had given me. Also, I thought it would be an excellent opportunity for Lucia to learn Guatemalan history, so I brought her along.

I knew that Rogelio, a man in his early fifties, was the father of three children who had all gone on to study post–high school, rare for a local family. For years, his family had owned a successful lakeside hotel and substantial home until the lake rose suddenly and submerged their livelihood. In a matter of days, they salvaged what they could from the rising waters and moved their base up the hill to a new property that they subdivided into a modest store and an even more modest home.

Instead of beginning his discussion with the usual narrative I had often heard—an overview of the history of colonialism and oppression leading to the "scorched earth" policy that razed over 600 villages and killed hundreds of thousands of people—he opened with "A neighbor betrayed me."

At the height of the war in the early 1980s, Rogelio was a young man of nineteen, a student helping his parents tend their store. During this time, the army passed through Indigenous villages, either looking for members of the guerrilla forces and the people who aided them with food and shelter or merely burning the villages to the ground. I was wrong to think the violence and political upheaval I'd seen on the Coxes' television when I first arrived couldn't reach our paradise; it already had.

When the army arrived at San Juan, a neighbor told them that Rogelio supported the guerillas, either to avert suspicion from himself or to receive a reward. Soldiers went to Rogelio's house in the hours of darkness and dragged him away to an outpost to interrogate him. They bound his wrists and ankles with wires and beat him. He rolled up his shirt sleeves and pant legs to show the deep indentations and scars still visible thirty years later.

I paused for a breath—for us all to catch a breath. I looked over at Alba to see the tears welling in her eyes. This was why she had asked me to interpret. How could she possibly relate why the hands that had provided for her family, that had held her since birth, were scarred?

Meanwhile, Lucia sat with a furrowed brow. *How will I explain this to her later?* I wondered. From the volunteer group, I saw bewilderment. I was sure that, like most Americans, they knew little of the history of Guatemala, much less of the US support of violence in the name of anti-communism. How would they reconcile what they were hearing with their notions of this country or our country? Would they think this was a random act of violence in a savage land, or would they see this as one of many such stories of systematic oppression throughout the world, throughout history?

Rogelio didn't confess to the soldiers. He did not know what to confess. He knew nothing of the guerillas and had never even left his village. As the army moved out of San Juan and on to other villages, they took Rogelio with them. After some weeks, he was given a plate of food with poisoned onions, perhaps the same type of poison used to kill the street dogs. He vomited and defecated until his insides were barren and foam bubbled in his mouth. The soldiers left him for dead until one saw him breathe and then gave him water.

A couple of weeks after this incident, his hands were tied behind his back once again. This time he was forced to stand on a chair. A soldier flung one end of a rope across a tree branch, tied the other end around his neck, and then kicked the chair out from under him. He twisted and turned, but there was no point; there was no extrication.

As he was being strangled, he had a vision often described by people with near-death experiences. Ahead of him, he saw a white light and was lulled into it. He passed through the light to arrive at a bucolic pasture filled with flowers. He knew that this was the place God had prepared for him. It was the most peaceful place he had ever been, and he would have been happy to stay there. For the first time during his talk, I saw him smile. A glow, a wave of joy passed across his face. He said that a figure appeared who told him that he was not done with life yet and must go back.

Not yet, Rogelio thought; he stayed in that field as long as possible.

Dangling from the tree, he flailed until he went limp. After he had not moved for some time, a soldier cut him down. The soldiers were planning what to do with his body when Rogelio began gasping for air. Startled, the soldiers jumped back. After his surviving two attempts to kill him in as many weeks, the soldiers thought that the hand of God must be protecting Rogelio, and so the torture and execution attempts stopped.

Rogelio unbuttoned his shirt to show us the scar around his neck. I could not speak to translate this. I did not look at Alba. I did not look at Lucia or the group either. I held my head down and sat in silence until he buttoned his shirt and continued with his story.

After that incident, a lieutenant favored Rogelio and started treating him almost as a pet. He gave him food and took Rogelio around with him. For four years, Rogelio remained a captive with this company. Individual soldiers came and went, but the whole time, he was at the service of one lieutenant. I thought there must be scars from this period that he could not show. At some point, Rogelio found an opportunity to escape and fled back to San Juan.

Rogelio concluded with an account of an occurrence years later. He had to go to a government office in the city to do some paperwork regarding a land petition. When he was escorted into the office for his appointment, he was shocked to see that the bureaucrat handling his case was one of his torturers. During the interview, Rogelio sat trembling in the chair, afraid of what would happen if he recognized him. Instead, the functionary politely offered him coffee and asked him perfunctory questions to complete the forms.

If it is hard for me to imagine the man I know Rogelio to be now as a victim, it is just as hard for me to imagine the other men I meet as perpetrators. After a long, bloody civil war followed by no accountability or reconciliation, victims and perpetrators alike go on with their lives to the degree that they can. The person sitting beside you on a bus or across from you at an office could be someone who has hurt someone you love. Likewise, you may be unaware of your daily dealings with your victims.

One of the volunteers asked about the neighbor who reported him. Rogelio shared that he still regularly runs into him but has never confronted him about the lie that nearly cost him his life. Instead, he chose to put his faith in God, forgive his neighbor, and move on. This was unfathomable to the volunteers and me alike. Sure, our Christian religion teaches the importance of forgiveness, but not impunity. Perhaps Rogelio as an individual can move on, but what impact does this have on the public? What happens when those responsible for genocide blend back into civil society?

After we thanked Rogelio for his story, Lucia and I took the path back down to our house. She launched into questions. "Why was the army looking for people? Why did the soldiers do that to him? Why was there a war? Why doesn't he report his neighbor?"

I replied simply, "The war happened because the government and the people who were in power wanted control of the Indigenous people's land, so they either killed them or forcibly moved them off."

"Would it happen again in Guatemala? Are our friends here going to be taken away?"

"I hope not. During the war, right-wing governments were in power. They say that the same groups that backed those governments were supporting Jimmy Morales now."

"Would that ever happen in our country?"

"It already did. Our government killed or moved most Indigenous people off their lands."

"But would it happen again?"

"I don't think so now—at least, not in the same way. But our government has told people they can't live in certain places because of their race. Also, our government has moved people, mainly those who were not White, because they wanted to use their land for something else, like a highway or a dump."

"But what if Trump is elected? He is right wing, right? Will our friends at home be okay?"

"Look, there's no way Trump will be elected. He's in the news a lot because he had a TV show and says crazy things that get a lot of attention. Of course, there is still racism in our country, but I can't imagine that we would have the type of war that Guatemala did. I can't imagine we have to worry about our neighbors. The people we love are safe."

While I had the misguided naivete to think that people in my country would be unscathed, I was also wrong in thinking I had sequestered us in a place protected from the political violence that seemed so far away. The persecution and displacement of people could easily return to Lake Atitlán as it did to the United States.

Why did I think I was immune? Because my race, class, and citizenship status have protected me in the United States as much as in Guatemala, was I naive to think I could show Lucia the beauty of Guatemala while also shielding her from the ugliness—to let her see the difficulty of people's lives but protect her from suffering herself? Would we not always have to worry for people we love?

40
THE OTHER SIDE OF THE HILL

ONE SATURDAY MORNING, Lucia and I headed out to the Kachiquel villages of Santa Catarina Palopo and San Antonio Palopo on the eastern side of the lake to see some of their ceramic studios. Guatemala is world famous for textiles, not ceramics, so this pair of villages was unusual. In the 1950s, US missionaries taught the Kachiquel firing and fashioning techniques using local clay. The Kachiquel designed molds and patterns to adapt the ceramics for the gringo market.

We took the hour-long lancha ride to Panajachel and then walked through town to catch a pickup truck that would take us to Santa Catarina Palopo and on to San Antonio Palopo. On the back of the truck, plank boards served as seating, and rebar served as handgrips. Riding along the rural but paved road (our side of the lake did not have pavement between towns), I observed that this side of the lake seemed different—older, a little more populated, more developed, but with fewer tourists. As we passed through Santa Catarina, I noticed the deep indigo of the women's huipiles in these Kachiquel villages, unlike the red huipiles in the Tz'utujil communities on our side of the lake.

When we arrived at San Antonio Palopo, we were let off at the large white church atop the hill. Without knowing where we were going, we meandered down, looking first for a place to eat. We found a decent restaurant in a hotel with a large patio overlooking the lake. After we ordered, we stood at the railing, taking in the view. I studied the lake every morning while drinking my coffee and knew every house and hill from my perch; however, I had never seen it from this vantage point.

Lucia pointed directly in front and asked, "What does that hill look like to you?"

"Uh, I don't know. A hat?"

"I knew you were going to say that! It's a snake that ate an elephant."

"Huh?"

"Since you are more than ten years old, I knew you wouldn't get it right."

"Huh?" again.

"Taska told me about this. It's what the first scene in *The Little Prince* was based on. There's a drawing that looks like this view. The book says that anyone ten and under can see things as they really are, but anyone older doesn't have the imagination to see the truth."

Of course, I knew of this classic novel by Antoine de Saint-Exupéry that, despite its simplicity or perhaps because of it, was one of the most renowned works of literature of the twentieth century. It is the story of a boy who, with his rose, lives on a small asteroid with even smaller volcanoes. He leaves the asteroid to explore the universe, meeting many characters in the worlds he visits. In the end, he realizes how much he loves and misses the rose, but there is no return.

This was one of the books Lucia and I read together when we crawled into bed and hid under the pabellón to protect ourselves from the swarms of bugs that came out at night. It seemed appropriate to read it in Guatemala because there was a theory that de Saint-Exupéry, a World War II pilot, conceived the prince's home when his plane crashed in Guatemala and he had to stay in the country for several months, recuperating from his injuries. He convalesced in Antigua, where there were three volcanoes, two active and one inactive, as in the book. The baobab trees in the book are similar to the ceiba, the national tree of Guatemala. The rose supposedly symbolizes de Saint-Exupéry's wife from El Salvador, a country also purported to be the inspiration for the book's setting.

Regardless of whether the hill looked like a hat, a snake with an elephant in its belly, or an inactive volcano, it appeared different from this side of the lake. Looking at something I gazed at every day but couldn't wholly see made me think about other things I had not fully seen from my limited viewpoint.

For nearly three years, I had perseverated on how Wade and I had met, fallen in love, and then fallen apart. I ruminated over my side of the story, but what did he see from his side of the hill? When I moved to Seattle to be with Wade, I was overwhelmed by the overcast sky and waited what seemed like years for the sun to return. Did he see the sun set when I went west to be with him? Did he feel smothered by clouds? When I went for that walk soon after moving to Seattle and the rain washed away my tears, what did he see when he looked out his window? Did he see a coming storm? Did he turn and look around his apartment, note the piles of boxes, his bachelorhood pushed to the side?

When we were married, I tugged at him nightly at dinner, trying to engage him, explaining that I just wanted to have a conversation about whatever. I once grabbed him by the shoulders, shaking him, half-playfully and half-seriously, pleading, "Please, just love me!"

In Guatemala, hearing him talk to Lucia via Skype and try to connect with her reminded me of all the times I had tried to connect with him. On good nights, Wade and Lucia told corny jokes. On bad nights, she was tired and distant, and I heard him tug at her for crumbs about her day, her interests, her friends, her life. He was trying to grab Lucia by the shoulders, silently saying, "Listen to me. Love me. Don't forget about me."

And I know she did listen, love, and remember. She clung to him hard when he came in December. She spent time researching silly jokes to tell him during those nightly calls. She cried in my lap when we first arrived and begged me to not love anyone but him.

He never wanted to hurt me, but he had. He must have had an enormous hole in his heart to be separated from his daughter. I never wanted to hurt him, but I had.

I constantly probed Lucia to understand her side of the hill. In Seattle, she was living on a little planet, surrounded by everyone and everything she held dear, and in Guatemala, she had crashed into a desert, with only one adult and a few random animals to guide her way. Her complaints were about the day-to-day hassles—kids teasing her at school, vendors trying to rip her off, not understanding the teachers—but she didn't tell me she wanted to leave. She didn't express love or hate for the country or for our life as a whole.

Perhaps she was too young to look across her life and have perspective. Perspective requires distance.

Unlike Lucia, I was old enough to have perspective. Perhaps it was not she who was the little prince but I. As the little prince was tamed by the rose through his tending to her, I was tamed by tending my daughter. Love isn't just a sentiment; it is a bond that results from the care you put into someone. Love engenders responsibility. My wanderlust of the previous twenty years to explore other worlds conflicted with my calling to be the mother my daughter needed. I thought I could do both, but it was looking more like I couldn't.

After lunch, we walked down from the center of San Antonio to the shore dotted with ceramic studios and shops. We wandered into a handful of family-owned studios past the public areas where items were displayed for sale, without asking permission, to check out the kilns, molds, and samples at various stages.

Among the reasons I brought Lucia to Guatemala was for her to be more aware of her place in the world and be more sensitive to other people and cultures. Even so, I used what in the US would be called our "White privilege"—or what would be known in Guatemala as our "gringo ignorance"—to make ourselves comfortable and to invade spaces we had no right to be in. In doing so, I did not show her what it means to be Guatemalan; I showed her what it means to be a White person in Guatemala.

Toward the end of the afternoon, I was tempted to stay awhile, bask another day or two in this vantage point. Lucia would have appreciated a break from San Juan. I had a credit card and internet access. We could have surely found a decent place to stay. However, I felt a need I couldn't explain to get back to San Juan, back to my side of the hill. We loaded into another pickup truck, wound down a mountain road, hiked through a town, boarded another boat, sped across a lake, stopping at each village along the way, docked in San Juan, and walked up another hill to get to our home on a pile of rocks.

41

BLOOD ON THE FLOOR

"WHY IS THERE BLOOD on the floor?" I asked Ines when she handed me a form to sign for a referral to the public hospital.

"Another woman has had a bad *aborto*," she responded. Since the same word is used for both induced abortion and miscarriage in Spanish, I was uncertain about the woman's situation.

Ines explained, "She took some herbs from a *curandera* [folk healer] to stop her pregnancy, and now her bleeding won't stop. There is nothing we can do except send her to the Hospital Nacional in Sololá. She is the third woman we have seen in the same situation in the past two weeks."

"Can we find the curandera to find out what she is giving the women? Maybe at least knowing that, we can find a treatment."

Ines paused, appearing to edit her thoughts before replying, "Jan, this is all we can do."

I had worked with Ines long enough to trust her assessment of the situation.

"If a woman wants to stop her pregnancy, is there anything we can do in the clinic?" I asked. Though I knew expats in San Marcos who had gone to Antigua for illegal abortions provided by a Guatemalan gynecologist, I also knew this was out of reach for local women. I assumed that with most of our funding coming from US churches, this might be an issue for our donors.

"There is nothing we can do to help a woman stop her pregnancy, nor can the other clinics or hospitals, since abortion is against the law. All we can do is offer to pay for her transportation to the hospital if she is in grave condition," Ines told me.

The hospital was half a day away and would include tuk-tuks, a pickup truck or bus, and a choppy lancha ride. If a woman was hemorrhaging or had an incomplete abortion, this was her only option.

"Are these abortos that common? I don't remember any of these cases a few months ago."

"The Ministry of Health ran out of family planning methods, so now we are seeing more abortos and more pregnant women."

"But we have family planning methods."

"Not enough."

"Can't we get more?"

"ALAS [the NGO that supplied birth control to private providers] only gives us the amount that we use each month."

"Well, that doesn't make sense. We need more than we use. Obviously we don't have enough to meet the demand. Isn't there any way to get more?"

"Herlinda and I are going to a training on adolescent pregnancy sponsored by ALAS in Antigua next week. You can come as well and ask them then."

Signed referral form in hand, Ines and Tomás carefully escorted the woman out of the clinic, down the crooked, rocky path to the road, and into a tuk-tuk, the first leg of her long journey to the hospital.

In the late 1990s, when I was teaching English at night in migrant farmworker camps, one of my students, Estela, asked me to talk to her friend waiting inside the house. Estela introduced me to Marta, a woman in her early thirties seated on the couch with four young children who were thinner than air. Despite Marta's head being turned down, I could see the bruises on her face. Estela said her friend had been beaten by her husband and wondered if I could help her. My day job was training local health departments on domestic violence, so I thought I knew some resources to connect her to.

Marta's silence told me that there was more to the situation than what Estella had said. I asked Marta if we could speak privately. We went to a back bedroom and sat on the mattress on the floor where she and her four children slept. She covered her mouth with her hands as she shared her story with me.

Marta was from a small town in Mexico. She'd married Francisco at fifteen to get out of the house to make room for her younger siblings. In just over a dozen years, they had six children. Money was tight. Together, they could not earn enough money to feed their family, so they decided to go north to find work. Three years previously, Francisco, the children, and Marta, pregnant with her seventh, walked across the border. They suffered hunger and thirst along the way. Three months passed from when they left their home in Mexico until they arrived in North Carolina. By the time Marta gave birth to her youngest daughter, Carolina, she was ten pounds lighter than when she had gotten pregnant.

"You have seven children?" I asked. "Where are the other three?"

"They are still at home with their father. There is no space at Estela's house for all of us. Also, if they stayed here, they wouldn't be able to catch the bus to school."

"Marta, what happened?"

"Francisco was not like this before. Life was hard in Mexico. We left out of necessity, but life has been harder since coming here. He works as a landscaper, and I work at a dry cleaner, but it's not enough. Francisco started drinking because he is ashamed and scared. When he drinks, he hits me."

"How can I help you?"

"I need to make my period start," she whispered as she looked away.

I naively responded, "I'm sorry, I don't think I understand. Your period should start every month unless . . . Are you pregnant?"

"I don't know. I need my period to start so I can go home."

"Marta, is that why Juan beat you? Because you are pregnant?"

The following day, we were at Planned Parenthood, waiting for the results of her pregnancy test. When I interpreted the news of her positive results, she broke down and cried.

"I can't have any more children. We can barely feed the ones we have."

Marta was no more than a few years older than me and had already spent half her life pregnant and caring for infants.

"Do you want to have the baby and then give it up for adoption? There are some programs that can help with that."

"I can't miss any work at the laundromat because we need every dollar to survive. I can't be pregnant."

"Marta, do you want to have an abortion?"

After a long pause, Marta said, "There is a nun at my church, Sister Kitty, who told me that if I force my period to start, I will go to hell. But going to hell is fine with me if that means my seven children can eat."

"Marta, Sister Kitty never has to worry about where her next meal is coming from. She made a choice to not have children. You never had that choice before, but you do now."

Marta never said the word "aborto." I was concerned that I might be manipulating her into something she did not want.

"Marta, if you want an abortion, I can arrange it for you, but you have to say yes."

"Sí."

I picked her up from Estela's house a couple of days later to take her to her appointment. She asked if we could stop at her home on the way so she could pick up some things—including the gun, so Francisco wouldn't shoot her. That I would be going to an abortion clinic with a gun in my car freaked me out. Marta didn't have a key to the house because she had run out with only the clothes on her back and the four children who were not in school, so we crawled through the window. Breaking into someone's house to steal a gun to take to the abortion clinic nearly sent me over the edge.

So that I would not have to see the gun while she was packing her bags, I excused myself to the bathroom. There I saw drops of blood on the floor. Her blood. Propped against the wall was a piece of rebar spotted with dried blood. Her blood as well. I thought I was going to vomit. I had been traveling around the state, talking to domestic violence programs and clinicians who worked with victims of abuse, but I had never seen their blood. *How could anyone survive this?*

At the clinic, I went into the procedure with her to interpret. I held her hand and told her how brave she was. The ultrasound revealed that the fetus was not moving. It was already dead.

"Marta, it is a good thing we are here. If you had miscarried at home, you could have died, and then your children would have suffered even more."

Through her sobs, Marta told me, "I'm not going to hell, and my children will eat."

I thought, *No, she is not going to hell. She is already there.*

I arranged to meet Ines and Herlinda at the ALAS office in Antigua early Saturday morning for training on adolescent pregnancy and to ask ALAS how our clinic could get more birth control. I took Lucia with me to Antigua, thinking we would have a fun sortie, perhaps hike Volcán Pacaya once the ALAS meeting was wrapped up. But as was the case on our trip to Xela a few weeks earlier, Lucia became sick soon after we arrived. This time she only had a low fever and some diarrhea—no vomiting. Our Friday night in this charming city was spent cuddling in our room and reading books rather than exploring the craft markets or people-watching in the plaza.

On Saturday morning, Lucia was stable but weak. I felt guilty about leaving my ill ten-year-old alone in our room, but I knew that Ines and Herlinda would be waiting for me at the ALAS office and expected me to advocate for the girls in our town. I dosed Lucia with Tylenol, stocked her with food, charged her phone, and downloaded a couple of movies to keep her occupied while I was out.

Ines, Herlinda, and I attended the training alongside a dozen other Indigenous women, promotoras who dispensed subsidized birth control methods out of their homes. Though the promotoras could earn a little money, they were intrinsically motivated to serve the women in their communities. I could tell that they were from different parts of the country because each wore a different style of corte and huipil. If this training was to have a national reach, I wondered how this handful of women could possibly be expected to serve all the teens in need.

The training began with a presentation on sexual abuse of young girls in Guatemala. As in the rest of the world, most girls aged ten to fourteen who experience abuse are victimized by a family member or someone living with them. I thought it was sadly ironic that families were afraid to allow their girls to play in the streets when the most dangerous place to be was home.

The trainer shared the correlation between girls in this age group who are pregnant and those who are raped. In reality, girls this age cannot grant consent, so all these pregnant girls have been violated. In the previous year in the departamento that includes Lake Atitlán, eleven ten-year-old girls had given birth—girls the same age as Lucia. Counting backward, most ten-year-old mothers were only nine when they got pregnant. Since most ten-year-olds haven't started menstruating, there must have been many more girls violated who never got pregnant.

I thought about what secrets lay behind that statistic. Having worked in rural health in Guatemala, I knew the official number of births to young girls is an undercount. The Ministry of Health only knows what births are reported to the local government health center. Many communities do not have a health center, and many avoid reporting births or infant deaths to avoid government investigations.

I also thought about my dear ten-year-old daughter shielded in our hotel room for the morning, watching movies and reading books. The only man who had lived with her was her father, whom I trusted more than any person in the world to protect her. We were her gift as much as she was ours.

The Ministry of Health recognized that these pregnancies to young girls were a problem that needed to be addressed. I agreed. I did not agree with how they defined the problem and how they chose to address it. Each birth to a young girl costs the government approximately $200. By spending money on family planning, these births and these costs could be avoided. This was why the Guatemalan government and other agencies granted money to ALAS to expand birth control to girls aged ten to fourteen.

"I don't understand," I asked. "Why doesn't the government spend the money on stopping the girls from being abused? Why should a young girl take responsibility for protecting herself from pregnancy when no one is protecting her from being raped?"

I had entered this meeting upset that there was not enough emphasis on providing birth control, and now I was angry that there was too much.

The ALAS trainer acknowledged the unfairness of the government's actions but claimed that they could not turn down the opportunity to protect girls—if not from abuse, then at least from pregnancy. Herlinda, who had been a family planning promotora for ALAS for years, told me about her pregnancy as an older adolescent.

"In my case, I made a mistake by falling in love with a boy who left me. I was lucky that my father did not throw me out of the house and gave my son his name. Now when women come to my house for injections or pills, I do what I can to help them. We can't do everything, but this we can do."

I understood her point, but my overarching thought was to wonder how much more blood would be spilled on the floor before girls were protected.

42

IN WHAT WORLD?

ANOTHER WEEK BROUGHT ANOTHER TEAM. This time, rather than being good-hearted church folks from the US South, this team comprised two physicians from Quebec—Camille and Claude, a gynecologist and a pediatrician, respectively.

Camille and Claude declined my offer to provide an orientation before their arrival because they insisted they knew enough about medicine. They also refused my request to donate funds to the clinic, as was the practice for other volunteers, to cover the cost of hosting them.

"We are offering our time for free," they wrote to me. "That should be enough. Also, we are bringing a suitcase full of medicine and supplies."

It was true that what they were bringing was valuable, but what we needed most was cash. After a church that had been an ongoing supporter decided to redirect its ministry to another worthy cause (i.e., to not fund us anymore), ODIM had a huge budget hole to fill. I was more concerned about running out of funds to pay the staff than about running out of medicine to give the patients.

The Canadians were not bringing cash, but I thought they could indirectly benefit us financially. If they could help us build our women's and children's health services, then we could generate revenue through contracts with US churches and NGOs to serve the schools and local churches they supported. The Canadians were right; we needed their help.

The first part of the plan was for Dr. Claude and Dra. Camille to start the week by training the Mamá y Yo Saludable promotoras to assess infants' health and development. Then Dr. Claude would support the clinic staff with practicing our new child-health protocol. The team had adapted a medical history template for children that I found from the States. They added questions on bullying and earthquake safety and removed questions on seat belts and guns. Tomás spoke for the team by saying, "Tuk-tuks don't have seatbelts, and children are rarely in other vehicles. Also, only soldiers and police have guns, so there is no need to mention them. These questions would alarm and confuse our patients."

The second part of the plan was for Dra. Camille to support Ines and Herlinda in performing pelvic exams and pap smears. The nurses needed to conduct a certain number of exams under a gynecologist's supervision to be certified by ALAS to provide women's health services, which would give us the added benefit of having access to more birth control methods. Under Dra. Camille's supervision, they could become certified to do pap smears.

Prior to the Canadians' visit, Ines shared her frustration with me: "The ALAS gynecologist has told me several times that she would come to supervise and certify us, but at the last minute, she always cancels. She says that we are too far away from Antigua for her to come."

"How long has this been going on?" I asked.

"Three years."

If Ines and Herlinda could manage to get to Antigua, why couldn't she come to us?

Excited about these opportunities, the team prepared for weeks. Ines and Herlinda organized and supplied the exam rooms, and Tomás and Tulita spread the word at the churches for the women and children to come. The promotoras worked overtime to see all their patients before the Canadian physicians arrived so they could dedicate themselves to the training.

When I went to pick up Dr. Claude and Dra. Camilla from their hotel early Monday morning, the day after they arrived, they were unprepared, complained of jet lag, and wanted to linger for another cup of coffee. I was anxious to get them going because the promotoras were meeting us at Chuitinamit in San Pablo at eight o'clock, which meant they had to wake early to feed their families and get someone to watch their children. When we showed up nearly an hour late, the twenty promotoras crammed into the salón did not comment on our tardiness. However, Alba, who was there to translate for the physicians from English to Tz'utujil, gave me a quizzical look, as she often did when she needed help understanding gringo behavior. And as I often did, I shrugged back at her and gave an awkward smile.

Though the Francophone physicians could certainly greet and hold a short conversation in English, it quickly became apparent that they could not manage a presentation in English. Seemingly indifferent to Alba's need to understand them, they started stringing together whole sentences in French. After a few minutes of this, Alba stood back and stared at them in disbelief. Fortunately, Hannah was there to jump in, having learned French from living in Montreal. Since the promotoras had finished primary school, they all understood Spanish. The training quickly transitioned from being translated from English to Tz'utujil to being translated from French to Spanish.

As I had feared, for the rest of the week, a clash continued between the aloof Canadians and the clinic staff, who valued connection above all else. The Canadians arrived late and left early to do sightseeing. "Can't you see the sights are the people?" I wanted to ask. I did ask if they would treat the staff to lunch, as was the custom for the other teams.

"Why would we pay for a big lunch?" Camille asked me.

"So that you can get to know the staff. Also, they have less time to go home for lunch since they have to take time for you," I responded.

"But we are not very hungry at midday," Camille replied, seeming to miss my point.

"We would rather just eat our bread and cheese. If someone would like a piece of bread, we can share," Claude offered.

I wondered if the disconnect came from our limited ability to communicate in English or if there was a chasm in our understanding of why they were there. Even when Alba and I accompanied them in the tuk-tuk ride between the clinics, they continued to speak only in French, separating themselves from us.

However, as with the other teams, they did breakfast at Gilda's. When they learned that my house was behind Gilda's salón, they walked around the corner and onto my porch early one morning as I was rushing to get Lucia ready for school. Camille walked through my porch and poked her head into my three rooms.

"You live here? It's plain, but what a picturesque view you have. Can I photograph your house?"

I half-jokingly responded, "Only if you invite me to your home to take pictures." I didn't want my life and child to be part of her holiday week in Guatemala.

Camille looked at me like once again she did not understand what I was talking about. After she snapped a few pictures, I said, "Look, I need to finish helping Lucia with her hair so she can go to school. Sanjuanerita is opening soon, so we have to hurry."

"I'll see you there. I'll have my second coffee here so I can enjoy the view," she told me. Lucia gave me the same confused look that Alba had. Once again, I shrugged and carried on.

That night, Lucia and I went to Daniella's new house for dinner. Lucia enjoyed another break from my cooking, and I enjoyed a break from the Canadians. While Lucia, Emilio, and Aldo played volleyball with a balloon in the salón, Daniella, Edoardo, and I partook in a large bottle of beer on the patio.

"Oh, Dani, this cheap beer is so bad but tastes so good," I joked. "I miss having a cold one after a long day."

"The tienda around the corner from your house has Gallo, and the Super Q'ik even has boxes of wine," Edoardo said.

"I know, but I can't buy it. One of Lucia's classmates at La Salle saw me buy a beer and told the whole class that I was a *bola* [drunk]."

Daniella interjected, "That's terrible. That's why I send Edoardo to buy the beer. Actually, we need another." Daniella waved the empty forty-ounce bottle. Taking his cue, Edoardo picked up the bottle and went to the store to get another.

"Lucia said that she tried to 'defend' me by saying it was fine for me to have a drink, but her classmates told her that a woman can't have one drink without being a drunk. I'm trying to act like a regular Guatemalan mother as much as I can to not embarrass her."

"Jaaaaan, face it. There is nothing regular about you, and you will always embarrass your daughter," Daniella chuckled. She then scooted up to me and said, "Jan, I need your help with something rather personal."

"Yes, anything," I replied. "What do you need?"

Daniella slipped forward in her chair and dropped her head in her hands, her long, ash-brown hair falling forward. "Could you pick out my *piojos* [lice]?"

"Of course! Pedrina taught me how to do this with Lucia. The trick is to snap them with your fingernails." I laughed as I started to dig my fingers into the hair around the nape of her neck. "I noticed Emilio now has a sleek new haircut. Piojos as well?"

"Ay, sí!"

After a moment, I admitted, "Dani, the piojos are the same color as your hair. I'll never get them all. Look, when Lucia had piojos last year, I tried everything. The only remedy that worked was ivermectin. Let me get some for you from the clinic."

"You know I only like natural remedies, but I'm willing to try anything in this case. It's been weeks dealing with this. Thank you so much!"

"And you know that asking me to pick your scalp has moved our friendship to a new level of intimacy," I teased.

As I started to tell her about the crazy Canadians, we heard a thump and a scream. We ran into the salón to see Lucia lying on the ground crying because Aldo had slipped and fallen on her. I tried to console her, but the pain was intense. There was no ice to press against her injury, so I asked Daniella to watch Lucia while I ran to the clinic to get ibuprofen and a bandage. I also lifted a few ivermectin pills for her family. I returned to find Lucia's wrist had swollen, and she could not move her fingers.

I thought perhaps the Canadian pediatrician I was just complaining about could help. I knew he had moved from the hotel to stay with a Guatemalan family, but I was not sure where the family lived. Lucia and I went to what I knew was the street of his host's house, which like the other houses was indistinguishably tucked away behind the lamina fences. As Lucia's pain increased, I grew more desperate. I frantically ran up and down the street, banging on the tin walls, yelling out for "*el médico gringo.*" Eventually, Claude appeared at a doorway.

With only the moonlight to see by, he examined Lucia. He could not discern whether her arm was broken, so he advised me to get an X-ray. The only facility on the lake with an X-ray machine was in Santiago Atitlán. Since the boats did not run at night, we would have to rise early in the morning to go.

The next day, Lucia was still reeling in pain. I ran to Sanjuanerita to tell Alba that she would have to handle the Canadians without me. There, I also wrote Lucia a referral for Hospitalito, a private hospital in Santiago Atitlán, so that we would be seen more promptly and so that we might not be charged the gringo rate, which was several times what locals pay.

We took a tuk-tuk and then a lancha to Santiago Atitlán, where we had to take yet another tuk-tuk to the hospital. With so many modes of transportation taking so much time, I don't know how anyone seriously ill or injured manages to get to the hospital.

When we walked into the hospital, we ran into Otto, who also worked in the dental clinic there. He vouched for my referral to the receptionist, who moved up our turn with the doctor, though she still charged me the gringo rate. My local credentials could only take me so far.

Also, by coincidence, we saw Leticia—the mother of Felipe and the director of Centro Maya—with her older son, Alvaro, along with half a dozen other children with various disabilities in the waiting room. She brought the children to Hospitalito once a month for therapies. Some of these children looked as if they needed weekly, if not daily, therapy and would have difficulty making such a long journey. However, this was all that was available to them.

The anxiety I had felt the night before over being unable to take my injured child to urgent care and my annoyance that morning about having to pay the gringo rate for the lancha and the doctor was replaced by gratitude that my child was healthy and that she had access to any possible care she might need. Though I was constantly short on cash, in reality, money was no issue for me. With my credit card, we could always hop on a plane and be back in Seattle within twenty-four hours. *How do Leticia and the other mothers manage?* I wondered.

The X-ray revealed that Lucia's wrist was severely sprained but thankfully not broken. The doctor put a cast on her arm and gave instructions to come back in two weeks.

After breakfast on Friday, the last day the Quebecers would be with us, Camille came down from Gilda's salón to talk to me while I was showering. My small towel wrapped around my front and clutched in the back, I walked out onto the porch to face her, likely showing my rear to the fishermen below.

Camille launched into an explanation of how she would not be going to Chuitinamit because she had not had enough time to do her shopping, so she needed to spend the day buying souvenirs. Therefore, we should cancel the women's health jornada since she would not be available to supervise the nurses. I retorted that we would not cancel simply because she did not want to go. We had advertised at the churches and paid for a truck to drive around town announcing the event. Likely, women from around the region had risen long before dawn to wait their turn in line. Plus, Ines and Herlinda had been waiting for weeks to have a chance to practice doing pap smears with a physician's supervision.

"We planned this because of you. Even if you don't come, we'll still have it," I insisted. "Now let me rinse the conditioner out of my hair."

During my bike ride to San Pablo, I dreaded the conversation I would have to have with the staff and the conversation they would have to have with the women. *How do I explain to them that Camille flaked? That they still matter to me? Should I advise them to do their best, knowing that their best would still mean that there could be some women whose cancer would be undetected?* I didn't know whether it was better to risk that a few women might have undetected cancer today than for all the women to distrust us and never return, which would mean that we'd never detect their cancers or other diseases in the future. How could I start a preventative health program when I couldn't prevent disasters like this?

I was living in a world where someone I thought of as a colleague thought of me as a tour guide, my home as a public park, our work as a vacation, and my town as a place to pick up souvenirs. A world where an injured child could get first-world medical care in a poor country if her mother was White and had plenty of money, while an Indigenous baby must rely on the scant training of an illiterate comadrona for a chance to take her first breath.

I felt conflicted. I wanted to show Lucia how Guatemalans lived, and I demanded to be treated as a local. Yet when it suited me, I easily reclaimed the privileges and perks associated with my position in life. It was hubris to think that just because I lived in a cinder-block house with no running water, or that I tried to live within my means, that I shared the locals' lot. Perhaps I was closer to the Canadians than I had thought.

43

DANCE OF THE MOORS AND THE CHRISTIANS

COMING HOME FROM WORK the week before *Semana Santa* (Holy Week), I stumbled upon a performance in the plaza in front of the church. It seemed that most of the town had gathered to watch. About twenty masked men swayed and circled each other. Half wore white masks and blond hair, and half wore dark masks and dark hair. A man dressed as a black bull and a boy as a little red devil weaved in and out of the two sets of adversaries. Costumed in bolero jackets and knickers of sequins and feathers, they looked like bullfighters in drag. The dancers were accompanied by flutes and drums and appeared to use the music as an intoxicant rather than a cue for pace or play.

I wondered who these masked men were, whether they were from the village or a traveling troupe. Curious, I snaked through the spectators, asking about a dozen people if they knew the meaning of this show. None did.

Confident that Nehemias would be able to explain, I asked him about this in our next Tz'utujil lesson. He told me that this dance of the Moors and the Christians is from Spain and is a folkloric reenactment of the conquest of the Iberian Peninsula and the expulsion of the Moors (Muslims).

From what I already knew about what happened in the Iberian peninsula during that time, that dance should have been named the dance of the Moors, Christians, and Jews. From the eighth century until the fifteenth century, these three peoples cohabitated in the same space, and the interplay of their cultures led to advances in architecture, art, science, philosophy, and the theological evolution of each of the three monotheistic religions.

In the late fifteenth century, King Ferdinand of Aragon and Queen Isabella of Castille, sovereigns of two kingdoms on the peninsula, were married in order to consolidate the power of what would eventually become Spain. These "Catholic Monarchs" did not dance well with others. In 1492, in an effort to create religious purity, they expelled the Moors in the south, forced the Jews into ghettos, and gave them four months to either convert to Catholicism or leave. To ensure orthodoxy of the converts and stamp out heresy, they established the Spanish Inquisition, killing and torturing thousands. This all occurred in the same year they financed Columbus's quest that eventually led to the conquering of the New World. While the Catholics enjoyed their purged and pure Spain, they would, at the same time, defile another world.

The Spaniards viewed the Indigenous population of the New World as heathens, ignorant of God, and needing to be brought, if only nominally, into the fold of Christianity. Therefore, local beliefs were incorporated, and gods were rebranded to fit a Catholic schematic. The Spaniards brought this dance of cultures and conquest to Guatemala in the sixteenth century as a means of Christianization. The Maya assimilated the dance into their existing cosmology, and long after winning independence from Spain, they still practice it.

Were the men in this dance reenacting a history that perhaps they did not know—acting out a tale that they did not understand? Did they realize the metaphor of this dance as it related to their own conquest by the Spaniards? Does it even matter, since they are remaking this dance into their own?

As was the case of the dance of the Moors and the Christians, the daily dance of cultures I saw in the area of Lake Atitlán where we lived had three partners: the Maya, the Ladinos, and the gringos.[31] These three peoples coexisted in this place: the Maya for thousands of years, the Ladinos for

---

[31] As mentioned in chapter 3, many Maya people lump Ladinos and gringos together into the category "Kaxlán." I consider these separate cultures.

close to 500 years, and the gringos have had an increased presence in recent decades.

Though it is true that the Maya lived in city-states during the height of the classic pre-Columbian civilization, by the time the Spaniards reached Lake Atitlán, that was over. Most people lived scattered around the lake. It was the Spaniards who forced them to consolidate into the settlements they have now.

The Spaniards vanquished their religion, customs, and even their names. The Maya had a complicated naming system that included their calendar name, father's name, father's and mother's names combined, and nickname. A person's name identified family relationships, personal characteristics, and how that person came to be in relation to space and time. This is now lost.

The few contemporary Indigenous given names I have heard (e.g., Ixmucane, Ixquic) are from the *Popol Wuj*. As was the case of enslaved people in North America, their masters' surnames were bestowed on many Indigenous people. Surnames assigned to Indigenous people also included Hispanicized derivations of Mayan words that described these people's labor, not who they were. For example, according to Nehemias, Cholotio, a common surname in San Juan, is from the Mayan word for brickmakers.

Though in Petén I had been called Juanita, when I interviewed for my job at ODIM, I offered staff the option of calling me either Jan or Juanita. When I walked into the clinic on my first day of work, I was surprised to see Bienvenida a la clínica Jan written in construction-paper cutouts taped on the wall. Though no one said it outright, I inferred that this preference to use my English name was a token of resistance to Hispanization. How ironic that my culture would Hispanicize them the instant they crossed the border to the US, dubbing them with a label they have resisted for hundreds of years.

Though the Tz'utujil language is more prevalent, Spanish prevails. Spanish is the language of formal communication. The written realm of the clinic was nearly entirely in Spanish—medical records, patient forms, health-education posters, meeting agendas, reports, etc. Our staff meetings were conducted in Spanish, and Spanish was the language that connected me to everyone in my life except Kenneth, Hannah, and Lucia. However, everyone in my sphere spoke Spanish as a second language except for Dra. Faustina and Dr. Otto, the dentist. We were all reaching out to understand each other.

Still, Tz'utujil is the language of community. Sounds of Tz'utujil were everywhere. The man who drove by in a truck announcing when the water would be shut off did so in Tz'utujil. The staff meetings, though conducted in Spanish, began, ended, and were peppered throughout with chatter in Tz'utujil. The lady who came in every morning to sell her homemade *atole* (corn drink) did her business in Tz'utujil, asking only me in Spanish if I wanted a cup. The patients received all the services in their own language unless they were being seen by the doctors, but they could still ask Tulita to interpret.

However, English is the language of control. As a US 501c3, ODIM had to comply with American laws and regulations. Though nearly all the organization documents were in Spanish, the official budget was in English, as were board-of-directors meetings and minutes, grants, donor correspondence, and volunteer relationships. As my father used to explain the "golden rule" to me, "The man with the gold makes the rules."

My office was situated between the exam rooms of Dra. Faustina and the Tz'utujil nurses. As the sounds of their consults wafted over the partial walls separating our spaces, sometimes I would close my eyes and take in the contrasting tones. The Tz'utujil language has a combination of short and long, singsongy vowels and deep-throated, guttural clicks, and Spanish has short, staccato syllables and rolling "r's." I imagined Tz'utujil as the flute and the Spanish as the drums, both playing together, each with their own part.

I wondered what images English invokes for nonspeakers. I read that the prevalence of the "sh," "s," and "th" sounds makes English sound like hissing. Do they see us as serpents slithering on the ground or coiled in a tree, waiting to bite or to offer a piece of damning fruit?

Language and, for women, dress are vestiges of the Maya culture, and they proudly wore both. While girls and young women might wear

Western clothes, a proper woman would never leave the house without being fully put together with her corte, faja, and blusa or huipil. Though Maya women were masters of weaving, it was the Spaniards that taught them embroidery. The feathers they once adorned themselves with became birds stitched onto their clothes. Even the unique traje típica of each town is thought to have originated from a Spanish command that the Indigenous identify where they came from.

The communities they were forced to live in and the clothes they were forced to wear became part of their identity. In contrast, the Ladinos distance themselves from anything that might lead them to be mistaken for Indigenous. Instead, they prefer to buy American thrift-store castoffs from the *paca* shops. Purchases of traje típica by gringo visitors keep these art forms alive.

Roman Catholicism and North American Protestantism compete for souls and their place in society. Each has made its own mark on politics, filled its own niche, and both have woven and been woven into the Maya cosmology. Around 500 years ago, the Spaniards brought Roman Catholicism to this region, in part to coerce allegiance to the crown so that they could abscond with the Maya's riches. They leveled Maya pyramids and used their stones to build churches on sacred sites. A tall hill outside San Juan, once the site of a Maya altar, was topped with a cross and statue of the Virgin Mary. In the famous market town of Chimaltenango, a Catholic church was built on a holy Maya site—by Indigenous laborers who, in turn, fooled their Spanish masters by incorporating Maya symbols in the architecture.

Around a hundred years ago, the North Americans brought evangelical Protestantism, in part to coerce allegiance to corporations so that they could abscond with the Maya's resources. Prominent evangelicals, including Pat Robertson and Jerry Falwell, influenced US policy in Guatemala and in the early 1980s backed Efrain Rios-Montt—the soldier turned evangelical preacher turned dictator—in his genocide of thousands of Maya and the seizure of their lands in the name of anti-communism. The propagation of the "prosperity gospel," the belief that God bestows financial blessings on those who follow His will and donate to the church, has enriched Guatemalan megachurch leaders.

Guatemala is a leading destination for short-term mission trips by North American Protestant and Catholic churches. Too often, those who want to help the poor for a week do not understand that the poverty in Guatemala exists in part because of the policies and actions of their own (our) country. They do not stop to consider that perhaps Guatemala would be better served by their spending a week in the US advocating on behalf of more equitable policies and reallocating their travel funds to finance projects developed and staffed by Guatemalans.

Yet Roman Catholicism and North American evangelical Protestantism also had progressive influences on culture and politics. From a syncretism of the Christian doctrine of original sin from which humans need salvation and the Western political concepts of liberalism, social democracy, and class struggle, liberation theology sprang out of the Latin American Catholic church.[32] Liberation theology recognizes the structural sin of oppressive governments and opportunistic enterprises. It aims to liberate or save the poor by creating a just society. Catholic clergy and laypeople who espoused this ideology helped propel the transition from authoritarian regimes to democracy in Latin America.

Compared to Catholicism, Protestantism has allowed women greater participation and prestige because they can hold higher offices in many of their churches. It is also appealing because of its decreased use of alcohol, greater democratic participation in decision-making, and the savings of not being involved in costly *cofradias*.[33] Catholics and Protestants alike still

---

[32] Chiappari, Christopher L. "Toward a Maya Theology of Liberation: The Reformulation of a 'Traditional' Religion in the Global Source." *Journal for the Scientific Study of Religion*, Vol. 41, No. 1 (Mar., 2002), pp. 47-67.

[33] *Cofradias* are religious brotherhoods established during the conquest and colonial era in Central America and Mexico to propagate Catholicism. They are a syncretism of Indigenous and Catholic customs and beliefs. The brotherhoods serve as keepers for relics related to saints and bundles of traditional relics, and also have civil and political status.

turn to Maya spirituality to find auspicious days in the calendar, consult healers, honor the sacred landscape, or when they feel their religion has failed them.[34]

Traditional Maya spiritual expression was influenced by Catholicism and Protestant Christianity, but rather than adhering to the instruction of the friars and priests, many Maya assimilated the Catholic saints into their pantheon of deities and used the candles and incense intended for mass for their own ceremonies. Also, the Maya have employed the strategies, systems, and structures of Ladinos and North Americans to advance their religion and culture. Maya spirituality was officially recognized by the government in the 1996 Peace Accords. Maya priests and spiritual guides have formed professional associations and, for a fee, teach their cosmovision and *costumbres* (practices) to tourists.

One of ODIM's principal donors, Connie, arranged for a Dances of Universal Peace troupe touring Guatemala to visit Chuitinamit. According to Connie, their participatory dancing, singing, and chanting were influenced by new-age sentiments and Sufi practices such as the whirling dervishes. In Guatemala, they call what they do "movement with music" rather than "dancing" because, she claimed, the evangelicals forbade dancing. (I have never heard about this prohibition from Guatemalans.)

I had seen Connie with her pink ukulele, her long, swishy skirt, and her tinkling anklets sing happily with staff at a few of our events and did not doubt her intent to do something meaningful. However, I questioned her understanding of the team. Connie had previously insisted on conducting a workshop with staff and the promotores on recovering from the trauma of the civil war. This sickened me; I felt that it was wrong for an older American woman—whose country was responsible for much of the trauma induced

---

[34] Hinojosa, Servando Z. 2018. "The Limits of Conversion: Evangelical Experience and Enduring Maya Principles in Highland Guatemala." *The Latin Americanist* 62, no 4:568–585. https://doi.org/10.1111/tla.12215.

when she was a young woman—to tell people, many born after the war, how they should heal. Nevertheless, since she was a member of the board of directors and a donor, we had to accommodate her.

On the day of the workshop, Dra. Faustina, Dr. Otto, Hannah, and Kenneth made excuses not to attend, but all the Tz'utujil staff was there. The staff listened politely, and I sat to the side, squirming. I assumed from Rogelio's story and countless other stories I had heard in Petén that in that salón were people whose families had informed on each other, had fought in the army against their own people, and who had lost everything because of the interests of the Ladinos and the gringos—the same peoples who had skipped and were conducting the training. None of this was acknowledged. Instead, Connie talked about the atrocities with pity and showed the staff how to release stress by applying pressure to the chakras in their hands. They delicately pinched each other's hands and snickered in Tz'utujil until Connie was done.

When Connie asked to close the clinic again, this time for the dance group, I was afraid of repeating another awkward encounter. Noting the skepticism on my face about the dance group, Connie insisted, "We have been doing this for years with the ODIM team. Really, they love it. The highlight is when we sing and dance to the Hebrew song 'Shalom Shabbat, Shabbat Shalom,' which means 'Peace on the Sabbath, Sabbath of Peace' in English."

I imagined a bunch of aging, trippy hippies imposing their Deadhead dancing on the staff and worried that this would be yet another group that wanted to use our team as part of their feel-good foreign experience.

Again, knowing that the dance troop would make a donation and needing to fill that budget hole, I blocked out time for this communion. As the dance troop, staff, and promotores gathered in a circle in the salón, the Americans gave lots of deep looks directly into the Guatemalans' eyes, heartfelt thanksgivings, and sincere hugs with an extra little squeeze. Kenneth stood outside of the circle, not sure if he should join in or step aside. After the first song, I had some budget work that pulled me away, so I hid in my office.

Connie was right, though. Our folks loved it. From my office, I heard the entourage lead a full-blown kumbaya power hour with fiddles, tambourines, and even the pink ukulele. When it came time for "Shalom Shabbat, Shabbat Shalom," there was spirited singing, clapping, and stomping.

Just before the last of the three encores of "Shalom Shabbat, Shabbat Shalom," I asked Oscar to come into my office to help me with my spreadsheet. Kenneth saw an opportunity to leave and popped into my office as well. I quipped to Kenneth that this was why God invented punk rock—to provide a counterpoint to such saccharine sincerity. Oscar looked confused, so I tried to explain the tenets of punk rock to him.

As Oscar put on the most diplomatic grin he could muster, I noticed a smirk emerge, so I asked him, "Why are you smiling like that?"

He hesitated but finally confessed. "You see, 'Shalom Shabbat, Shabbat Shalom' sounds like 'I have sex with myself; you have sex with yourself' in Tz'utujil, so everyone is laughing because they are singing and dancing about masturbation, and the visitors don't realize it."

My office exploded with laughter. I joked to Kenneth, "Now, that's punk rock." Once again, the Maya had taken what was put upon them and made it their own.

After the last encore, Dra. Faustina passed my office on the way to her exam room and saw Kenneth and Oscar guffawing, me giggling in my chair. She walked in to ask what was so funny. Since she was Ladina, she did not know the double meaning of the song she had been singing. Knowing that she was a demure evangelical, I whispered into her ear what Oscar had shared. She chuckled, "¡Dios mío!"

I often reflected on this dance between the three cultures in our region of Lake Atitlán and in the clinic. Would the coming together of the Tz'utujil, Ladinos, and gringos, the convergence of our ideas and cultures, yield something new and glorious, or were we doomed like the performers in the dance of the Moors and the Christians to continue to act out a history that we did not understand?

Maybe moments when we can laugh together are the best to hope for.

44

HOLY WEEK

THE DAY BEFORE THE HOLIDAY BREAK, Maestra Elvira asked her class to draw a picture of what Semana Santa meant to them. What it meant to Lucia was a vacation that she had been begging to take for weeks—a tour-group hike with Mommy from Xela to San Juan. She would also be able to do what we couldn't during the last trip to Xela: go to a movie theater, eat Indian food, and shop at a mall.

However, she had been in Guatemalan schools long enough at this point to know that she should not draw such a personalized picture and instead should take a cue from the other children. She looked at her classmates seated around her and saw nearly identical depictions of the same scene: Jesus ascending Mount Calvary with a cross on his back, followed by his disciples. Naturally, Lucia had to add her perspective to her portrayal. When she submitted her work at the end of class, Maestra Elvira gasped and dropped her jaw. Lucia had drawn Jesus as a woman and all his followers as robots.

When she told me about this after school, I laughed and exclaimed, "I love you."

She knew exactly what she had done.

Lucia explained, "Jesus wears the same clothes as Princess Leia, so why couldn't Jesus have been a woman? Since people are supposed to blindly follow Jesus, his followers are kind of like robots. Also, none of us were there, so how does anyone know what Jesus looked like or if there weren't robots? What do you think, Mommy?"

"Well, I think Jesus was probably a real person and probably a man. However, Christ, or whatever it is that connects you to God, you can see any way you want. If you see Christ as Princess Leia, so be it."

On Palm Sunday, we joined our hiking group at the tourism agency in Xela for an orientation. Ashley and Becky, our novice guides just out of college, warned us about the difficulty of the itinerary and explained the ground rules. The route would take us fifty miles through the mountains over three days, sleeping and stopping in villages along the way. The first day would be the most arduous, nearly eighteen miles. We would each have to carry our own sleeping bag and supplies, plus a portion of the food for the group. If someone veered off the trail to pee, she or he had to leave a tissue on the trail as a sign. One of the guides would always be at the head and the other at the tail to ensure that no one got lost.

Ashley and Becky then invited the group members to introduce and share a bit about themselves. Our fellow hikers included a score of fit gringos from North America and Australia, most of whom were half my age and had trained for and traveled to Guatemala specifically for this excursion, and a couple of doughy, middle-aged Ladino couples who bragged about their competitive running. Becky muddled a few phrases in Spanish to accommodate the Guatemalans, but they assured her that they understood her English.

Ashley remarked that no child had ever done this hike with this agency and said to us, "You are very brave for trying this." The others nodded in agreement.

Are we brave or foolish? I wondered, gazing at the other hikers, who all looked like models from an REI catalog. They were outfitted with the latest, lightest gear, while we were in street clothes and did not even have backpacks. I was lugging plastic shopping bags filled with our clothes and the previous night's purchases, and Lucia was holding the sleeping bags borrowed from Daniella and Lana that they had found in the paca. Ashley offered to have our purchases sent to San Juan with the truck that would be bringing her and Becky back to Xela and lent us a couple of old, heavy packs to carry what we needed. My bag was additionally weighted with the

Lucia's allotment of provisions. I was fit for a woman pushing fifty, but I was still a woman pushing fifty, who, with an extra load on her back and a ten-year-old child in tow, would have to keep up with strapping, young hikers. *Foolish . . . or crazy?*

When Lucia hoisted her pack on her back, the weight caused her to bend over, but she righted herself. Just a few months previously, she'd complained about walking from San Juan to San Pedro, and now she was willing to try this venture. Whether foolish or crazy, I was proud.

As Lucia and I walked back to our room for the night, we were stalled by what at first appeared to be a funeral procession slowly moving down a street laden with pine needles. At the front were women in traje típico, their bowed heads covered with white lace veils, their hands clasped in front. They were followed by men clad in purple robes, some who were swinging lanterns of copal incense. Behind them, men in black suits carried on their shoulders a glass coffin encasing an alabaster figure of a man and adorned with fresh roses. The whole group was moved along by a brass band playing a march.

Like the rest of the country, Xela had begun nightly processions to mark the days of Semana Santa in which the passion of Christ and the pain of his mother, Mary, are portrayed with floats. Cofradias, parishioners, altar boys, and priests parade across intricately designed *alfombras* (carpets) of flowers, fruit, pine needles, and colored sawdust, stopping regularly to sing and pray. As people around the country marched through their villages, commemorating and connecting with the suffering of Christ, we would march through their communities, choosing suffering and sacrificing the comforts of home as a pastime.

Early the next morning, we started the first day of our journey. We passed through the heart of the Guatemalan highlands—corn-covered pastures, forested mountains, and Indigenous villages I did not know existed. When we stopped for bio breaks, Becky and Ashley led bonding exercises, such as "What is your favorite book?" These round-robin personal revelations among strangers, or even friends, would be odd to my Tz'utujil colleagues. In their view, it is not what is unique but rather what is shared that connects you to a group. Still, I enjoyed talking in English about a wide range of books and topics. I appreciated the chance to step outside the demands of the clinic and the grind of daily chores and blithely get to know new acquaintances.

Even so, awareness of where we were and self-consciousness about what we were doing made me uncomfortable. To bury our poop, the guides carried a spade likely purchased at an outdoor-furnishings store at a cost of more than a day's wage for a Guatemalan. Men carrying their weight in sticks strapped to their foreheads on a tumpline had to share the path with Kaxlán using metal-alloy walking sticks to stabilize their footing. We had all exuded incalculable amounts of carbon just to feel close to the nature we were destroying. Was it wrong to participate in a group that was ignorant of the suffering around them?

By midday of mostly ascent, the middle-aged Guatemalans were exhausted and declared that they could not take another step. They blamed the high altitude, not their fitness level, for their fatigue. Becky called for a truck to drop them off at our destination for the day, leaving Lucia and me as the only laggards. The wait for the Guatemalans' ride and the slower pace of the mother–daughter duo delayed our group's arrival at the K'iche' village, which neither Ashley nor Becky could recall the name of, where we would spend the night. At the late hour, only a handful of folks were still in the streets—children carrying bags of detergent home for the night's washing and men having an after-dinner chat on the corner.

Like many Latin American towns, in the center was a plaza and a church, but rather than a municipal or government building, there was a *centro de justicia Maya* (Maya justice center). The varying Maya groups and communities have had their own justice systems since before the Spanish conquest. Since the conquest, the Maya have struggled to have their rights, including their ability to self-govern, recognized by the powers that be. The media often disparages Maya justice, telling of public whippings for minor offenses and ignoring stories of restoration and reconciliation. No matter what someone has done, no one is cast out.

In 1999, a proposed package of constitutional amendments that would have granted rights to the Indigenous—such as bilingual education, protections for communally held lands, and to be subject to customary law—was voted down by the population at large. Still, the people have not succumbed to the Guatemalan government. They continue to practice their customs and honor those they see as their leaders.

Knowing this history, I saw the centro de justicia Maya as a sign of the independence of this anonymous village. As such, I was not surprised when I saw that our lodging for the night was a separate hall the community had built to host hiking groups, equipped with cinder-block walls, flush toilets, and a tiled floor. There would be no pit latrines or sleeping on dirt floors with animals for this group. This Guatemalan version of glamping may have emerged from years of realizations that tourists' visions of "roughing it" looked more like camping than campesino. I suspected they wanted to earn extra money for the community and maintain their privacy while giving the tourists their accustomed accommodations.

That night, we dined on overcooked pasta and passed around a bag of trail mix. A cold beer would have been amazing. Instead, I settled for a ten-minute turn with Lucia in a temazcal—a sweat bath the Maya use to clean filth and sin through fire and water. Ashley led us to the temazcal behind the hall. It was a low adobe dome with a short tunnel entrance that made me think of an igloo. Temazcales are often built in the shape of a uterus to represent the experience of being spiritually and physically reborn.

Lucia and I crawled through the flaps at the entrance and into the "womb." In our hot igloo, I used the one bucket of hot water allotted to us to wash off the grime of the day and soothe my exhausted child; the sin would have to come off another way. Sooner than we wanted, Ashley returned with the next two hikers for their turn. Lucia and I went back to the hall and zipped ourselves into a single sleeping bag, sealed for the night.

The second day was as grueling as the first, and we barely managed to keep up with the group. Becky led the way, followed by the other young tourists, the Guatemalan couples fresh from their rest, and then us along with Ashley. The periodic water and snack breaks were an opportunity for the stragglers to reunite with the leaders, meaning that those who stayed in front had ample time for repose, while Lucia and I scarcely had a moment to take off our packs before we had to put them on again. I tried every tactic I could think of to motivate Lucia to keep going and distract us both from the throbbing pain in our backs and legs. We sang, told jokes, played naming games, and asked Ashley a multitude of questions.

In what would be our next-to-last stop for the day before reaching our destination for the second night, Lucia and I paused to polish off a liter of water. I stuffed the empty bottle into my pack. After tightening the drawstring and clicking the flap of my bag into place, I looked up to see no one but my child. The group was gone! I yelled at Lucia to throw on her pack and run.

Though we hurried as fast as we could, we could not catch up to the group. We encountered three or four forks in the path and each time took the way that appeared the most traveled. After a while, I looked down to see that I was merely standing in a space between trees and not on a path.

Lucia spotted a pair of Indigenous women collecting *leña* (firewood). She ran up to them, asking in Spanish, "Have you seen any White people carrying something on their backs?" The women looked confused. I wasn't sure if they did not understand Spanish or why a group of gringos would be in the forest or how a mother and child could be lost. I hoped that even if the women could not help us find the group, they might direct us to the village where they would be headed.

"Where is the town?" I asked.

"Which town?" one of the women responded.

I had no idea. "A town where White people might be spending the night?"

I sounded like an idiot.

"Down the mountain," the other answered, pointing through the trees with pursed lips as her hands steadied the load of sticks on her head.

After fifteen minutes of our absurd pursuit to find a town where White people might sleep, Lucia cried, "Mommy, I'm scared. Let's go back."

Yes, that would be better, I decided. If someone came back for us, we needed to be on the right trail. We backtracked to the site where we were abandoned. It was getting late, and with the dense tree canopy, it grew dark sooner than sunset. While we waited, Lucia became more frightened. Her voice was shaky, and the tears were ready to spill. I had to stay calm to prevent her from completely falling apart. I crossed my legs and pulled her into my lap, holding her like a baby. I suggested we watch a movie on the partially charged Kindle while we waited; however, *Akeelah and the Bee* was not much of a distraction for either of us. I knew I did not have much time before panic ensued.

Close to an hour later, we heard a distant yell. We yelled back. Ashley, charged with holding up the rear flank, ran up to us, breathless. At the last break, someone finally noticed we were missing, and she came back to find us. She was very apologetic, but I was furious. I downplayed her negligence to keep Lucia calm. When we reunited with the group, I could see waves of relief wash over their faces, and we were greeted by hugs.

This second night, the village where the White people stayed was Santa Catarina, which is on the lip of the mountains around Lake Atitlán. Lucia and I had passed through Santa Catarina numerous times, entering and exiting the road down to the lake. Once again, we slept in a salón built for tour groups adjacent to a family's home. We celebrated our last supper together around a fire on our hosts' patio, sharing tortillas and beer rather than bread and wine—but still in communion. We toasted marshmallows, introduced s'mores to the Australians, and sang with our host, who performed Mexican boleros on his guitar.

Becky roused us at four o'clock in the morning to ready ourselves for the hike. After an hour of descent on that switchback road, which Lucia and I had often braved on buses, we turned onto a large plateau in the rocks to see the sun rise over the lake. While Ashley and Becky heated a pot of water to prepare coffee and oatmeal, the rest of us curled into our sleeping bags and stared up at the stars. Clouds hovered over the water as the light slowly broke through. We gradually made out the shapes of seven volcanoes on the horizon to the east.

In the distance, smoke and fire emerged from Volcán Fuego, the active volcano in this chain. It felt like we were safely floating in the heavens, with the fires of hell burning far away. Our bellies were full; we were warm and safe. On this third day, I felt that a stone had rolled away and we were emerging out of a dark cave.

After sunrise, Mercedes, an officer of the Policía Nacional from San Pedro, came to escort us to San Juan as a precaution against robbers. While Ashley and Becky packed our breakfast items, I went over to talk with her.

Originally from Chiquimula, a departamento in southeastern Guatemala, she had been serving in San Pedro for twelve years and, in that time, had been separated from her three children in Chiquimula with her family. When I asked her whether she could get a transfer to her hometown to be with her family, she told me that all Policía Nacional serve in a place that is not their own community. I recalled what I had heard about how the army deployed soldiers into communities that were not their own so that they would not feel conflicted about oppressing them, or worse. The "demilitarized" national police had taken the same tactic. Perhaps the rationale was more about keeping people in line rather than keeping the peace.

After chatting with Mercedes for a bit, I walked back to my pack, where Lucia was still eating, to put our sleeping bags away. Suddenly, the guy standing by us yelled, "Drop to the ground!" I grabbed Lucia by the wrist, threw her down, and fell on top of her.

Becky had asked Mercedes to hold her pistol, and not one to argue with the person paying a generous fee for her moonlighting, Mercedes complied. In a millennial moment, Ashley took the gun and waved it around, striking various poses for Becky to snap photos to post online. When our guides realized that the more mature travelers in their midtwenties were appalled by their behavior, they realized their mistake and begged, "Would you guys not post this or mention it to anyone?"

Though Mercedes was there allegedly to protect us from Guatemalans, it was Ashley, the stupid gringa, who had been the only threat to our lives over the past three days.

The remainder of the trek took us down a rocky path on the side of the mountain. By the end of the morning, we emerged on the hill by San Juan where the Spaniards had leveled a Maya altar and placed a cross and a Virgin Mary statue. After concluding our journey with a stop at a fair trade coffee cooperative in San Juan and another stop for lunch and a swim in San Pedro, Lucia and I returned home for much-needed long showers and rest.

The next day, Good Friday, Lucia barely left the bed, utterly exhausted and utterly proud of herself for completing the hike. She was already preparing her story to tell her friends in Seattle when she went to visit Wade in a few weeks. I wondered how the story of this trip, and Guatemala in general, would be conveyed when she was back in Seattle. Although I felt I was gaining traction at work and was much less worried about Lucia now that we had found a school, home, and friends that we liked, I knew she was still overwhelmed by Guatemala and missed Seattle. *Would the visit home make it hard to return here?*

While she recuperated at the house during the day, I surveyed the activity in San Juan. Most of the population in this Catholic-majority community was preparing for the main procession of the week—the commemoration of Jesus's death on the cross and the climax of his suffering. The men decorated the street with carpets of colored sawdust that would be ruined hours later while the women provided refreshments or sat on the stoops, chatting. I walked along the procession route, checking out images of Jesus made with vegetables and of Mary made with flowers. The floral and fruity smells intermingled with the earthy scents and cooking smoke.

Several times, I went home to check on Lucia and pleaded with her to join me in taking in the vivid scene.

"You should come to the center. The carpets they're making on the street are amazing. I've never seen anything like it."

"Ugh, I'll just look at the pictures."

"I saw a lot of your friends there. Emilio and Yuriel are helping some of the men with their stencils. Maybe you could help them too."

"No, I don't care. I don't want to see Yuriel," she moaned.

"Evelyn and Ofelia are on a corner watching. We could bring some drinks for them."

"No."

"Please, you may never get another chance to see something so extraordinary."

"No, I'm too tired. I just want to rest," she insisted. I realized I had already pushed her hard that week, so I let it go.

Later that night, as we sat down to eat, we heard a wailing sound.

Fearfully, Lucia asked, "What is that? Is it an animal?"

"No, it sounds like a woman screaming. It's coming from whatever's going on over there," I said, referring to the evangelical retreat center next to our house. "Hey, let's go check it out."

I was surprised that she agreed. We snuck over the rocks and hid in the bushes that separated our property to investigate. We saw about a dozen people in an open salón holding a vigil. The leader was rousing them by calling for the Holy Spirit to come, speaking in tongues, and casting out demons. He laid hands on a teenage girl brought to him, and then she vomited and fell over. I feared that snakes would be pulled out at any moment. When one of the worshippers looked over at us, we ran down the rocks back to our house, nervously laughing.

Once we were back home, Lucia asked, "Mommy, what was all that about? What were they doing to that girl? Why did she puke and pass out?"

"The preacher said he was casting out a demon, but really what he did was give her a chance to let out her pain."

"What do you mean?"

"She may have had some pain inside her. Really, we all have pain inside. The way we let it out depends on the culture we live in. These evangelicals think of this pain as a demon, and the way they try to get rid of it is to cast it out like it is a parasite on the soul."

"That sounds freaky. Our church at home never did anything like that."

"I know, but a lot of other churches in the States do. That's where they learned this from."

"But that girl? What happened to her? Is she going to be okay?"

Attempting to reassure her, I said, "She was probably caught up in the excitement of the group. People in groups like that can get hysterical or act in ways they normally wouldn't alone. I'm sure she will be fine."

"Mommy, have you ever gotten hysterical in a group?"

"I don't need a group to be hysterical. I seem to be able to work myself up without any help."

"Mommy!" she snapped.

On Saturday, Lucia had recuperated enough to go to a sleepover at Stela and Lana's house. Easter Sunday morning, I rose early and alone. I walked up to town to survey what I assumed would be the grandest celebration of the week. Instead, I found the streets empty of people and clear of the sawdust and pine needles that had bestrewn them the previous night. It was the quietest day I had seen. I wondered if the contrast with the earlier part of the week was because the people identified more with the suffering of Jesus than the resurrection.

While I was out, I stopped at the Super Q'ik, the only open tienda in town, to buy chocolates and a plastic wind-up chick for Lucia's makeshift Easter basket. I placed them in the plastic bowl I had lined with dried grass. I wanted to make sure that Lucia knew the Easter bunny had found her, even though Santa Claus couldn't. Later that morning, I pointed to the bowl on the table.

"Lucia, look. The Easter bunny brought you a basket."

"Oh," she said and then furrowed her brow. "There's not much candy in it."

"Well, I think this is all the Easter bunny could find here," I replied.

I recognized the irony of quality chocolate being prohibitively expensive, and therefore not carried in stores, in the region where cacao originated.

She smiled for a moment, and then her face turned to a frown again. "I wish we could do the Easter egg hunt with our neighbors like we do every year."

"I know you miss your friends. I'm sorry."

"I always got a lot more candy at the Easter egg hunt than I got in my basket."

As I had every year, I insisted, "Easter is not about the candy."

"Then what is it about?" she asked, as she had every year.

And as always, I had a hard time explaining the reason.

I had grown up hearing that the meaning of Easter was to honor Jesus's ultimate sacrifice to save us from our sins, but that made no sense to me as a child and even less to me as an adult. Why would God, who is supposed to be the definition of love, condemn us and then condemn his child? I knew the term "Easter" was derived from a pagan goddess and that many of the American customs that Lucia loved, such as visits from the Easter bunny and egg hunts, were related to pagan fertility traditions. Still, this explanation sounded hollow to me as well.

I settled on saying, "I think it is about reconciliation. Jesus's resurrection is a symbol of healing the rift between God and humanity."

But that didn't feel right either. Why would there be a tear in the relationship between God and humanity, and why would it take one person's death and resurrection to heal that? What kind of Christian was I if I couldn't explain the basic tenet of my religion in a manner that was authentic and sensical? If I had to draw my own picture of what Holy Week meant to me, what would it look like?

Maybe there is another way to look at this time.

The *Popol Wuj* asserts that humans were created to revere both the gods and the calendar. The Maya's 360-day haab calendar guides planting, harvesting, and hunting—activities that depend on the sun's movement. The holy cycle of birth, growth, and death is honored because it is essential to survival.

During the solar year, the Maya view the equinoxes as dangerous and chaotic times. The autumnal equinox occurs during the height of the rainy season when the Heart of the Sky, also known as the one-footed god Huracán, unleashes torrential storms. The wayeb', the five days between haab years, coincides with the vernal equinox and the end of the dry season, when the scorched Heart of the Earth yearns for the cooling rain.

Before the conquest, the Maya marked this wayeb' with ritual celebrations marking the death of one year and the birth of another. The Tz'utujil community of Santiago Atitlán continues a coming-of-age tradition for young men. In one day, they trot fifty miles together from the highlands to the coast with their empty packs. On the verdant coast, they rest briefly. They scavenge for and load their packs with the fruits of the season. With only a night's rest, they make a two-day return up the steep hills. The blood and blisters from the burden on their breaking backs express the pain they carry inside them, a pain brought about by intense human suffering, pain their people have borne for hundreds of years.

After an arduous three-day, hundred-mile peregrination, they are greeted with gratitude and revelry. They get drunk, dance, and wail with the whole town. They grieve the death of the old year. The pain of the past is suddenly released through their rituals of sacrifice, death, and grief. Wet with the first rain of the season, they embrace the life to come.

After the conquest, the Maya hid their wayeb' traditions within the Catholic celebration of Holy Week since they occur around the same time of year. As with many other Maya beliefs and customs, a veneer of Christianity was painted over it, but the heart remained the same. Though the evangelical churches' celebrations were different from the Catholics', they also provided a theater within which the people could act out their grief and pain in wild, ecstatic dancing and emotional singing.[35]

---

[35] See note 15.

When I learned of wayeb', I thought first of how Lucia and I had experienced our period of chaos, our perilous journey that week. Though going half the distance and bearing half the weight of those young Tz'utujil men who trekked to the coast and back to Santiago Atitlán, we had our own odyssey filled with suffering and rejoicing.

Upon further reflection, I came to another understanding. My whole time in Guatemala was my wayeb'. The nine months we had spent here thus far had been filled with chaos and peril. This was a liminal space, a transition from one life I had left behind to another that I had yet to build. Lucia and I were both grieving the death of our little family. While I was mourning what I thought our lives would be, she was mourning the life she had.

Maybe the picture I needed to draw wasn't what Holy Week meant to me. What I needed to put to paper was what our lives would be in the next haab.

45

BRINGING LIGHT INTO THE WORLD

NAVICHOC FINALLY INVITED me to attend a birth after putting up with my pleas for weeks. While I was lounging by the pool with Lana after the girls had gone horseback riding, Navichoc called to tell me that a pregnant woman was now seven centimeters dilated and the baby would likely be born later that afternoon.

Within a couple of hours, I met her outside the woman's family compound. She motioned for me to hurry.

"Ya es tiempo." (Now it's time.)

I followed Navichoc into a back room made of mud bricks, exactly the type of buildings washed away in Hurricane Stan. The room had one small window that opened onto the shared patio between the two other structures on the compound and a low-voltage bulb dangling from the ceiling and shaded by a scrap of cloth. As I entered, I seated myself in a tiny wood-and-metal chair in the corner, likely discarded from a US kindergarten classroom and somehow ending up here through a series of transactions.

Directly in front of me stood a small table with a pile of supplies Navichoc had dumped out upon her arrival. On the other side of the table, a young woman and her husband lay on a queen-sized mattress. The husband was holding his wife's head and torso and helping her with deep breathing. He was Q'eqchi', not Tz'utujil, so Navichoc bounced between Tz'utujil and Spanish, not for my benefit but for his. A bloodstained sheet was draped from the ceiling over the bed as a protective barrier from the heat radiating down from the hot tin roof, yet I still felt like I was in an Easy-Bake Oven. I thought about my little sister's pink canopy bed, which I was envious of when I was a teen. Doubtless, this young woman could never even imagine such a thing.

I assumed that I would be a quiet observer relegated to my kindergarten chair in the corner. Navichoc promptly told me that since Ofelia was not available to assist her, she expected me to help. She handed me gloves and pointed out the instruments and supplies too fast for me to absorb all their names in Spanish. She crawled onto the foot of the bed and knelt at this woman's pelvis between her upturned knees. The woman's mother came in, asked Navichoc in Tz'utujil who I was, and then sat on the bed's edge for a moment. She darted in and out of the room to stir the soup, stoke the fire, flip the tortillas, and watch her youngest of eight give birth. There was still a whole family to feed that evening.

"Ya viene" (It's coming now), Navichoc called out. I stood to peer over their backs and saw the baby starting to crown. Navichoc directed me to grab the fetal Doppler to monitor the heartbeat during the passage down the canal. I began to hand it to her, and she said, "No, you do it! Get the gel, squirt it there, stick the wand on the gel, and jab deep."

So, I too crawled on, to be the fifth person in this bed. With one hand, I followed Navichoc's instructions and watched the heart rate on the monitor rise and fall with the contractions. With the hand not holding the Doppler, I held on to a stranger's thigh at the most intimate moment of her life. I still didn't know her name and felt awkward doing this. How could I have thought to impose on such a personal, private moment?

The fetus was stuck and needed extra help moving along. Navichoc directed the husband to put his hands down the woman's two tank tops and stimulate her nipples to release oxytocin to strengthen contractions. Not only was the woman wearing two tank tops, but she still had on her corte, though it was loosely draped around her waist. She was lying on a torn trash bag, presumably to keep these sheets from being stained, and she made no sounds other than deep breaths.

Days before my due date, my mother flew in so she could meet her granddaughter right after the birth, and I packed a bag with soothing CDs, aromatic candles, and clean cotton pajamas to take to our highly equipped birthing center. I wanted the ambiance of natural childbirth but the assurance of technology. However, when the time came, I wanted no other sensory input and no one but Wade by my side. We left my mother to wait anxiously in our apartment and all the supplies in the bag.

In the silence of our room, I could hear his stomach rumble.

"Why don't you grab some lunch?" I suggested. "I think Almita is taking her time in finding her way out."

"Well, if you don't mind, then yeah, I'll go. I'll be back as fast as I can," he promised. "Do you want anything?"

"Are you kidding?" I joked. I needed him to go get his strength. I needed him.

The midwife was in and out, alternating between checking in on me and another client in labor, so I was alone in my room for a while. Labor progressed slowly, but motherhood was coming quickly. My hypothetical fears about whether I could bring Almita safely into the world and about whether I would be a good mother were about to be confirmed or debunked.

When Wade returned, he held my hand quietly as I voiced my concerns between the contractions and moaned at the ever-increasing pain. If he ever doubted me, he never said so. I felt he had as much faith in me as I did in him.

The pangs eventually felt so sharp that the midwife suggested I relax in the Jacuzzi in my private bathroom. Wade stayed by me while I was in the Jacuzzi, holding my hand even though he was awkwardly contorted on the floor.

"Ow, my back hurts," he complained.

"You think your back hurts?" I said back. This was one of those silly moments we laughed over and told Lucia about years later. In reality, he did his best to be supportive while containing his nervousness.

While I was sitting in the hot tub, gritting my teeth, and persevering through the worsening labor pains, the midwife who had provided my prenatal care had gone off duty, so another, whom I had not met, tended to me. She told me that she'd studied astrology and could do a rough chart of our baby-to-be. Though Wade and I considered astrology nonsense, we agreed to listen.

Based on how the planets would be aligned in a few hours, she predicted that our baby would roam the world (not knowing that we both loved to travel), be dedicated to humanitarian causes (not knowing that we both had public service careers), and would maybe run an orphanage (I don't know where that came from).

When the Jacuzzi cooled to tepid, I added more hot water, causing me to overheat. Wade helped me out of the tub, and then the intensity of the pain suddenly increased. A few minutes of agonizing contractions were enough to toss out my fantasy of natural childbirth and demand an epidural—NOW!

After what seemed like hours of pushing since the sweet drip had not only ceased the pain but also slowed the labor, our daughter was born. As soon as she was out and her breathing passages were clear, the midwife moved to hand the naked baby to me.

I said, "No, let her father hold her first."

I had held her for nine months and knew that once she was in my arms, I wouldn't let her go. I wanted him to have this experience of giving our baby her first loving embrace. As he cradled her in his arms, tears rolled down his face—a perfect little girl. After a few minutes, he handed her to me, her tiny left fist curled by her face. And no, I didn't let her go.

In the final few pushes, Navichoc called out for scissors and an *abrazadera*.

Damn! I wished I had paid more attention when she went over all the instruments in Spanish.

"It's blue!"

Which of the two blue things on the table does she want? Okay, the blue clamp probably is needed before the blue suction bulb.

"Hold her leg! Keep the Doppler going! Hand me the oil!"

Navichoc used vegetable oil to lubricate the vulva and mouth of the vagina.

"Give me the *pera de goma*."

Oh, God, I have no idea what that is.

"The *other* blue thing."

Why didn't she just say that?

At the moment I turned to find it on the table, the baby slipped out—a perfect little girl. Navichoc grabbed that other blue thing from my hand and hastily started working on the baby.

"Rub the feet! Rub the feet!"

Though I had never heard of this, I gently slid my thumbs along the baby's wrinkled soles.

"No! Harder! Like you are tickling them."

Afraid I might hurt these tiny toes and ankles, I rubbed as hard as I could while Navichoc kept goading me to do more. She cleaned the mouth and nose, evaluated the baby from head to tickled toes, and applied erythromycin ointment to the eyes as a preventative measure.

"Now, swaddle the baby in this towel and hold her."

Wait a minute. "Doesn't the mother want to hold her?" I asked.

"No."

I held the little girl for what seemed like half an hour, though it was probably less, while Navichoc delivered the placenta. She told me that while the woman was pregnant, she had fallen at least three times on the slippery cobblestone streets. Staff at the health center, where she had received prenatal care, had told her that the baby would likely be born with defects resulting from her falls. This poor girl was terrified to see her baby. I held the infant with no name of the couple whose names I did not know and described how darling and alert she was.

"¡Qué bella! ¡Qué preciosa!"

Eventually, the father came over and gazed at his new daughter, tears rolling down his face. Q'eqchi' men cry at first sight of their baby girls as much as Seattle men do.

After the placenta came out, the woman's mother handed Navichoc a tub with scraps of cloth, to select one with which to wrap it for burial. The placenta is considered to be the root of a child. Where it is buried is where the child is connected. When this was completed, I gave the baby back to Navichoc, who washed her with toilettes, diapered her with a rectangular cloth and a long tie wrapped several times around her waist, and then dressed her in a pink onesie pajama. All those layers in all that heat.

Navichoc held the baby up and cooed as well about how adorable she was. The young woman could only skirt her eyes in that direction, so Navichoc handed the baby back to me. Then the grandmother and Navichoc helped redress the new mother. They removed her two tops and put on two more. Her corte was likewise taken off only to be replaced by another. As soon as she was presentable, half a dozen women and children poured into the cramped room to see the baby. The grandmother kissed the baby in my arms, in *my* arms.

"Ay, qué bella."

At last, the new mother acquiesced. She took her baby and wept at the sight of her perfect child. The baby took to nursing easily; the new family was now complete.

Navichoc, being all business, instructed these new parents that the baby must get the hepatitis A vaccination within twenty-four hours. She called the health center to check the vaccine availability and whether they were open. The grandmother and Navichoc slid a pair of pajama bottoms on the new mother to get her ready to go to the health center before it closed that afternoon. Navichoc then packed up her things while I took a few photos. As we walked out the door, the grandmother paid Navichoc with a jar of soup and a stack of tortillas.

Navichoc said as we were leaving that when she had first arrived, the young woman was screaming in pain, but her mother told her that she was bothering the neighbors and if she continued, she would send her to the hospital, the worst possible place to give birth for an Indigenous woman.

Spanish-speaking Ladino doctors and nurses in Guatemala are notorious for treating Indigenous women like animals. For example, in Petén, the hospital nurse threw a bucket of cold water on one woman I knew because she was "a dirty Indian." At the closest hospital, women in labor are warehoused in a ward of about twenty beds and are not allowed to have anyone with them. The doctors move down the row of beds in an assembly-line fashion, delivering babies who are taken away instantly and placed in a separate nursery. This was part of the motivation to build a casa materna in San Juan—so that women can give birth safely, with dignity, and with their families.

Within a few hours of my giving birth, my mother flew into our room, followed by Wade's father, who had brought her to the hospital. She had gotten the note I left in the early morning saying we were on our way to the hospital and had been pacing in our apartment ever since.

"How beautiful she is!" she gushed.

The next day, Wade's family and closest friends visited us, bringing balloons, cards, and warm wishes.

A long line of nurses I can't remember gave me stacks of forms to complete, tip sheets to read, and reminders of appointments to make. I couldn't stand or even pee on my own. How was I supposed to do all of this and take care of a baby? After a couple of days in the protective confines of the birthing center, three meals a day delivered to my room, and obtrusive vital-sign checks in the wee hours, we strapped baby Lucia in the car seat, covered her in a pink blanket given by the hospital, and went home.

Our family and friends returned to their lives, and Wade and I were left to figure out together how to be parents.

One day, I came home from the clinic to find Lucia coloring a large poster.

"What's this?" I asked.

"We are supposed to make a poster describing what we offer to the world. We started in class and have to finish it at home."

"How's it going?"

"All the other kids did the same thing. They wrote their names at the center and drew lines to words around the edge like '*amable*,' '*cordial*,' '*simpatico*,' and '*agradable*.'"

"Don't all those words mean 'nice'?"

"Yeah, I wanted to do something different."

"I understand why. 'Nice' isn't the first word that I would use to describe you."

"Mommy, you're mean!"

"Oh, you know I'm kidding. Show me what you've got there."

Lucia's held up her poster, which was predominately colored black. "This is the earth," she said, pointing to the blue-green circle in the center, "and this is my light." She pointed to the tiny yellow dot in the middle of the circle.

"And those letters scattered around the edges? What are they?"

"They spell out 'What I bring to the world.' I figured that since they were in outer space, they would be floating around."

Indeed, the world is blessed by the light she has brought to it.

46
THE FALL OF THE PUFFED-UP PLUMED BIRD

THE TRANSFER TO La Salle incurred the cost of a new uniform, extra school supplies, tuition, and enrollment fees, which totaled more than a hundred dollars. Again, tapping into my savings, I could manage; however, given that this amount was about 20 percent of my monthly salary, how could a Guatemalan family possibly afford this? Particularly for a family with several children, this sum was out of reach.

In the States, school uniforms are purchased online or at least through a catalog. But in San Juan, the uniform had to be made by a tailor. The administrator could not give me a phone number for the designated tailor so that I could make an appointment but instead instructed me to go to his place of business directly. The tailor was also a coffin maker, so I looked for the shop with model coffins in the front window.

Since I could not call to make an appointment, Lucia and I stopped several times by his shop, which was also his home, for her to be fitted. We then had to go several times again to pick it up.

On one of these trips, we swung by Daniella's new house to drop off the sleeping bag she had lent me. On the way, Lucia and I purchased slivers of *sandia* (watermelon) at the corner *frutería*, the only place in town where I could buy produce outside the morning market hours.

As Lucia bit into her slice, she whined, "Ew! There's a bug in my sandia."

"Look, we are in Guatemala, and unfortunately, you are going to have to get used to bugs," I told her. Just then, *SQUISH*. I stepped into a massive pile of dog shit that encased my sandal and oozed between my toes.

Lucia cackled. "Mommy, we are in Guatemala, and unfortunately, you are going to have to get used to poo."

Damn, she's right.

I limped the few remaining steps to our destination, where I took off the shoe and began banging it against the neighbor's wall. Lucia ran up the stairs to knock on Daniella's door, all the while laughing. As the whole family came to the door, the clump that encased the shoe fell into the narrow alley between the houses. They were disgusted to see me hobble to their pila to rinse my foot and the remaining chunks off my shoe. Granted, this was where they had to wash their dishes and clothes.

I slipped the wet shoe back on my foot and climbed the stairs to the landing where the family and Lucia were standing. As I turned to go after handing Daniella her sleeping bag, I slipped and lost my footing. I tumbled down the concrete stairs and fell on my ass, splat into the pile of shit that I had just banged off my shoe, causing the feces to spray back up into my hair. Lucia, Daniella, Edoardo, Aldo, and Emilio were aghast. Something between a deep laugh and a wail welled up inside me and erupted. The onlookers stayed silent for a moment in shock and then joined me in the cachinnation.

I did not realize that both my legs had scraped along the concrete in the fall until I stood and saw the bloody abrasions. Covered in blood and feces, I did not know how I would make it back through town. My ten-year-old was too humiliated to be seen in public with me and forbade me to pick up the uniform, even if it meant we would have to wait another week. Wincing from the stares of passersby, I limped through back streets to the clinic, where I let myself in to clean and bandage my wounds.

The following week, I was able to pick up the uniform, but we discovered the P.E. shorts were too small. Again, I had to go by the shop several times to request an alteration and even took to knocking on the tailor's home door and speaking to his mother. Meanwhile, Lucia's teacher reprimanded her for not wearing her uniform.

I was finally able to come upon the tailor during my midday rush to Chuitinamit. As I was about to explain what was needed, up rode a tuk-tuk with an ailing elderly passenger. His family lifted him out, carrying him by the arms and legs, and brought him to the shop to be fitted for his casket and burial clothes before he died.

"NO! I was here first!" I barked.

Oh, God. What have I become? A woman who shoves a dying man out of the way.

Weeks later, Lucia brought another note home from school saying that an NGO was sponsoring her class to plant trees the next day and that the students should bring their machete, a water bottle, and dress appropriately. I could send Lucia to school with a water bottle, but a machete? I didn't have one lying around, but Gilda lent us one. It seemed like Lucia had only recently reached a grade where in Seattle she would no longer have to use round-edged scissors. I couldn't imagine Seattle parents sending their children to school with a two-foot-long blade.

When I came home for lunch the next day, I was surprised to find her already there. Hot and hangry, she was covered in scratches.

"Why are you home so early? What happened to you?"

"The sponsors of the tree planting thought they were taking just the sixth-grade class, so each kid would have six or seven trees to plant. Instead, the administrator sent the whole school, so we each had only one tree to plant. Once we were done with the trees, we went home."

"What do you mean you went home?"

"Well, it only took about thirty minutes. All the kids went home instead of going back to school."

"Why are you so scratched up? What are all those bumps on your skin?"

"I had to crawl around in the dirt and got eaten by bugs. All the other kids wore long pants and long sleeves, so they didn't get scratched up. Why did you have me wear shorts and a T-shirt? Why didn't you know I should dress differently? You're the mom!"

Yes, I'm the mom, but I'm not all-knowing.

The lack of predictability in the school schedule hindered my ability to be fully present at work and fully participate in school. The Catholic school was constantly closing for holidays with only a day's notice to the parents. For the town fair that was only one day, the school closed for three days to prepare and then another three days a week later to commemorate the fair.

On several occasions, Lucia came home with a note stating that the following day there would be a family dinner, a parade, or some other community-building activity that would help me become familiar with the children and their parents and to help them become familiar with us. In nearly every case, I could not attend because I did not have enough time to make plans. And if I could participate, the event usually started at least an hour late. I asked Maestra Elvira for more advanced announcements, but she thought her notes were sufficient. I went to the administrator to plead my case.

"Don't you know what the academic year is? When school starts and stops? When there are holidays and events?"

"Well, of course we know," he replied.

"Then why do you not tell the parents ahead of time?"

"Because they will forget."

Perhaps that is true. Day planners are not common in Guatemalan households.

"Okay, well, if you know what the schedule is, could you please at least tell me so that I can make plans?"

He looked at me like what I was asking for was unreasonable. I imagined this was the look my mother would have received if in 1978 she had told my sixth-grade principal that I required a vegan, low-sodium, kosher, gluten-free, and nut-free diet due to my allergies and my family's lifestyle and belief system. Was I an *exigente* (demanding) gringa or a crazy woman?

Both?

I had demanded to be reimbursed when I pulled Lucia out of Nuevo Amanecer and insisted she be admitted to La Salle even though I did not have the requisite paperwork to enroll her in a Guatemalan school. Despite my claim that academics were not important, I pressed for her to be placed in a higher grade so that she would be challenged and would be with children who were more her intellectual peers. Despite my claim that social development was a priority, by putting her in sixth grade, I'd placed her in classes with older children who were entering their awkward adolescence and leaving their carefree childhood. I dropped into recess or disrupted class to check on my child whenever I felt like it, indifferent to the effect on the teacher or students. I was demeaning to my child, to the school, and to the support services of the community. I demanded that an administration that accommodated the needs of the other parents and students change to accommodate my needs. When I brought her to the clinic, I expected the staff to help keep my child occupied while they could not be with theirs.

I was worse than an exigente gringa or a crazy woman. I was an arrogant jerk.

If there were such a thing as sin in the Maya worldview, it would be pride. In a culture that values harmony in community and creation, a person who thinks of himself as better than others needs to be brought back down.

Repeatedly in the *Popol Wuj*, prideful characters are easily tricked, and their pride leads to their defeat. After the destruction of the mud people, the *Popol Wuj* tells of the fall of the bird Vucub-Caquix (Seven Macaw), also known as the "Puffed-Up Plumed Bird."

Before the first dawn, when the earth was lit only by the moon, Seven Macaw boasted about himself so the wood people would worship him.

He bragged about the brilliance of his silver-and-gold face, his sparkling, jeweled eyes, his teeth of jade. He declared that when he went forth from his throne, he brightened the face of the earth. He claimed to be the sun and the moon and to have far-reaching vision, but this was not the case. His vision did not reach beyond where he sat. He was not truly the sun or the moon, but he puffed himself up by way of his plumage. He desired only grandeur and transcendence before the real light of the sun and moon were clearly revealed.

Huracán, the Heart of the Sky, saw evil in this prideful one who acted according to his desires. Honoring Huracán, the Hero Twins, Hunahpu and Xbalanque, set out to bring him down. When Seven Macaw was in a nance tree, they shot him in the jaw with a blow dart, causing immense pain in his teeth. The twins then conspired with two elders to trick Seven Macaw into thinking they would repair his teeth and eyes. Instead, they replaced his jade teeth with ground maize and plucked the precious metals and jewels from his eyes. Thus, the basis for his pride was taken away.

My jeweled eyes saw the truth; my jade teeth made wise edicts; and my gold-and-silver face illuminated everything before me—or so I thought. My hubris led the way until Huracán sent his agents to bring me back down.

Not even counting my ass splat into dog shit, I had been humbled. The extra costs were beyond my budget. The unpredictable schedule prevented me from planning. I couldn't figure out what the school expected from me. The food was unfamiliar and upsetting for my child, and the bullying she experienced because she looked and spoke differently was incessant. I was a highly educated woman with stable employment that subsidized my childcare, was fluent in the "official" language, and could easily afford the best private school in town, yet I was still flailing.

I realized I had not extended the same pity I felt for myself as a single mother to the mother of the boy who once hit Lucia in Nuevo Amanecer.

Worse, my situation as the sole parent with no support resulted from my own decisions. Lucia had a loving father in Seattle, whereas many other parents on their own were in a situation that was forced upon them.

In Seattle, one in five children lives in a home that speaks a language other than English. Many parents from these homes do not have my education or socioeconomic class and could not presume to make the demands I did. How do those parents navigate our system? The response in the US seems to be that if we merely make websites and brochures in other languages and provide interpreters, we have done our due diligence. However, as a foreign parent in Guatemala, I learned that the language barrier was the least of my concerns. The breakdown occurred because the entire system was constructed for the Guatemalan family and circumstance—as it should be, but that wasn't my system or preference. I didn't understand it, and mostly I resisted it. Again, I had the power and means to do so, but what about the families who don't?

Since I was aware, or thought I was, of the plight of immigrants and advocated for them in the US, I thought I was not one of those obnoxious Americans. I was more evolved, more understanding, wiser. But now that I was the "other" and not merely advocating for the "other," I was using the same exact White privilege I scorned.

By puffing up my plumage and believing only my skilled eyes could see the truth, the right way things were supposed to be done, I was incessantly in chaos and conflict, both internally and externally. I did not need to be tricked into opening my real eyes or casting my light in a different direction. My fumbling led to my fall.

47
WHAT LIES BETWEEN THE SEA AND THE SKY

"MOMMY, THERE'S NO school today," Lucia announced as I handed her the uniform that I'd pulled off the clothesline. "Can I go to work with you?"

"What? Why's the school closed?" I asked.

"It's some saint's day," she explained.

"Why didn't you tell me last night? Why wasn't there a note from your teacher?"

"Maybe she forgot to give out the notes," Lucia answered my second question. "Can I please go to work with you? Please?"

"Wouldn't you rather play with Karin and Felix?" If La Salle was closed, they would be home too.

"No, I'd rather go with you. *Please*. I don't want to be here alone."

There was no guarantee that the kids would be available all morning to play, and I didn't know whether could Gilda watch her. I went through my plan for the day to figure out what to do. Since it was Friday, there was only the morning clinic at Chuitinamit in San Pablo. Kenneth would be with Oscar in San Juan, tallying up the month's receipts, so he wouldn't be bothered if I brought Lucia for a few hours.

"Well, I suppose you can help Herlinda in the pharmacy. You have to hurry, okay?"

"Thank you! I promise I won't get in trouble." Lucia dropped the uniform and slipped into her shorts and T-shirt as I finished washing the breakfast dishes in the pila.

At Chuitinamit, Lucia stayed busy and on task. Straightaway, she made packages of vitamins to distribute at the schools. She helped Tulita with filing the backlog of patient records. She then helped Ines wash the flores de Bach vials. She didn't seem like the same girl who couldn't sit still and who wandered off to bother the staff or livestock. I thought she might finally be adjusting to life in Guatemala.

Only the week before, she had been excited to be one of two kids from her class to be selected to recite a poem at the town's Tz'utujil literary festival. She had written her poem about a papaya. She tried to downplay this honor by saying the boys in the class thought it was lame and the other girls were too shy to read their poems. Still, she was proud. Ofelia helped her translate her poem from Spanish to Tz'utujil. Gilda and Gaspar coached her pronunciation of the deep-throated clicks. Navichoc lent a traje típica belonging to her youngest daughter. On the day of the event, I sat at the front of the crowded library and whipped out my camera to capture Lucia's moment. I was proud too.

After spending the morning at Chuitinamit, we caught a tuk-tuk ride to San Juan with Ines and Dra. Faustina. I asked them whether they knew what saint was being celebrated and commented that it had not affected the number of patients in the clinic. They both replied that since they were evangelical, they didn't keep up with Catholic commemorations.

We passed a group of youth wearing La Salle school uniforms and eating cantaloupe slices from a corner fruit stand. I turned to Lucia and asked, "Are you sure you didn't have school today?"

"Those kids are in básico. They still have to go to school in the afternoon." I knew that La Salle, like other schools, used the same building to hold elementary school in the morning and middle school in the afternoon, but I thought it was odd that the school was closed for only half a saint day.

After lunch, when Ofelia came to the house, I headed out for my Tz'utujil class at a small language school just down the shore on the lake.

As with my Spanish teacher, Lourdes, my Tz'utujil teacher, Nehemias, and I sat across from each other at a little table, chatting for hours. Nehemias was also an artist and amateur ethnographer. He claimed that if he ever had the funds, he would record all the grandfathers and the grandmothers to capture their stories and their old, non-Hispanized words that were slowly slipping away. My language lessons were like a survey course on Maya mythology.

He told me about Lucia's nawal, aq'ab'al.

"Aq'ab'al signifies polarity, the dawn and the dusk, the cold and the heat, the light and the darkness. It is two sides of one coin, two energies that are contrary and at the same time in harmony."

I wondered whether Lucia would suffer extremes or if she would be able to hold together the contrasts of her nature.

Nehemias continued, "The polarity of aq'ab'al is represented in its animal—the owl—and colors—yellow and orangey red. The nocturnal bird bears witness to the transformation of night to day at dawn, which is signaled by the hues of the sun. Aq'ab'al is a good day to give thanks to Ajaw [God] and ask for forgiveness of human errors. Unfavorable characteristics of aq'ab'al are failures and suffering. Sometimes they suffer diseases from their own irresponsible acts. They have the tendency to not tell the truth. They can form enemies and betrayals. Their pride and arrogance cause them to want to be the center of attention. Innovative, noble, magnetic, and powerful, they are strong before their enemies. They have valor and the energy to solve problems. They maintain a youthful spirit."

Everything I heard about Lucia's nawal rang true to me. She has been the greatest joy in my life, the light by which I see more clearly, yet I was often frustrated and overwhelmed by her.

On my walk home from my Tz'utujil class, I passed Evelyn's house, where I saw her in her school uniform, playing with her siblings.

"How is Lucia?" she asked me. "Why wasn't she in school today?"

"Today wasn't a holiday?" I asked.

"No, why?" Evelyn said as she jumped on one foot.

What a rascal, I thought. I hurried home to confront Lucia about the lie. She was hanging on the limb of the large tree by the house.

I called out, "I saw Evelyn, and she told me that today wasn't a holiday. Why would you say that you didn't have school? How am I supposed to trust you?"

Lucia launched into excuses. "Mommy, I was tired of being teased. I just needed a break. I wanted to spend time with you."

I could see that she was sincere, but I was still upset with how she had lied to me.

"Well, you need to go apologize to the teacher and administrator right now. It's almost five. If we hurry, we can get there before they close at five thirty."

"Nooooo, please don't make me do that."

"Look, you need to take responsibility for your actions. It won't be bad. The administrator seems like a nice man. I'm sure he will understand."

We knocked on the administrator's door a few minutes after five. He politely greeted us and invited us in. He dismissed the staff that was mulling around so that we could talk privately. Lucia clearly and bravely owned her actions. He kindly gave her a short lecture on honesty and then forgave her. As they were talking, I thought about Lucia's deceit, especially in relation to her nawal. Her spunk had kept her going through our time in Guatemala, even if it annoyed me at times. Her lie was a way to spend time with me, but it was also to exert her will.

Early in the mornings, before Lucia rose, when I could only hear and not yet see the lake, when I saw the black sky but no longer heard the winds from the night before, I would sit on my porch and wait for the new day. Only when the yellow and orangey red appeared in the east was I able to see the celeste above and cobalt below. Between those opposing blues, those opposing views, broke the massive figures of the volcanoes Santiago and San Pedro. And behind them was a sliver of sun, the light between the sea and the sky.

48

SICK AND STUNTED

IN SURVEYS THAT ODIM conducted in San Pablo and San Juan, between 40 and 60 percent of the children were found to be stunted from chronic malnutrition,[36] and nearly all the homes' water sources were contaminated. The Mamá y Yo Saludable program provided some basic foods, and the volunteer teams brought suitcases full of vitamins, but filling children's bellies with supplements and nutritious food will curb malnutrition only if the water they drink and use to wash their food is potable.

To address access to clean water, we started healthy-homes education and provided families with easy-to-maintain water filters. To monitor children's health, we finally implemented our well-child protocol. This was an unusual practice in a culture where people tend to only go to a clinic when they are sick.

As we were developing our protocol, I negotiated a deal to do well-child screening with a local NGO that provided scholarships to students. Including medications and tests, I calculated that the total cost of an average consult was eighty-five quetzales (eleven dollars), so I insisted the NGO pay that amount for their scholarship students rather than the subsidized twenty-five quetzales we charged our other patients. They agreed to pay only twenty-five quetzales and said they would purchase

---

[36] Chronic malnutrition is when the height-for-age is more than two standard deviations below the World Health Organization Child Growth Standards median.

the medications at a private pharmacy. So that we would not displace our regular patients, I required that the scholarship kids have a limited number of slots each day designated for them.

In the first month, the scholarship children filled all the designated slots, and we were paid a significant sum. Nearly all the children we screened were diagnosed with at least one ailment, including malnutrition, skin infections, and intestinal parasites. Dra. Faustina and the nurses wrote scores of prescriptions for the families to give the NGO to fill. I thought we had accomplished something new and positive. However, after a few weeks, the number of children who visited the clinic dwindled, and eventually, they stopped coming.

I contacted the NGO to find out why, and no reason was given. Eventually, they stopped returning my calls just as their scholarship children stopped coming to the clinic. I later learned that the NGO was not buying the needed medicine at private pharmacies as they had promised to do. Since nearly all the children screened required medication, there was a gap in care. The parents were now aware of their children's ailments but had no way to pay for the cure. Once the other families learned of this, they did not see any reason to send their children to the clinic, so the project ended.

For a while, I blamed this NGO for not supporting kids they committed to. Now I blamed me. These kids weren't just their responsibility. I should have found another way to accommodate them by rearranging our schedules, going to their site, or allowing the medications to be included in the price. Instead, I delegitimized what I had been promoting.

One day during this time, I was resting in the hammock at home during my lunch break when I saw Lucia walk onto the patio, held up by Adela and Evelyn and trailed by three other girls. I jumped up to ask what was wrong.

Adela told me that Lucia had gotten sick in class and felt faint. I took her into my arms and brought her to the hammock to ask how she felt.

Lucia told me that her stomach hurt and that she felt weak. Switching to Spanish, I thanked the girls for their help and reassured them that Lucia would be fine so that they could go.

In the move to San Juan, the final bout of lice ended, but recurring stomach ailments for Lucia began. Since we ate the same food and drank the same water at home, I assumed that the snacks at school were to blame. Lucia insisted on being like other kids by buying her snacks from the vendors at school and drinking tap water, though I packed fresh fruit and a bottle of purified water.

After lunch, I took her back to the Sanjuanerita clinic, where I was to meet with the staff to review our well-child visit protocol and discuss what we should do about the scholarship kids. I asked if we could postpone the meeting so they could attend to Lucia. I thought these pains might be similar to the stress-related stomach pains Lucia had experienced in Seattle, but I wanted to make sure.

Ines took her temperature and pulse, and Herlinda weighed and measured her. Dra. Faustina examined her, tapping her belly to determine whether she had gas or parasites. In doing so, she heard the authentic rumblings of a disturbed system.

"Ay mami, ¿qué te pasa esta vez?" (Oh, dear, what has you this time?)

I looked through Lucia's thick medical file lying on the table. She'd had six visits to the clinic for bug bites, a couple of bouts of diarrhea, lice, fever, and now stomach pains. Dra. Faustina's file on Lucia did not even include her sprained arm or the times she was sick when we were in transit. I plotted her height and weight from the records of each of her visits on the well-child growth chart. She was thin but still in the normal weight range, though barely.

Dra. Faustina recommended that I send a stool sample to a private laboratory in San Pedro to test for parasites. I walked Lucia to the toilet and pressed her to give a stool sample in a little cup I held. Since the clinic had an agreement with the San Pedro laboratory to provide services to our patients at discounted prices, I wrote a referral for Lucia and certified it with a stamp from Tulita's desk. I dropped Lucia off at home and asked

Gilda to watch her. Then I rushed to San Pedro in a tuk-tuk, cup in hand, and begged the technician to examine Lucia's sample before she left for the day. She saw the desperate look on my face and graciously took the cup to the back.

The lab owner stepped out to attend to me. I handed him my referral form, and he gave me their intake form to complete. After he glanced over what I had written, he told me the fee would be 150 quetzales, the full price. I argued that since he had an agreement with the clinic to take the patients at a discounted price and my daughter was a patient, he should also charge us the same amount. He looked at me as if I were saying, "The sky is blue, so fruit is sweet." How could this gringa girl be a patient at Sanjuanerita?

"How do I know you didn't forge the name of the clinic administrator?" he dared to ask me.

"Because I *am the clinic administrator*!" I declared. "If you still want to receive referrals from our clinic, then you will have to recognize my daughter as one of our patients!"

What a hypocrite I was. I did not want the scholarship kids to disrupt the clinic's normal flow, yet I threatened to cancel a clinic contract for my kid. I demanded that the scholarship NGO either pay a higher fee for a consult or not have access to our medications, yet I availed myself of the free medicine at the clinic.

I hurried home, where Lucia was resting and waiting. I was able to care for her that night, but I'd probably have to take her to work with me the next day. I knew I had taken advantage of the staff and my role as a supervisor by having her at the clinic during school closures and sicknesses. However, working from home was not realistic because the bulk of my job was on-site management and the internet at home was even more sporadic than at the clinic. Again, I was cheating my job and my child. I could not expand my reach to cover it all.

Lucia may have been the sick one, but maybe I was the one in danger of becoming stunted.

One day in early June, Lucia burst into my office at Sanjuanerita to explain that while Maestra Elvira was out for the day, instead of having a proper substitute teacher, the school recruited two eighth-grade boys to fill in. Shortly into the lesson, the boys started arguing, which turned into a fistfight, which turned into a mob fight when the sixth-grade boys jumped in. Lucia said they were screaming, punching, throwing things, so she got up and walked out of the class and to the clinic. This on top of the constant bullying and teasing she received was too much. She was done with La Salle.

Every reasonable option for school had been tried and had failed. If Lucia were in the US, she would be ending the school year in June, so I was fine with her stopping formal school in Guatemala. I would piece together more tutors in addition to Ofelia to keep her occupied until I figured out what to do next. In the span of twelve months, Lucia had been in six school situations, counting Seattle and the language school. I knew she was sick of school and sick in general.

The next day, I went by La Salle to inform them that Lucia would not be returning. Maestra Elvira was surprised and, surprisingly, saddened.

"Can she come by to say goodbye?"

"Hmm, no." I knew that would not happen, so there was no point in mincing words.

Regardless, the next day Maestra Elvira called me to inform me that the class wanted to bid farewell to Lucia and would be coming to my house late morning the following day. I left work early because I didn't want the class at my home without me there. When the whole class arrived, they were bearing a large cake. Lucia changed into her La Salle shirt to show she was still part of the group. On cue from Maestra Elvira, the children assembled in a circle around Lucia and, one by one, proceeded to tell her what a good friend, student, and inspiration she had been and then gave her a sweet hug. Most of the girls presented her a gift, a card, or a poem, and all the boys apologized for bothering her and gave a begrudging half hug. *Why could this not have happened months ago?*

The boys scarfed down their cake and started doing stunts with the hammock. Lucia, Adela, Evelyn, and the other girls gathered in a circle on the porch floor and chatted. Lucia was part of the group. She did fold in, though she may have been caught in the crease.

As the festivities wound down, the girls washed all the dishes while the boys continued to play. Lucia later told me that at every school event with food, the girls were instructed to do the dishes while the boys played. When Lucia complained about this sexist division of labor, Maestra Elvira told her that the boys would make a mess and do it slowly, so it was better to not even bother to ask them. Lucia then proceeded to show how she, too, could make a mess and wash dishes slowly.

Despite the adversity, or perhaps because of it, she had grown. She could see that in each school situation, either in the US or in Guatemala, kids are the same. And yes, Lucia was sick of school, sick of not belonging, sick of feeling alone, but she was not stunted. At least, that was my hope.

49
FISH-EYE VIEW

NEHEMIAS SHOWED ME one of his paintings in his new style, *vista de pez* (fish-eye view). Seen from the watery perspective of a fish, the subject was a man with enormous feet lying asleep in a kayak. His feet were elephantine because he had refused his calling—denied his don—to be a bone healer. According to Nehemias, anyone who refuses to accept his or her don will suffer.

In this world of dreams, the water and the air blurred into each other. Swirling swatches of colors in the sea and the sky were punctuated by dots of white representing the bones he had refused to heal. With feet so swollen that he could no longer walk, he would never recover or rise until he accepted his role as a healer.

Flor was one of the diabetes promotores and also had a job cleaning the Chuitinamit clinic. Her young daughter had an eye infection that damaged her cornea so much that she was in danger of losing her vision completely. Flor had stopped sending her daughter to school because she was afraid that she might accidentally fall or be hit and blinded permanently. The only treatment available was from a specialist in Guatemala City. The bus fare alone far exceeded what she earned, so paying for a private doctor and medication was well beyond her means. This child's life trajectory was that she would not receive an education and perhaps still lose her vision, thereby condemning her to a life of poverty.

A nurse from one of the visiting medical teams was interested in helping the girl pay her expenses, so she set up a fund of about $500, a little more than I would typically pay for a long weekend getaway in Seattle. With a combination of eye patches, glasses, and drops, the girl could save her eye and recuperate her vision. As her fears settled, Flor allowed her daughter to go back to school. Within a few months, the girl transitioned from being glued to Flor's side to playing with her brother while her mother cleaned.

Later, Tulita brought me the case of a seventeen-year-old girl who had lost an eye when she was only ten. Another benefactor associated with the clinic had paid for a glass eye for her. Perhaps even if she could not see normally, she could be seen normally. In the seven years since, the child-sized eye no longer fit her woman-sized body. She was a pretty young woman with thick, silky black hair that draped over half her face. She pulled her hair back for me to see. The prosthetic eye looked like a marble in her droopy eye socket.

The previous year, the girl's mother had been given twenty dollars to replace the prosthetic eye. Instead, she paid for the school fees and supplies for her other children. Knowing firsthand how expensive these fees and supplies could be, I understood her case. The eye was important but not urgent, whereas the fees had to be paid, or the children would miss a year of school.

"I don't think we should give her more money for an eye since she didn't spend the last money we gave her correctly," Tulita suggested.

"We have a fund set up for cases like this," I lied to Tulita. "The woman who donated to help Flor's daughter wants to help any child with an eye problem. Let's give her the money, and I will deduct it from the fund." Tulita reluctantly went back to her desk to retrieve the 150 quetzales. I understood her point of view. In a town filled with poverty, filled with need, we did not have enough to help everyone. However, not everyone was sitting in front of me. I could help one young woman whose mother was trying to balance the needs of all her children.

My vision had been blurred, and it didn't take a specialist or medicine to see that. For years, I had a vision—an illusion, really—of what I thought my life should be about. I wanted to be a missionary who found purpose in helping other people. I wanted to be part of what Padre Cirilo called "*el sueño de Dios*" (the dream of God). I wanted to bring heaven on earth by helping create a just world where every life is equally valued, where no mother has to make difficult choices between her children or about her children. But it was more than that. My first experience in Guatemala showed me that as a foreigner, I could only do so much.

I longed for partnership and purpose. But I was on the surface of the earth with everyone else, not in Eden. I had not been gifted an Adam, but I had been gifted a Hero Twin to share my life's work. I had thought that my Hero Twin was my daughter, a projection of me, but I was wrong. Lucia is as much her own person as me, Wade, or anyone else. I needed to think of my midwife's prediction about Lucia's destiny as having common elements with mine and Wade's, yet it is unique rather than shared. She would have to find her own purpose. My Hero Twin is not her but merely another side of myself. I have to draw upon the different parts of myself to pursue my dreams, just as I have to let my daughter grow up and have dreams of her own.

All mothers have to make choices on behalf of their children. No good works I or anyone else do will change that reality. My hope was that Lucia would fold into Guatemalan life, befriend local kids, learn the language, disavow materialism, shun popular culture, and thrive. I wasn't sure if any of that was happening, but I did know she was suffering. I was worried about walking the line between building resiliency and traumatizing my child. Now I needed to choose differently. I needed to choose her.

I could emerge out of the water and into the sky. It was time to see clearly. It was time to go back to the States.

After I told Kenneth, I pulled the staff together to let them know I was leaving. Tears dripped down my face. Even after a year back in Guatemala, I lacked the language skills to articulate the nuances of my feelings.

"Please look at what is in my heart rather than just hear what is coming out of my mouth," I pleaded and then proceeded to tell them what I saw come out of their hearts and into their lives.

They had all made sacrifices for their children and striven to set a good example for them. Dra. Faustina took a step down from running a hospital to be a provider at a small clinic to earn a stable salary for her daughter to go to the American school in Panajachel. Tomás was separated from his wife but kept his job at the clinic rather than going to the city where he could earn more money, in order to be near his children. Herlinda and Ines had started in clerical positions but had gone to nursing school on Saturdays, studying at night, doing their rotations in other parts of their country, sacrificing time with their children to show them the value of education and the importance of ambition. Navichoc was a one-woman show in organizing comadronas in San Juan. She was grooming her daughter to follow in her footsteps and take on more responsibility with the casa materna that would be opened soon.

They each had obstacles—physical, economic, social—that I never had to face because of accident of birthplace. I confessed that I felt weak for not being able to do what they do every day. I apologized for letting them down.

Ines responded that they all had their families to help, but I was alone. She could not do what I was doing either. Navichoc said that she saw up close how much Lucia was suffering, how lonely she was. They each told me what I had brought to their lives. Alba said she learned from my administrative skills, and Dra. Faustina said I had brought a higher standard of professionalism to the clinic. Tomás appreciated learning about the pharmacy and laboratory, despite his initial resistance. They had been looking into my heart all along.

After we finished our conversation, they went back to their posts, and I walked into Kenneth's office where he was waiting to debrief with me.

"How did it go?" he asked.

Instead of answering, I said, "Hey, I have an idea. I can come back to Guatemala once I have Lucia settled in school, stay for a couple of months, then go back to Seattle, and come back again. This way, I could extend my time another six months."

Kenneth looked at me with a blank expression.

"I can't do that, can I? It's ridiculous to think I can go back and forth. It's not fair to the people here to not let them go."

Shifting from boss to pastor, he counseled, "St. Augustine said that one of the first steps of discernment is to know where you want to be. Are you here, or are you there?"

"My daughter needs to be in Seattle with her father and her friends. She also needs her mother with her. And I need to be with her. Every day." Still feeling a twinge of attachment, I continued, "But it is super hard. You know how much I love everyone in that room. I think they were sincere. They all love me too. It has been so long since I have felt that."

"Well, if I can quote another religious leader, David Mackay said, 'No other success can compensate for failure in the home.'"

The knot in my stomach, the lump in my throat, and the water in my eyes all exploded out of me so hard I had to gasp for air. I slipped out of the chair and onto my knees, where I heaved sobs, sobs that I had not cried since I'd sat on the steps of our townhouse while Wade picked through his things that I had thrown out the window. Most men I have known would have been scared by this outpouring of female feelings, but Kenneth squatted down and put his hand on my back while I emotionally vomited.

When the water dried from my eyes, I finally saw clearly. Kenneth, in a sense, captured what this had all been about. When the tree that was my marriage fell, the roots thrown in the air and the crown crashing to the ground, I felt like a failure. I thought about how my nawal, no'j, was a bird that spreads trees. When my home was destroyed in one place, I migrated south with my seed to build another. In doing so, I had put my desires before Lucia's needs, therefore failing to protect her from the hardships of Guatemala. I was being a bird who wanted to fly away when my daughter needed me to be a tree for her.

50

BIRDSONG

HAVING COME TO PEACE about leaving, I was able to enjoy more of Guatemala without the pressure of trying to make it home. When Alba told me that her brother Raul would guide a volunteer team from Texas up Volcán San Pedro, I asked if Lucia and I could tag along.

To spur Lucia to dare another excursion with me, I told her about climbing San Pedro with Daddy years ago when we first started dating.

"It was the toughest physical activity either of us had ever done. I don't know if it really was harder than the hike you and I did from Xela or if I was just out of shape."

"You were probably out of shape," Lucia said.

"Anyhow, I hear that it is different now. There's a truck that takes you part of the way up, and the path has been cleared. Are you willing to try?"

"If it means that I get to brag to Daddy that I did something that was hard for him, then *yes!*" she laughed.

"Rascal."

When I did the hike with Wade, we met our guide, a stout Tz'utujil man, at the edge of town just after seven in the morning. The guide had insisted that we leave by six, but I wanted to wait for the restaurant to open so that we could eat a hearty breakfast. While Wade and I were weighed down with backpacks full of water and snacks, our guide carried only his machete and a few tortillas wrapped in a bandana. He warned us that the hike would be strenuous, but I bragged that I routinely did the StairMaster at my gym.

It wasn't long before the path was covered in vegetation. The guide hacked a new course with his machete where he could. Wade and I both struggled to keep up. The hike transitioned to a climb as the ascent became steeper, so the guide used his machete to cut steps into the side of the volcano cone. Then, as the climb transitioned to a crawl, I had to grab vines and grasses to pull myself up. Every movement forward required every muscle. The guide was frustrated with his laggard clients. He warned us that if we didn't hurry, the clouds would be at the summit, and we would not have a photo-worthy view of the lake.

During a water break about three-quarters of the way, I plopped down and told Wade, "I can't do it anymore. Why don't you just go ahead without me? I can wait here until you come back down."

"No, Jan," he said, "I'm not going to leave you, even if it means we don't finish. Just rest for a few minutes. There's no rush." And so, he waited patiently until I regained enough strength and stayed with me the entire way.

We reached the summit midday, and as the guide had predicted, the cloud cover was so heavy that we could see no more than a few dozen feet in front of us. We didn't care, though. We didn't climb the mountain to see the view; we climbed to see if we could. An hour into the descent, the guide asked if he could leave us because he was late for his other job. As soon as we assured him that we could get down on our own, he darted off like a deer down the hill. What the guide claimed would be a morning jaunt we finished in late afternoon.

The next day, still exhausted from the hike, we took off for Cuba, even though we could barely walk. I had to hold on to Wade's belt loop to go up stairs, and he had to lean on my back for support to go down stairs. We complained about the aches and pains, but we didn't regret the journey. We were off to our next adventure.

As with the guide on the hike with Wade, Raul suggested we get an early start so that we would make it to the summit before the afternoon clouds rolled in. Lucia and I rose at four in the morning to meet him at the dock in San Juan. At this point in our time in Guatemala, Lucia and I had taken many bus trips at four in the morning, so we knew the drill—what to pack the night before, how to navigate through Gilda's property in the dark, and how to wait patiently for transport. When Raul and the lancha showed up half an hour late, we boarded quickly and headed straight to the dock of the house where the team was staying. Even though they'd had extra time to be ready, when we reached the house, the dozen mostly middle-aged Texans were fumbling with their gear, struggling to cram food and water in the packs, and chugging their coffees before stepping into the lancha.

In the nearly one year we had been on Lake Atitlán, this was the first time I had been on a lancha at this hour. The Maya consider this time, the liminal space between night and day, sacred. The time between being asleep and being awake is when God can slip in through the "open crack of our consciousness."[37] This is when dreams become most vivid and then vanish. Though from my porch I could hear the lake at night and see the rippling reflection of the moon's illumination, I had not experienced the transition of the water from choppy waves in the late afternoon to the placid surface in the morning. I wondered *if this change was the chaos moving out or the calm coming in. Was this what stilling looked like?*

We disembarked at a dock on the other side of San Pedro that didn't exist when Wade and I were there, because the water level was much lower then. After catching a lift in a pickup partway up, we started along the now well-worn path as the first rays of sunlight were breaking.

Raul and I chatted in the lead of the group while the Texans hustled to keep pace. I learned that, like Alba, Raul had studied English with hopes

---

[37] See note 15.

of getting a good job. He wanted to be a biologist. He seemed to know every plant and animal we crossed, but realistically, he knew that being a tour guide was likely the best job he could get.

He and I took turns looping back to make sure those at the end of the line were not lost.

"The altitude change makes it tough to breathe," I assured them. "My daughter and I have had months to adjust, and y'all have only been here a few days." Meanwhile, Lucia, bored with waiting on the group, darted ahead and came back to tell us what to expect.

About halfway up, we stopped at a rest station equipped with a latrine and picnic tables. We watched Guatemalan families pass by on their Sunday outings—women in flip-flops and small children carried on their fathers' shoulders. While the group welcomed the rest, Lucia and I borrowed Raul's binoculars to look out through an opening in the trees down at San Juan in the distance.

"Hey, I've never seen San Juan from this angle," I told Lucia.

"Let me see! Let me see!" she cried. After a few moments of scanning the area, she announced, "Hey, there's our house!"

"Come on, now it's my turn again!" I insisted. I found our house too and then moved my gaze along the shore of the lake. I spotted a house with shiny solar panels on the roof. "Hey, I found Kenneth's house. I think that moving dot on the porch must be him."

When we started back on the path, Raul and I pulled ahead for a while and entrusted Lucia with keeping up the rear. With the chatter of the group far behind us, the chirping of the birds grew audible. One by one, Raul named the calls. The caldera lake and surrounding cinder cone volcanoes have dozens of species, each with unique calls. Like the people in the region, some species make their homes permanently there, some migrate north each year, some are taken against their will and held captive, and some are dying out.

Hearing a familiar deep, slurring song, I said, "That's a quetzal, right?"

"Yes. You know the bird calls?"

"Well, just that one." The quetzal, the national bird of Guatemala who lent its name to the currency, is distinguished by its iridescent green body, red breast, and unusual call.

Because we repeatedly had to wait for the group to catch up, we did not reach the summit until early afternoon, and just as happened the last time I had climbed this volcano, it was covered in clouds, so we couldn't take in the view. And also like last time, I didn't care. Lucia and I accompanied Raul in escorting the team during the tricky part of the way down to make sure folks had their footing, and then we took off on our own, leaving them behind.

"I can't wait to tell Daddy that I climbed San Pedro and rub it in that it was hard for him and easy for me," Lucia boasted.

"Well, are you going to tell him about the new path and truck that took us partway?" I asked.

"Of course not!"

51

FERIA DE SAN JUAN

SAN JUAN CELEBRATES the feast day for its namesake, St. John the Baptist, on June 24. This saint's day is recognized in other places as Midsummer Day, roughly coinciding with the summer solstice.

How fitting that Lucia, a child named after the sun, was born on Midsummer Day. Her birthday was her favorite day of the year, even better than Christmas because all attention was on her. I wanted this one to be good for her because she had been so disappointed with the holidays of the past year. Halloween was a bust because she was the only child to dress up (and the only child) at a party at a bar in San Marcos. Thanksgiving was a disappointment because we ate in a restaurant instead of our home. Christmas was without Mommy or a visit from Santa Claus. Easter, which followed our exhausting hiking trek, had no egg hunt.

It was perhaps the worst day of the year to hold a party. I feared that the invited guests who lived in town would be caught up in the *feria* (fair) held to celebrate the day and that those who lived out of town would not be able to get in because of the crowds.

I set the time for her party at midday, purchased a piñata and treats in San Pedro, ordered a cake from the bakery, prepared the punch as Pedrina had taught me, and then held my breath to see if anyone showed up. First to arrive were Lana and Stela from San Marcos, then Karin and Felix from the house below, Verna from behind our home, Daniella and Emilio, Ines and Francis, then Ofelia and her sisters. I stood back to notice that we had five languages circulating in the conversations: Spanish, Tz'utujil,

Croatian, Italian, and English. This varied, multicultural group was not from the videos of Escuela Caracol that I had seen a year earlier but rather from the community we had created.

The guests presented Lucia with hand-drawn notes. She was gifted a combination of cheap plastic toys being sold at the feria and fine handwoven scarves and bags made by the girls and their grandmothers.

She really did have friends.

When it was time for cake, we gathered around to sing, "Feliz Cumpleaños." The tradition in Guatemala is that after the birthday celebrant blows out the candles, she takes a little bite from the side of the cake while the guests pretend to dare to push her face into the cake. Before the guests could begin taunting her, Lucia did a face-plant into the cake, smearing and splattering everywhere.

The guests were shocked by her gall, and there were wails of "Oh, Lucia. How could you?"

Despite the nose, mouth, eyes, and hair contact, the guests were not about to let a good cake go to waste and merrily finished it off. The sugar-infused ruckus, propelled by the candy from the piñata, continued for a while longer. Eventually, the sugar crash kicked in, and the guests dispersed.

For her tenth birthday the previous year, I'd held a grand party at a circus arts facility. I tasked Wade with picking up the designer cupcakes I had ordered. When we opened the box at the party, they had melted in the June heat. Seeing that I was frustrated with her father for the mistake, Lucia picked up a cupcake and smashed it on her head. All her friends followed suit. At her eleventh birthday party, I was as appalled as her guests, but I saw her sparkle once again and admired how she can use humor to make the best of a tough situation.

After the party mess was cleared, we decided to walk up the hill and check out the feria in town. For weeks, itinerant food and game vendors had been claiming the most traversed streets and corners in town. Now every landing was loaded with peddlers selling assorted goods, such as shoes, back scratchers, pirated DVDs, and churros. Packed with folks from neighboring villages, the narrow streets were even tighter. The reigning princess of San Juan presided over the fair. Around her were a half dozen "princesses" from other towns, each wearing a sash, a crown, and the traje típica of her respective community. A few Ladino couples danced to reggaetón music blasting out of speakers as tall as they were while the Indigenous townspeople watched.

In the center of town were carnival rides, likely castoffs from a county fair in the US. The trucks must have brought them disassembled down that curvy, unpaved road. Lucia begged me to let her on one of the rides. Among the attractions was a small, hand-turned Ferris wheel. I looked closely and saw that some parts were held together by rope. There was no way in hell I would let her get on that death trap.

On the other side of the plaza, where the crowd was thinner, were the bumper cars. That, I was willing to do. We stood in line to wait for our turn while the current group took theirs. Right away, I noticed something odd about how the current group was playing. There was minimal movement across the rink but a lot of bumping. The cars were clustered and could not pull away from each other. Then I realized what the problem was. Except for a handful of tuk-tuk drivers in town, no one knew how to drive, and most people had probably not even sat in the front seat of a car to watch another person drive. They had no idea what they were doing.

When the current group's time was up, the people waiting made a mad dash to the cars to replace the people getting out. The line must have meant nothing. Lucia and I bolted to a car on the far side. I told Lucia that she probably knew more about driving than anyone else in the rink and that she could take over the track. At eleven years old, Lucia obviously didn't have her driver's license, but she knew the basics: steer the wheel, push the pedal, don't hold back, but be prepared to get knocked. If she didn't already know before, she'd certainly learned this past year. She sped around the track, surprised at her ability to move forward and rebound from the bumps, and didn't let her car get stuck in a mass of others.

I pondered how, like the cars, we had been bumped and banged, but we had also formed a beautiful community that loved us and that we loved. And that was something to celebrate.

52

CONFIANZA

IN OUR FINAL WEEKS in Guatemala in July, Lucia and I made another expedition to Petén, this time to visit the San Benito region where we had expanded the program when I worked there from 1999 to 2001.

A lot was riding on this visit. I wanted to show Lucia the villages that Marina, Lilian, and I had reached out to, and I was also introducing the team leaders, Dalia and Mynor, to the principal funder of the program, Beth, who had flown down from the States for this visit. Beth was an American woman I had known for many years who had discreetly donated tens of thousands of dollars based on her long commitment to women's health and my word that the funds were being used prudently to help those most in need. But perhaps the most important and most personal reason for this trip to Petén was that I wanted to finally put to rest the remembrances that had been haunting me since I left.

On our first day there, I felt my throat begin to close and my chest tighten. I worried that the air-conditioning on the overnight bus had given me a cold. I downed a strong coffee, hoping the warmth would help my breathing and the caffeine would help my brain as I translated during the luncheon that Dalia and Mynor had organized in Beth's honor.

Dalia shared a PowerPoint presentation and beamed with pride when she talked about applying fluoride to children at schools, building low-smoke and wood-efficient stoves, campaigns to rid people of parasites, and providing women's health care. Mynor said that their accomplishments also included having management in local hands (i.e., no longer depending on international volunteers), training scores of promotores and comadronas, and serving hundreds of people who had been abandoned by their government.

Their joy dissipated, though, as they recounted a dispute over birth control with the new Italian priest. In the 1990s and early 2000s, the Catholic Church was the largest provider of birth control in the region, but the times had changed. The revolutionary priests and catechists had been replaced by an old guard who wanted a return to conservative values, including keeping women in their place. In Las Cruces, the conflicts over family planning led to the catechists evicting the health team from Casa de los Estudios, which was why they had moved before my last visit there.

At least the Las Cruces team had received enough notice to find another property to relocate the clinic and training facility. In contrast, the contention came to a head for this team when the priest locked them out of the clinic and kept all the medicines and equipment inside. The priest insisted that if they continued to dispense birth control, he would find others who would not. Despite his proclamation, he couldn't find a nurse or promotora willing to staff the clinic on his terms, so it remained closed. After being kicked out of the church's clinic, the health team struck out on their own, starting again from scratch.

My gut tightened at the thought of trying to explain to Beth why the equipment and medicines purchased with her contribution remained under lock and key by the priest and were not being used. I wanted her to see that the investment she made was in the team who had been trained and not the goods purchased.

The plan for the following day was to hold a women's health jornada in Rey Balantún, a village I had not returned to since leaving Petén in 2001. I was anxious that this was the community Dalia and Mynor had chosen to visit because my last memory of Rey Balantún was of a rumor that Doña Marina had relayed to me. She'd heard that if "that gringa" (me) went back, they would stone me, presumably because I represented the Catholic Church. The divisions between the Catholics and evangelicals that became politicized during the war had come to this region, along with the people these divisions had hurt. The evangelicals had extrapolated from US missionaries that flooded the area that the pope was the anti-Christ and that the Catholic Church was conniving to bring on the apocalypse.

In that same vein, I thought about how in the early days of the program, I had stopped by another of the evangelical communities, El Aguacate, to drop off a note to the mayor, who was also the pastor of the Assembly of God Church. I was requesting to meet with the village's improvement committee to discuss their participation in the program. In the time before cell phones, the only means to request a meeting was to hand-deliver a letter. Upon hearing that I was looking for him, the mayor fled, afraid that I was carrying the sign of the beast.

I instead delivered the letter to the head of the improvement committee and arranged a meeting for a week later. Feeling that I would need backup, I asked Doña Marina to accompany me. She was not only a comadrona and a promotora but also the pastor at her local Assembly of God church. I thought that she could speak with them directly, evangelical to evangelical, about the ecumenical nature of our work and assuage their fears.

After Doña Marina and I made our presentation the following week, the committee members politely indicated that their acceptance of the program was contingent on whether they thought I was working for the devil. I was stunned, but I knew I needed to try to salvage the situation. I told them that Doña Marina and I would wait in the truck while they debated this, and if they decided that indeed I was, I would have no hard feelings and would continue to greet them as I drove by. However, if they did decide that I was not an "agent of the anti-Christ," we would return later to plan our first project.

Doña Marina and I walked down to the truck and climbed into the back to catch a breeze. It was hard to chitchat with her as we awaited the committee's verdict about me. Out of nowhere, Doña Marina asked me if I had ever been in love. I was a bit taken aback. I had made it a practice to never talk about my life as a young, single woman dating in the US. Culturally, I thought explaining the continuum of relationships I had been in would seem alien to a mother of seventeen, married at the age I'd had my first kiss.

Thinking of Stuart, I said, "Yes, I was in love, very much so. He made so many promises to me. We were going to get married. We were going to travel the world. Wherever we were together would be home. A few weeks before our wedding, he broke it off and broke my heart. Since then, I have not been able to trust another man."

"Juanita, that is exactly how these people feel. So many organizations have come making promises and have broken their hearts. It is easier to deny you with an excuse about religion than to believe in you and be hurt again."

After an hour, a committee representative came to the truck to tell me what they had decided: they couldn't decide. Despite Doña Marina's insights, I was beyond frustrated. We bid farewell and headed out.

As I had promised, though, every time I drove by El Aguacate thereafter, I waved at the people by the road. Whenever I saw women walking with empty jugs to fetch water, I would stop and offer a ride to a finca a couple of miles away whose owner granted access to his well. At the finca, I chatted with the women about the weather, their lives, or whatever while I waited for them to fill their jugs. Being thought of as someone who makes broken promises that lead to broken hearts was worse to me than being called the agent of the anti-Christ.

Months of these happenstance encounters led to a slow building of trust. El Aguacate joined the program the following year. Our first project was to build a tank that could store enough rain during the *invierno* (winter) to last them all year.

In those early days of setting up the program, it was Lilian who accompanied me on the visit to Rey Balantún. When we first arrived and took a few steps out of the truck, three children, their hair brittle and rusty from malnutrition, bowed their heads to me. The mayor told me that as a respected elder (I was thirty-two at the time), I was to touch the tops of their heads to bless them. I did as instructed, but I was afraid the children would think that I had some magical property.

After our business with the mayor, a distraught mother asked Lilian and me for help with her twelve-year-old daughter, who was bedridden with cholera (which means an emotional rather than an intestinal disorder in Guatemala). The government doctor covering this set of villages had given the girl a vitamin B shot—a common treatment for whatever ails— that had no effect. As we approached her house to check on the girl, I asked the mother when the problem started.

"About the time she had the miscarriage a month ago."

Lilian and I read each other's thoughts in a glance. Everyone had been so focused on getting the girl to eat, drink, or leave the bed that no one asked why a twelve-year-old girl was pregnant. I kept the mother outside, making my best bad attempt at small talk, while Lilian prepared a cup of chamomile tea to take inside to the girl for an honest heart-to-heart. I never knew the details of the secrets they shared, but afterward, the girl got up and came outside.

During the hour-long ride to Rey Balantún along the bumpy dirt road for the women's health jornada, Dalia explained the history of the villages the program served.

"They did not exist until the end of the armed conflict in 1996. To provide land to displaced people as required by the peace accords, the government acquired cheap land from *finqueros* [large farmers]. The land was cheap because it was basically uninhabitable. There's no water source except for a lagoon, which is hours away on foot."

I added, "Because Petén is naturally a rainforest, all the land's nutrients are stored in vegetation. When the campesinos slash and burn the land to grow their crops, they end up destroying most of the nutrients. This land isn't suitable for multiple years of crops."

"Why do they continue to live here, in a place where humans can't survive? Why don't they give up and move to the city for jobs?" Beth asked.

Mynor shared the story of a village man who had attempted to make a life in Guatemala City with a guaranteed job as a security guard waiting for him.

"He asked for a few quetzales from everyone in the village just to pay the bus to the city. When he got there, he nearly starved while he was waiting for the security company to pay him. His family nearly starved in the village because he was not there to work the field. Eventually, he was assigned to guard a Coca Cola distribution truck. The fancy gun he carried was worth a lot more than the cash the driver had. He was shot at several times to steal his gun. He gave up and went back to his community."

Dalia added, "Some people sell their land and use the money to go north to the US, but if they are caught and deported, or worse, kidnapped, they have nothing when they come back."

When we reached Rey Balantún, I searched among the gaunt women sitting on benches and standing outside the vacant house where the jornada was being held to see if I could recognize the girl Lilian had cared for or the children who once bowed to me. I did not. Several women remembered me, but none mentioned the threats to stone me from long ago. After all these years of promises kept, they had let go of their fears.

We set up our makeshift clinic in an abandoned house with a tin roof, no electricity, no water, and lots of bats. I couldn't imagine the horror of being bitten by a bat *there* during a pelvic exam, so at my behest, we pulled our shirts over our heads for protection and swooshed out the bats.

Beth, Lucia, and I offered to help in whatever way would be useful. I did the patient intake, asking intimate questions about *flujo* (discharge), *picazón* (itching), and *olor* (smell). Lucia respectfully noted the women's answers in their medical records. Since there were no lab tests, every woman who had any signs or symptoms of infection received two big bags of antibiotics (one for her and one for her partner) called *la bomba* (the bomb) to treat every possibility. Beth's job was to strategically point the flashlight in the dim room where the pelvic exams were conducted.

"I didn't know that all cervixes look different," she later told me.

"Neither did I," I replied.

"There was a woman who had eleven children, and her uterus was hanging out."

"Yeah, she told me in the intake that four of her eleven children died."

"Did you see that woman with a Cesarean scar that ran from her pelvis up to her sternum? She was butchered!"

"Oh, no! She didn't mention that in her intake."

I wanted to go back into town, grab that priest by the neck, and shove his face in a few of these pelvises to see the results of denying women control over their bodies.

As we were finishing an intake in the late morning, baking under the tin roof, I began to feel dizzy and nauseous. I stood up, took a few steps, and then collapsed on top of Lucia, knocking her to the ground. The next thing I remember is lying in the truck cab while Dalia checked my blood pressure and Mynor adjusted the air-conditioning vents.

Lucia crawled onto the seat next to me. "Mommy, I know you will be fine, right?" Her smooth little hand wrapped around mine.

When I started to feel better, Dalia helped me out of the truck and onto the porch. I spent the rest of the day on the ground outside the house, flat on my back, with my knees perched up in the same position as the women being served inside.

After we returned to San Benito, I asked Doña Marina to refer the women in need of surgery to an organization that could help, and I asked Lilian to go back to Rey Balantún to talk with the women about their rights to not be abused. After all these years and even with a college degree in social work, there was little that Lilian could do in these rural villages apart from bringing tea and listening to stories.

The trust that took me years to build was reciprocal. I knew that Doña Marina, Lilian, and now Dalia and Mynor cared for me as much as I cared for them. I wondered if, after only a year with ODIM in San Juan and San Pablo, I had built these types of close relationships. *Had I formed the same sort of friendship with Ines and Navichoc that I had with Lilian and Doña Marina? If I go back there again in fifteen years, will anyone remember me? Would anyone catch me if I fell?*

53
THERE IS A LIGHT THAT NEVER GOES OUT

A COUPLE OF days later, the tightness in my chest evolved into bronchitis, and I lost my voice completely. Lucia was once again scared for my well-being, because I could only communicate by writing in a notebook. Tears filled her eyes.

"Mommy, please be alright."

I tried to reassure her with little notes and big hugs, but I was afraid—not of being unable to speak but of the feeling that I had lost control over my life. Was losing my actual voice a metaphor?

Rather than exploring new parts of the country as I had hoped to do, I decided to slowly make our way back to Lake Atitlán. We stopped for a few days at a backpackers' destination—Finca Ixobel—near the town of Poptún. I wanted to rest and allow Lucia to do group activities like horseback riding and exploring caves without me so that she would not be bored.

When I had lived in Petén, I used to go to the finca when I desperately needed to shun the curious gaze of the Guatemalans. I always felt strange. The way I dressed, my coloring, the food I ate, and the fact that I was a single, childless woman in my thirties were constant sources of questions and comments by the people in community meetings, on the bus, at church, everywhere. This must be how Lucia felt. Back then, I'd wanted a space where I could blend in, even for just a weekend.

The finca had been staffed mainly by young international travelers trading a few weeks of work for room and board. All-you-can-eat, family-style vegetarian dinners brought the travelers together to swap stories, share bits about their respective countries, and plan their next stops. I could drink beer, wear shorts, be a little saucy, and flirt shamelessly without a watchful eye on me that could affect my standing as a lay Catholic missionary.

This time around, I asked the staff if we could lodge in one of the treehouses I used to sleep in, thinking it would be fun for Lucia and a reminder for me of my adventures once upon a time. As we approached our accommodation, I saw broken boards dangling from a tree—what was left of my treehouse from long ago. In fact, very little remained from that time. Most of the scattered, makeshift treehouses had been replaced by sturdy cabanas. The staff consisted of locals there for a wage and not a story. Guests dined on their own at the full-service restaurant. And staff directed guests to guided tours at a set hour rather than encouraging impromptu explorations of the surrounding area.

After a day of rest, I finally had the strength to explore the main grounds of the finca with Lucia. In our walk, we came upon a large macaw locked in a cage beside a corral of horses. He was brilliant. A strip of yellow separated the red of his head and chest from the blue of his wings and tail.

I commented to Lucia, "I wonder if this bird was caged to keep as a pet, to protect him, or to hold until they sell him."

"Why would you think they are going to sell him?" she asked.

"Because the last time I was here, someone had brought to the owner a baby monkey whose mother had been killed. The owner let the guests hold him while she was making arrangements to sell him. I held him too. He was wrapped up in a blanket and cried like a human baby, except that since his facial muscles were more developed than a human baby, his cries were more expressive."

"Oh, that's so sad!" Lucia said.

Gazing at the macaw, I commented, "Yeah, I know. I think it's wrong for wild animals to be trapped and sold as pets. I wonder why people can't just admire their beauty without having to own them."

I turned back to Lucia to see that she had opened the corral gate and freed the horses, who started to walk out of their pasture. "No!" I yelled at her. "You can't let the horses go!"

"But you just said people shouldn't trap animals and keep them as pets."

"Lucia, horses are different. They are domesticated," I attempted to explain. "We have to get them back in."

"That doesn't make sense," Lucia said, following me as I jaunted up to the horses strolling away.

"Okay, you remember what I told you and the girls from Nuevo Amanecer about evolution? Everything changes and everything is related. Well, humans helped horses change. They bred them so that they would help people. A lot of domesticated animals depend on people to survive," I explained.

The horses were outpacing us, and I feared that if I walked any faster, I would scare them away. Just then, I saw one of the finca workers walking down the road toward us. With my still weak voice, I called out to him that the horses were loose. He waved at me and told me not to worry; he would retrieve them. I grabbed Lucia by the hand and ran in the other direction so as not to startle the horses.

The setting I had hoped would help transform me had itself been transformed. I had expected to come back and find something I had left here. I did, and I didn't. Everything changes and everything is related.

We woke the first morning covered in bug bites due to a tear in the pabellón (Lucia had fifty-two on her legs), so I switched from the treehouse to a cabana. Just as well. Sometimes trying to relive the past does bite.

After a few days of recuperating at the finca, I was well enough to continue to San Juan. We went back into Poptún in the late afternoon to catch a night bus to Guatemala City. Sitting in the seedy waiting area at the station, something seemed off. The flickering fluorescent lights appeared green, and the blaring television looked blurry.

Lucia noticed white clouds floating across my eye. Since the grubby bus station did not have a mirror, I ran to a restaurant bathroom a block down the street to see pus accumulating in my lids and the corner of my eyes. *Damn.* The infection that had started in my lungs had worked its way up my throat and into my eye. The best I could do was get saline drops from a twenty-four-hour pharmacy and napkins from a tienda to dab my eye.

"Mommy, you'll be fine, right?" Lucia asked. She had just stopped worrying about me having lost my voice a few days before. I didn't want her to upset her again.

"Of course, it's just a weird eye thing," I assured her. But I felt a sickness, a different sickness, rise up inside me—the memory of the last time I had caught a ride in Poptún.

On the day after Christmas in 2000, when I was living in Petén, I boarded a shuttle to go to Belize to meet up with friends. Behind me sat a loud, rude North American man complaining incessantly about how the driver was late, how the bus was uncomfortable, how everyone was trying to rip him off, and how overall Guatemala sucked. I rolled my eyes, annoyed that I was stuck in front of this guy.

After an hour on our ride, just past Poptún and with another four hours to go, our driver stopped. He had us get off this van and onto another that already had passengers. The drivers of the two shuttles were consolidating their fares onto one to save money on gas. As I moved toward the last available seat of the new shuttle, behind the driver, the obnoxious man knocked me out of the way and took my place. Not up to engaging him further, I went to the back of the van and wedged myself between the piles of backpacks and the emergency exit door.

Nearly instantly, it was evident that this second driver was drunk, likely having not even slept after the festivities the night before. He swerved along the road, dodged a horse, and then veered onto a bank on the right, flipping the van onto its left side. As a result, the passengers fell on top of the man who took my seat. No one fell on me in the back, so I could reach around and let myself out of the emergency exit. I guided all the passengers out the small back door—all but one.

A few of the strapping, young, male passengers flipped the van upright, revealing the man who had taken my place still seated, blubbering nonsense. The window latch had ripped his skin from his forehead to his jaw. His face drooped over where his eye should have been; it was surely lost. I pulled my only clean shirt out of my backpack and lifted his face back into it place. I held on to his head as the same guys helped me pull him through the window.

The driver fled, and there was no way to call for help. As the only bilingual person on this tourist shuttle and having worked in health in the region for the past two years, I was in the best position to get care for this man. I waved down a truck and took him to the hospital in Poptún—a place where blood and filth covered the floors. While he was in emergency surgery, I went to the local Catholic church and showed my missionary credentials to ask for a ride back to the crash site. I wanted to retrieve this man's luggage to find his identification and to look for his eye. I couldn't find the eye, and only after the surgery pulled his skin back into place did I learn he had not lost it.

I found his Canadian passport, so I called the Canadian embassy to ask for assistance. I explained that their compatriot would die if he did not go to a private hospital in Guatemala City. However, he would never survive the ten-hour bus ride on a dirt road and must be flown. The embassy agreed to have someone meet us at the airport if I could get him on a medevac plane to the city. I arranged for the hospital staff to take us to our original departure point and wait with the man while I went to the bank with the airline manager to withdraw a thousand dollars from my credit card to pay for the flight.

The manager took me straight from the bank to the tarmac, where the plane was ready to depart. The hospital staff were lingering on the stairs to the plane's door, and the man lay on a sheet on the plane's floor. Assuming the plane would have a "med" with the "evac," I asked the airport manager, who had a thousand dollars of my money in his pocket, "Where is the doctor?"

He simply responded, "You're a gringa. Aren't you a doctor?" and walked away.

The hospital nurse said, "Here's the tube that goes in his nose. Here's the tube that goes into his penis. Make sure they stay there. Good luck." And we were off.

The pilot had to fly low, dodging mountains, so that the man's swollen brain would not hemorrhage. Soon after takeoff, he regained consciousness and began tearing at the bandages on his face and the tubes in his nose. I told him to stop, but he was delirious and didn't understand me. I crawled on top of him and pinned him down with all fours. I prayed that he would not rip off his freshly sewn face while we wrestled the entire hour of the flight.

A kind soul from the embassy met us at the airport with a proper ambulance and took us to a private hospital. Once I saw that he had been checked into an ICU ward, spoke with his doctor, and was assured that the Canadian government would help find his family and get him home, I took a taxi to some friends' house. I collapsed, covered in blood, on their stoop until one of them came home from work. For the next three days, I stayed by the man's side during the day, reading English-language magazines to him, and with my friends at night. I didn't know I had torn my ear until I showered at their home that night. I didn't know I had broken three ribs until weeks later. All I knew was I was in pain—physical, emotional, and spiritual.

After having failed so many times to save lives in the previous couple of years, the only life I could save was this Canadian, and only because he was from a country that valued his life. I saw too often how cheap life is, and I was torn by the inequities that result from the accident of birthplace.

Once again, I was in Poptún, catching a ride, this time with Lucia on a double-decker bus. As I now do on every bus ride, I made eye contact with the driver, visually checking his sobriety, and scanned the windows, looking for latches that could tear flesh so that I could cover them. The driver was sober, and these large windows had no latches.

As I shifted uncomfortably in my seat with Lucia sprawled across my lap, I realized that I hadn't taken Lucia to Petén or even to Guatemala to show her what I loved. I was there to feel the same rush I once had of living on the edge, of risking everything, of being in love. Yet a decade and a half later, it seemed as if so much had changed in Guatemala.

So much had changed in my life too. By insisting that the only way to recapture what I had lost was to go to Guatemala with my child, by chasing a thrill, I was as caged as the macaw. I had trapped myself into thinking there was only one way and one place where I could be happy again. Had Lucia opened another gate to free me?

Almost halfway into our route, I felt our bus go *BAM* and *BAM* again and again. On the second level, we felt the strong sway as the bus rocked, nearly flipping. I reached for Lucia but could not get ahold of her because I could barely see. The infected eye had sealed shut, and the other was filling with pus. She banged her head back and forth against the window and seat, getting a black eye on one side and a bruise on the other. Suddenly, the windshield and the front three windows on our level shattered. Other than a few people calling out, "Dios mío!" no one screamed, cried, or made any fuss. The little girl, maybe five years old, in the seat beside us was remarkably calm.

Was this something that people were used to? Or was it merely cultural not to call out because no one will hear, no one will care? Or was everyone too shocked to say anything?

When it seemed that the bus was stabilized, the passengers evacuated. We were nearly the last to leave. I didn't want us to be rushed out by others. We exited through the front doors and onto fallen trees. I could tell that we were on the side of a mountain, but in the dark, I couldn't tell where the trees ended and the cliff below began. I instructed Lucia to use all her tree-climbing skills to get out safely. She grabbed limb after limb, scrambling around the tree trunk. I followed her closely, not looking down until we could jump onto the road.

Out of harm's way, I asked other passengers what had happened. Supposedly, our bus had collided with a tractor-trailer carrying cattle, which collided with the bus behind us, which collided again with our bus. Our bus driver had fled, and the traffic was backed up for miles.

I saw a couple of people pulling passengers through the windshield of the other bus. A half dozen men stood in a loose circle, hands on hips, looking decisive yet doing nothing. Another half dozen men were marching back and forth, arms swinging, between the tractor-trailer and the two buses. They were directing a flatbed to pull the tractor-trailer off the road since that driver had fled as well. This time, I had no interest in taking charge. I sat by the side of the road in the drizzling rain, my arms wrapped around my daughter.

After the road was cleared somewhat, a bus headed in our direction was willing to take a handful of passengers. I shoved my way to the front of the line and used having a child as a justification as to why we should board. We took the last two seats in the back and were on our way to Guatemala City. I was surprised when we were taken to a bus station different from our intended destination and even more surprised when we got off not with an apology from the company but with an admonishment for using an electrical outlet behind a counter to charge my phone.

From Guatemala City, we took a cab to an Airbnb in Antigua. After showering, I found four ticks on Lucia and two on me. Before I could get tweezers, she plucked them off herself. I was filled with worry about whether she or I would contract a tick-transmitted illness.

I had wanted to show her the crystal-blue waterfalls of Semuc Champey, the Afro-Indigenous Garifuna culture in Livingston, and the houses on stilts in Rio Duce—the off-the-beaten-track sites that tourists proclaim is the "real" Guatemala. Perhaps, instead, my collapse, the crash, and our condition were the real Guatemala, and I had shown Lucia enough. She had seen the desperation and the resilience in the people there, in me, and in herself. The previous year, I might have insisted that we take advantage of the time in Antigua to hike a volcano, but this time we holed up in our room all day, watching dubbed movies on the Disney channel.

After a couple of days of TV and trips to the spa, we headed back to San Juan. Lucia started having a fever and body aches, and soon after we arrived home, she started vomiting. I gave her suero (oral rehydration therapy) that I had stockpiled at home. That night, she hallucinated, talking in her sleep and waking to tell me she was scared because everything was moving fast around her. I took Lucia to Sanjuanerita to see Dra. Faustina. Based on the ensuing rash, she diagnosed Lucia with Zika. My bronchitis lingered, my eyes were bloodshot, and I also developed the telltale rash and Zika.

Here I was again, leaving Guatemala after a terrible crash and a spate of injuries and illnesses, uncertain about what I had accomplished in my professional and personal life. However, the hindsight of fifteen years had shown me that my time before did mean something. The program I had helped start still endured. The insight I'd gained about the desperation of people's lives helped me advocate for immigrants in the US, and the friendships I formed enriched my life. This time, though, I was not leaving Guatemala as the same zealot I had been before. That Jan was still deep inside the rings of my tree, but the surface was breaking open with new and different growth. This time my focus was on being the mother my daughter needed.

Everything changes and everything is related. My year in Guatemala with my daughter was connected to my time before but different. Guatemala had changed. I had changed. My daughter had changed me, had tamed me. I could not predict the impact the year in Guatemala would have on my or my daughter's lives in fifteen years. And perhaps that is the point—to continue the journey. Even if it means switching buses along the way.

54

BIRD'S-EYE VIEW

SAN JUAN HAS A PARTICULAR STYLE of painting, *vista de pájaro*, or "bird's-eye view," that limns an overhead perspective. A legend regarding the inspiration for this style is that centuries ago, when the Spanish began their conquest and were killing other Maya groups, the Tz'utujil gathered in their capital, Chuitinamit, to decide what to do. Many of them transformed into spirits that lived in the air, the clouds, the lake, and the volcanoes to reduce bloodshed. Some morphed into birds and flew over to witness the atrocities of the Spanish invasion. The original bird's-eye-view paintings were a visual record of the horror these shapeshifters saw.

Among the many contemporary murals throughout San Juan are several in this style that continue to bear witness to tragedies, including the devastation caused by Hurricane Stan, as well as those that highlight traditions, like the healing acts of bone setters. For the tourist market, vista de pájaro has evolved in recent years into portraits of idealized bouquets of village life, such as a market scene or a kayak filled with flowers, fruits, and the crowns of a group of locals.

"Places have spirits," Nehemias said during one of our Tz'utujil classes. "There is a spot a few paces away that holds sacred ruins where new priests were once initiated. I went to a ceremony there led by a priest who had the gift of reading fire. He called the attendees to gaze into the fire and to make out what they could see. Birds appeared among the flames. Within moments, a flock circled them overhead and then dispersed."

Nehemias swirled his hands over his head, and I looked up to the sky.

"Why do you think that happened?" I asked.

"It was the power this place holds. The birds coming out of the fire were manifestations of the spirits that have been bound to this place."

Then Nehemias told me about how he had once taken a group of US university students there for another Maya ceremony. The priest advised them that they were treading on holy land and must comport themselves with reverence. All but one did. A young man stomped around and mocked the ceremony despite the warnings. Some invisible force seemed to grab his leg and slowly pull it toward a stone, forcing him to sit, as a parent would do to a misbehaving child. Terrified, he froze. The priest reminded him to show deference. As the young man settled down, his leg was set loose, and he comported himself well the rest of the evening.

The last story Nehemias told me was about when he took a middle-aged Tz'utujil woman to the site. As an evangelical Christian, she completely denied Maya spirituality. She showed her disrespect by kicking over rocks, spitting on the ground, and cursing each step. That evening when she returned home, she lost her mind and began uttering nonsense. The only word her in-laws could make out was Nehemias's name. The next day, her elderly mother-in-law went to Nehemias's house to ask for an explanation.

He said, "All I did was take her to a spot near here."

The old woman cocked an eyebrow and asked, "What spot?"

As he pointed and replied, "That place over there," the woman widened her eyes and asked him to wait there, as she would return shortly.

Her daughter-in-law had *susto*. Her spirit had been torn from her and had to be returned. The older woman hurried home and back, carrying a blouse from her daughter-in-law. She asked Nehemias to point out exactly where and what her daughter-in-law had desecrated. Walking around the pile of rocks, she beat the blouse against each specific spot where the younger woman had kicked, spit, or stomped to shake her daughter-in-law's spirit loose. Once it was released, she used the blouse to sweep the spirit into a pile. Finally, she gathered the spirit, swaddling it into the blouse like a baby, carefully picked it up, and took it back home to put back into her daughter-in-law.

Literally, susto is "fear" in Spanish but has an entirely different meaning in Guatemala. It is a condition resulting from a soul being torn out of its body due to a huge shock. Some twenty years ago, I sat at a kitchen table with Stuart, who had promised to love me the rest of his life, when he confessed it had all been a lie and then sobbed with his head in my lap. I felt like my soul was being ripped out of my chest, leaving an open wound from the top of my throat down to the middle of my belly. That week, I ground my teeth in my sleep so hard that when I woke, my jaws were locked, and I could not open my mouth. I could not speak for days.

Years after that event and weeks after canceling our trip, another man who had promised to love me the rest of his life sat across from me at the kitchen table and said that it had all been a lie, this time coolly, as if telling me we were out of laundry detergent. I ran out of the house and down the street so our daughter would not see me cry. Perhaps because of the need to hold myself together for my daughter, I could not fully respond. Rather than absorbing this shock throughout my body, over the following days, weeks, months, my soul fractured into thousands of little bits and fell into a pile of dust. Completely voided, all I could do was sweep the pile of dust from one spot to another.

Nearly two years after that talk around the table, I moved with my daughter and my box of dust to a Maya village on Lake Atitlán to retrieve my soul. As the lake, its people, and its life wet the dust, I slowly packed it back onto me, the way a child packs wet sand onto a sandcastle.

I was certain about going back to the US, but the sandcastle was not complete. Dry dust was still on the ground. It took six years to heal from my soul being ripped out the first time, so I acknowledged that I could not possibly recuperate from my soul being crushed to bits within just three years.

Through my twenties and early thirties, though I had no desire to be a mother, I had a recurring nightmare about a baby that deeply disturbed me. I had given birth to a baby with no father. We were in a large house with many passages and many rooms. For some unknown reason, I had to leave where I was, so I put the baby in a laundry basket for safekeeping. When I returned, my baby was gone, lost to me. I tore apart all the sheets and clothes in the basket but could not find it.

For years, I interpreted this dream to mean that I was too irresponsible to have a child. I was forgetful. I constantly lost everything—my phone, my keys, my wallet. I was terrified that if I ever had a child, I would not be a good mother; I would get distracted and misplace my baby, or worse.

Now when I look back at my dream, I see it differently. The baby was a new spirit growing out of me that I tucked away to protect and lost in the process, though I am still unsure who she is. Is she the part who wanted to be a missionary, travel the world, feel a purpose? Or is she the part who, after her family and her engagement fell apart, wanted to feel connected, loved, and at home? When I attempted to intertwine these parts of me in my marriage, they were smothered. The unraveling of my marriage didn't instantly release these hidden parts; rather they were torn about and became my pile of dust.

When I gave birth to my daughter, I felt like a piece of my life force had been shaved off. Since then, that shaved bit of life has grown into a tremendous spirit. The little soul that became Lucia has its own place, its own ties separate from mine that must be honored, or it will also be torn. When I think about the anguish that she went through after the divorce, especially the year in Guatemala, I feel anguish as well. Yet her needs are separate from mine. Her soul needs to be swaddled and protected in conjunction with but independently from mine. In my attempt to intertwine my needs with hers, I was smothering her as well.

A few days after hearing Nehemias's stories, I was washing dishes at the pila while Lucia pulled laundry from the line. I heard her coo, "My baby" at the clothes she held in her arms. I burst into tears once again, sobbing uncontrollably. *Is my spirit stuck on some rock?* I wondered. *Do I need to beat it loose? Should I wrap it in swaddling clothes and hold it like a baby? Or do I let it fly like a bird to catch a glimpse of what it can see?*

Since Lucia was naturally surprised by my reaction, I called her over to sit with me on the woven bench on our porch and told her Nehemias's stories. Lucia said the consequences for the Maya woman were worse than for the college student since she denied who she really was—denied her own culture. She had a tear at her soul rather than a tug at her leg. I reflected on the consequences of my own denial.

After a while, Lucia said, "My soul is leaving my body and is going to that little house on the hill. I can feel my soul flying over there."

"What does your soul see?"

"Just us sitting here talking."

"Do you want to call it back?"

"It will come back when it's ready."

Like the Tz'utujil, I am a bird person. In my work in the clinic, I have been able to go from one place to another, sharing what I learn, interpreting cultures, and facilitating understanding between them. I have navigated my life using the sun and the stars as my guide.

Like the Tz'utujil, I am also a tree person. I will plant myself in one place, spread my branches, and allow my little aq'ab'al to nest safely.

That week before we left, I commissioned a vista de pájaro painting from a local artist. Lucia and I are in a hand-carved kayak, dressed in traje típica de San Juan. Though only the yellow crowns of our heads are visible, I like to imagine that Lucia is laughing as she arranges the sunflowers while I labor to keep this kayak from overturning. I wanted an image to portray how the two of us had shared in the journey with the community. I wanted a witness. I wanted to hold something that held us.

Places hold spirits.

55

FAIRY-TALE MASHUP

IN ONE OF OUR LAST DAYS, I crawled down the rocks next to our house to find Lucia playing with the small Cinderella doll my mother had given her. Watching her dress Cinderella in petals, I remembered all those little doll shoes scattered in her room that I kept sweeping up, mixing with the dust, and how her little fingers put on and took off Cinderella's three dresses over and over again. She had this figurine along with three others that were lying in the dirt. I squatted beside her, my ponytail tickling my neck, picked up a stick, and started poking in the earth.

"Mommy, you take these two, and I'll be these two," she directed as she handed me the dolls.

"But why do I get the ones with the chopped-off hair and you get the nice ones?" I asked.

"Uh, just because," she huffed. "Now, you play the mommy and the little sister, and I'll be the teenager and her friend. The teenagers are going out, and you stay home with the little sister and clean up," she goaded, knowing that would rile me.

"Really? What fun is that?" I teased back.

"Okay, let's build a fairy house instead," she offered.

As we assembled a teeny shanty out of twigs, vines, and leaves, I recounted my flights of fancy as a child. "Lucia, when I was a little bit younger than you, I got my first record player for Christmas. My first record was 'Bibbidi Bobbidi Boo'—you know, Cinderella's fairy godmother's song."

"Oh, yeah, from that old cartoon movie."

"Well, it was already old when I was a child. Anyhow, I played it over and over again while spinning around in circles."

"Why? Didn't you get dizzy?"

"Not back then I didn't. I used to have a lot more balance. So, as I was saying, I had this Cinderella watch. Cinderella's arms were the hands on the watch and would come together at the stroke of twelve o'clock."

"Wouldn't her arms come together around every hour?"

"Oh, Lucia, let me finish. So, when I listened to 'Bibbidi Bobbidi Boo,' I would swirl as fast as I could. I'd pull my arms up over my head like hers and ask my fairy godmother to help me have my own magical transformation."

"Did you have a fairy godmother?"

"Yes."

I thought about how the fairy godmothers of my early life brought me to this place: Cinderella, Virginia, Lottie, Jane, Bibba, and Estela. I became none of these women. I became all of these women. I am becoming more fully myself.

And in Guatemala, I had other fairy godmothers guide me—Doña Marina, Navichoc, Lana, Daniella, Ines, and Gilda Just as I have carried in myself the women that influenced my coming of age, I will carry the women who influenced my coming of middle age.

In this mashed-up fairy tale I was living in, who was I? The intrepid heroine, the wicked witch, the old hag, or some combination of all? A couple of dark-haired princes have come, turned to pumpkins, and gone. I found a home in a foreign land and felt like an alien at home. I embraced humble strangers who became the dearest of friends. I tried to stir a change in others that instead changed me. I spent years toiling in barren fields and days in gardens feasting on fruits. I tried to give my daughter the best of me so that she can be the best of her.

Still, I ask myself, what is the price I pay for magic?

56

LEAVING

OUR GOODBYES STRETCHED for days. Ines, Alba, Herlinda, Navichoc, and even Josefina Cox invited us to dine with their families. The clinic staff planned another party at another lakeside restaurant. This time Lucia came with us when we packed into the back of a flatbed truck for the excursion. They gifted me a vermilion huipil típica from San Juan and a blusa típica from San Pablo, laced with embroidered birds. When the plates were cleared, as Lucia's La Salle class had done, each person stood and thanked me for the time we were together and shared how I had touched their lives. It was overwhelming.

We also made the rounds to bid farewell to our non-work friends. We had pizza with Daniella's family, who left for Italy a few days before us. Five years was enough for her family, but not for her. She was already planning to return to Guatemala within the year. Lana and Stela hosted us for an afternoon in San Marcos. Lana practiced her new psychic channeling techniques and told me how my last trip to Petén resolved the spiritual parasites that had clung to me. Oh, dear Lana.

Others popped by our house. Adela from La Salle made a long, teary speech about how she had never befriended a girl from another country and that Lucia had become very dear to her. Karin came up from the rocks below to make a similar teary speech.

"See how you have affected them," I said to Lucia. "You may not see it now, but I think they affected you as well," to which Lucia simply shrugged.

In our last full day in San Juan, I finally convinced Lucia to finish exploring the lakeshore with me. Until then, we had never ventured further than the house with the mare and her foal. We got a little lost in a maze of intermingled coffee trees and corn stalks.

Lucia and I climbed over a set of boulders. She was running ahead like a mountain goat while I struggled to keep up. I leaped to a rock and fell, badly scraping my hands, knees, and shins. When I cried out in pain, Lucia turned to see how I was. I quickly dismissed my injuries. I didn't mind my daughter seeing me fall, but I didn't want her to see me wince.

I looked up and saw Kenneth's house on the other side of a field.

"Let's see if Kenneth is home," I said. When Kenneth opened his door to see my bloody abrasions, he said, "What happened? Are you okay? Please, come in."

He offered a towel and his bathroom to clean my wounds and made us tea to calm Lucia. I once again thanked him for having enough faith to make the leap to offer me a job. I told him that I was troubled I had disappointed him, but he reassured me that was not the case.

This was our last goodbye in Guatemala. I knew that if I ever returned, he would be gone. I knew he would likely leave before long in search of what he could never find there. But I also knew that I would see him again one day.

Since dusk was approaching, he handed me a flashlight so that I would not lose my way, giving me one more opportunity to find light in the darkness.

We arrived at the airport with two suitcases and two backpacks, the same luggage we had brought, but what was inside was different. The used-up math workbooks had burned with the trash, the art supplies had been gifted to Karin and Felix, the English books and magazines were gifted to the San Marcos expat kids, and most of our clothes had been discarded. Instead, the luggage was filled with presents from people dear to us, gifts to our family and friends in the States, and mementos for ourselves. Likewise, the bodies we were taking back were more or less the same, but what was inside had changed. I had let go of the dreams that had gripped me for decades and opened myself to new possibilities.

We passed through customs without incident but had a brief delay in immigration. Our tourist visas, which were supposed to be renewed every three months, had lapsed by three weeks. In July, I was so busy wrapping up my work at the clinic, going to Petén, and dealing with the subsequent injuries and illnesses that I couldn't be bothered with leaving the country to renew our visas. Instead, I was willing to pay the fine, a little over fifty dollars, for overstaying our visas. I thought about how if we were Guatemalan and had shown up at a US airport with an expired visa, I would have been jailed, and my daughter would have been put into foster care until an immigration court heard my case. A year before, I'd felt cheated at the airport for receiving a lousy exchange rate. Now I feel like I am part of a culture that cheats families of their freedom.

In mid-August of 2016, Guatemala was in as much turmoil as when I arrived in July 2015. Likewise, the US seemed to be in bedlam. But for now, this fight would not be mine. For now, the fight would be settling back into Seattle, helping my tween navigate middle school, and making the most of this middle time in my life.

Lucia laid her head in my lap, as she loves to do on flights, and said, "Now you can read to me for hours."

And I did.

ACKNOWLEDGMENTS

THIS MEMOIR WOULD not have been born without the love, labor, and lifelong inspiration of many people.

First, I want to thank the people in Guatemala who welcomed me and my daughter into their hearts and their homes, including the staff and volunteers for Concern America and the Organization for the Development of the Indigenous Maya.

Second, my gratitude extends to the friends who accompanied me on the journey I recount in the book, both in visiting me in Guatemala and helping me heal: Susanna Block and her family, Jai Essenmacher, Christy Koch, Shilpa Kothari, Priti Lalka, and the congregation of Wallingford United Methodist Church.

Developmental editor Corbin Lewars did an amazing job of helping me to shape the random vignettes I drafted into an actual story arc and to see the (anti)heroine in my journey. In addition, I appreciate the copy editing and additional comments on the manuscript provided by Glen Cutting, Heather Eliason, Jai Essenmacher, Christy Koch, Eli Kern, Kellie McBee, Emily Sonne, and Hannah Woodlan.

Finally, I appreciate my former husband and forever co-parent. Though we did not share the journey initially planned, raising a bright, spirited daughter together has been an adventure greater than any dream I could have had.

ADDITIONAL REFERENCES

Bricker, Victoria R. and Harvey M. Bricker. 2015. "Linearity and Cyclicity in Pre-Columbian Maya Time Reckoning." In *The measure and meaning of time in Mesoamerica and the Andes*, edited by Anthony F. Aveni. Dumbarton Oaks Research Library and Collection, Harvard University Press.

Eberl, Markus. 2015. "'To Put in Order': Classic Maya Concepts of Time and Space." In *The measure and meaning of time in Mesoamerica and the Andes*, edited by Anthony F. Aveni. Dumbarton Oaks Research Library and Collection, Harvard University Press.

Gustafson, Lowell S. and Amelia M. Trevelyan, Editors. 2002. *Ancient Maya Gender Identity and Relations*. Bergin & Garvey.

Joyce, Rosemary A. 2000. *Gender and Power in Prehispanic Mesoamerica*. University of Texas Press.

Sexton, James D. 1992. *Maya Folktales: Folklore from Lake Atitlán, Guatemala*. New York: Anchor Books.

www.ingramcontent.com/pod-product-compliance
Lightning Source LLC
LaVergne TN
LVHW041739060526
838201LV00046B/865